PRAISE FOR
THE VIOLENCE PROJECT

"The most in-depth study of mass shooters." —*The New Yorker*

"Insightful and cautiously optimistic . . . the authors' nuanced portraits of mass shooters buttress the case that these tragedies 'are not an inevitable fact of American life; they're preventable.' This is a sensitive and knowledgeable treatment of one of America's most vexing social problems." —*Publishers Weekly*

"Groundbreaking." —**Voice of America**

"Reveal[s] striking commonalities among the perpetrators of mass shootings and suggest a data-backed, mental health-based approach could identify and address the next mass shooter before he pulls the trigger—if only politicians are willing to actually engage in finding and funding targeted solutions." —**Politico**

"[The] book identifies 34 potential solutions to the mass shooting epidemic . . . [it] focuses on understanding past mass shooters and preventing future ones by showing that our approach to mass shooters is flawed. By painting them as one-dimensional monsters, we avoid society's involvement. And that stops us from solving the problem." —*Minneapolis Star-Tribune*

"It's a reframing of our mass shooting problem, beyond the familiar and mistaken messaging that bullying, video games, and undiagnosed mental illness lay at the crux of the crimes . . . a reminder to open our eyes . . . It helpfully summarizes de-escalation techniques and it relays four Ds of crisis: dangerous, disruptive, dysregulated, or distressed behaviors . . . a courageous deep dive into a topic for public health that most researchers would rather forget." —*Mitchell Daily Republic*

"A must-read for every school employee . . . While there is no simple solution to the problem, the book has numerous helpful suggestions, including one for the media. Give only minimal recognition to the shooter by name." —*Morrison County Record*

"The Violence Project work is a statement of hope in a time when it is easy to feel that Americans have become so inured to gun violence that we simply accept it as standard operating procedure."
—*Pittsburgh Institute for Nonprofit Journalism*

"For teachers, business owners, parents, and health care providers, for anyone passionate about gun control laws, or anyone yearning to know more—this text is for everyone. *The Violence Project* tells you everything you need to know about the mass shooting epidemic in the United States and offers evidence-based solutions as to how this crisis can be abated. The authors discuss everything from live shooter drills to security products, explaining what works and what doesn't based upon their extensive research." —*True Crime Index*

"One major advantage of this book over others is that it directly addresses the 'So what can I do?' dilemma. Unlike journal articles and books that focus on state or federal policy efforts, this book offers a three-part approach to prevention. The book recommends steps we can take as individuals, institutions, and as a society . . . This book emphasizes concrete action, with links and descriptions of resources that can help facilitate these actions. In doing so, this book gives the reader a sense that mass shootings are preventable if we are willing to take a few basic steps to get started." —*Crime Prevention and Community Safety*

"This data could help put an end to America's deadly mass shootings."
—*The Independent* (UK)

"Groundbreaking . . . The book's conclusions were gleaned from a massive undertaking that's been years in the making . . . [*The Violence Project*] offers a detailed policy roadmap that Densley and Peterson believe could save lives." —*The 74*

THE
VIOLENCE PROJECT

HOW TO <u>STOP</u> A MASS
SHOOTING EPIDEMIC

JILLIAN PETERSON, PHD
& JAMES DENSLEY, PHD

ABRAMS PRESS, NEW YORK

Library of Congress Control Number: 2021934851

Paperback ISBN: 978-1-4197-5296-4
eISBN: 978-1-64700-227-5

Printed and bound in the United States
10 9 8 7 6 5 4 3 2 1

Abrams books are available at special discounts when purchased in quantity
for premiums and promotions as well as fundraising or educational use.
Special editions can also be created to specification.
For details, contact specialsales@abramsbooks.com or the address below.

ABRAMS The Art of Books
195 Broadway, New York, NY 10007
abramsbooks.com

For the victims

CONTENTS

CHAPTER 1
MONSTERS

Nearly six hours into the interrogation video of the Parkland shooter, there is a moment: The teenage boy has just confessed to killing seventeen people at his former high school. He sits slumped in a chair, barefoot, hands cuffed behind his back, one leg shackled to the floor. He's dressed in a pale blue hospital gown that billows open in the back whenever he leans forward, revealing a frame so slight that it seems impossible it could even hold a semiautomatic rifle, let alone use one to wreak the kind of terror this town has just witnessed.

"What do you think Mom would think right now if she was . . . ?" his younger brother asks. The police have permitted him into the interrogation room, hoping he might solicit a motive. His brother can't finish the sentence. Their mother, who adopted the boys as children from the same birth mother, died of pneumonia just three months ago.

"She would cry," both boys agree unanimously.

"People think you're a monster now," the brother says.

"A monster?" The shooter starts to shake.

"You're not acting like yourself," the brother goes on. "Why? Like we've—this is not who you are. Like, come on. Why did you do this?"

The perpetrator starts to cry. "I'm sorry," he whispers.

"I know what you did today," the brother continues. "Other people look at me like I'm crazy for even—and I don't, I don't care what other people think. Like, you're my brother. I love you. I want—I want you to—"

The shooter completely breaks down. There is a prolonged high-pitched cry before his body collapses in violent sobs.

The brother puts his head in his hands, then slams his hand on the table. He turns to the detective off-camera. "Can I hug him?"

The perpetrator, hysterical now, leans in. The brother quickly stands, walks over to his wailing sibling, and wraps him up in both arms.

—

It's instinct to cast aside mass shooters as monsters—their destruction is horrific and beyond comprehension. Collectively, they have claimed thousands of innocent lives and destroyed many more. Mass shootings are senseless, and they terrorize so deeply because they are so unpredictable, so inhuman.

That's why our societal response to mass shootings has been to wage war on the monsters. We've tried locking the monsters out. We've turned our schools into secure fortresses with metal detectors, bulletproof windows, and impenetrable doors. We've installed high-tech security systems in our workplaces, even stationed police outside our concerts and casinos to spot the monsters before they get in.

We've tried running from the monsters. Teachers time their students as they race through hallways single file to designated meeting spots where frantic parents will wait. We scan for exit points at the movie theater and sit in a seat on the aisle so we can be the first ones out the door.

We've tried hiding from the monsters. Hushed children huddle in fear in dark supply closets or hide behind bulletproof backpacks. Text messages alert employees to "shelter in place." Our workplace drills test how quickly we can stack chairs, dive under our desks, or crouch inside cabinets.

And we've even tried fighting the monsters. We've turned off the lights and practiced throwing our makeshift weapons—chairs, sharpened pencils, staplers, textbooks, binders, canned goods. We've named and shamed them on national television. We've hired good guys with guns to protect us from them.

America has been hunting monsters—even though they were among us before this—for more than two decades, ever since two high school seniors from Littleton, Colorado, murdered twelve students and one teacher before dying by suicide in what, at the time, was the worst high school shooting in U.S. history. Since that fateful day in April 1999, we've spent countless hours and billions of taxpayer dollars drilling, training, and preparing.

And still we are losing. The monsters aren't going away. In fact, there are more and more of them. And they are killing more and more people with each passing year. All the running, hiding, and fighting has failed.

It has failed because the monsters are not *them*. They are *us*—boys and men we know. Our children. Our students. Our colleagues. Our community. They're walking in and out of the same secure doors we are, past the same armed guards every day, like the rest of us. They're standing next to us when we rehearse for the next shooting. They're reading and watching the same media stories we are. They are not outsiders. They are insiders.

This fact may make mass shooters seem harder to stop. The reality is quite the opposite: It means we know where to find them, and with our research, we have learned how to reach them before they ever pick up a gun.

—

It was March 2, 2020, when we sat down with the childhood girlfriend of one of the most notorious mass murderers of all time. Little did we know that in just two short weeks, the entire world would be in the grip of a global pandemic and that the remaining interviews for this book would be conducted remotely. We did social distancing around the table as a precaution, but that only made the interview more difficult, because all we wanted to do was give this person a hug.

Our interviewee was understandably nervous—this was the first time she'd told her story to anyone other than her immediate family. It didn't help that we were meeting under the fluorescent light of a sterile university conference room, the type of place reserved for benign faculty meetings, not outpourings of emotion. Our interviewee was guarded, teary-eyed, her voice cracking. "When you label them monsters, you erase the ability for anyone to think someone in their life could do this," she told us.

She gripped the awkward teenage photographs and handwritten letters that she and the perpetrator had exchanged when they were young, years before he murdered more than a dozen people. They painted a very different picture from that in the newspaper clippings she also presented about the perpetrator—that he was born to kill, a maniacal psychopath, less than human. "We have to counter this narrative, realize and understand that people who commit acts of mass violence are human beings, human beings like you and me. Society needs to come to terms with that. Nothing will change until we do. We need to be able to recognize that someone in your life could do this."

For years now, we've been studying the people who commit these horrific mass shootings, the insiders who do monstrous things. We've interviewed five perpetrators of mass shootings in prison. We've met the families of mass shooters; their spouses, parents, and siblings; their child-hood friends and work colleagues; social workers and schoolteachers. We've sat down with surviving shooting victims, grieving parents, and first responders. We've even spoken to people who planned a mass shooting but changed their minds. In total, we've interviewed nearly fifty people directly involved in mass shootings. We've also pored over press and social media "manifestos," suicide notes, trial transcripts, and medical records—tens of thousands of pages of transcripts.

Our research is driven by a single, urgent, question: How do we stop the next mass shooting?

There is no one miracle cure, but there are things we can do today, and things we must do tomorrow, to end the mass shooting epidemic. That is why we wrote this book, and why we have genuine hope for a future where we can stop running, hiding, and fighting for our lives.

—

Throughout this book, we define a mass shooting as any event in which four or more victims (not including the shooter) are murdered with guns in a public location such as a workplace, school, house of worship, or restaurant. Four victims killed sounds somewhat arbitrary when you consider that all shootings are tragedies, that all victims deserve justice, and that what separates injury from death is often just a matter of aim or inches—but this is the threshold agreed upon by criminologists and the FBI.[1] Excluded from this definition are domestic shootings and gang-, drug-, and organized crime–related shootings—not because they are unimportant, but because the perpetrators of these crimes tend to target family members or intimate friends exclusively and have different profiles, motivations, and methods compared with shooters who select their victims more indiscriminately.

Using this definition, we find two things that are alarmingly clear about mass shootings in America: They are becoming more frequent, and they are getting deadlier. More than half of mass shootings have occurred since 2000, one-third since 2010. The deadliest year was 2018, with nine incidents, followed by 2017 and 2019, with seven each.

The death count per shooting is also rising dramatically. Sixteen of the twenty deadliest mass shootings in modern history occurred in the last twenty years, eight of them in the last five years—San Bernardino in 2015 (fourteen dead), Orlando in 2016 (forty-nine dead), Las Vegas in 2017 (sixty dead), Sutherland Springs in 2017 (twenty-six dead), Parkland in 2018 (seventeen dead), Thousand Oaks in 2018 (twelve dead), Virginia Beach in 2019 (twelve dead), and El Paso in 2019 (twenty-two dead). The names of each of these cities is now forever connected to scenes of death and destruction.

For decades, the toll of mass shootings has also risen. During the 1970s, mass shootings claimed an average of eight lives per year. In the 1980s, the average rose to fifteen. In the 1990s, it reached twenty-one; in the 2000s, twenty-four. The last decade has seen a far sharper rise. Today, the average is fifty-one deaths per year. At a time when the number of homicides overall was declining, the number of mass shootings was increasing.

Every mass shooting we experience eerily recalls the last. Initial media reports focus on the "tragic shock" of the crime and the chaos of the scene:[2] the rush of SWAT officers; the parade of ambulances and satellite trucks; bloodied and screaming survivors running through the streets; bodies on the ground; chains of survivors in the parking lots; families screaming out the names of their missing loved ones; friends hugging each other and sobbing. Then follows the "first witness reports," when survivors are interviewed for details of the crime and share raw, riveting, often contradictory accounts, which stations replay over and over again in the name of ratings.

Next comes the "identification of the shooter," dead or alive, from official sources, and the first appearance of talking head experts: researchers and retired police officers called on to speculate on motive or compare and contrast the "profile" of this shooter with the last. They respond to the public's need for a narrative with reasoning that feels digestible and holds the shooter individually responsible.

"Reports of the character of the shooter" follow, with the media going in search of anyone and everyone willing to comment on the life and crimes of the perpetrator, from his first-grade teacher to their next-door neighbor. By now, all major national news anchors and staff are on location, reporting on air with the crime scene in the background. The massacre is later "packaged" for syndication and broader consumption. Elaborate visuals such as maps and time lines are added, and the networks create their own "brand" for the incident, "breaking news" alerts complete with titles and a transition song.

Eventually, we get the "official response and official report," which brings some clarity to earlier conjecture, but in the absence of mystery, attention starts to wane. People stop asking "Why?" or calling for action. The news cycle moves on, and we move on—until the next shooting.

Mass shootings have become routine events in our lives. On October 1, 2015, following the shootings at Umpqua Community College in Oregon, when a student shot and killed his professor and eight students in a class-room, President Barack Obama went to the James S. Brady Briefing Room in the White House—a room named after a victim of gun violence—and said as much: "Somehow this has become routine. The reporting is routine. My response here at this podium ends up being routine."[3]

Our emotional reactions to mass shootings are dulled by repetition. Daily tragedy becomes ambient noise until, eventually, we grow numb to the pain. However, our fear of mass shootings is ever present. A 2019 poll found that a third of adults say they feel they "cannot go anywhere without worrying about being a victim of a mass shooting" and that they avoid certain places like movie theaters and grocery stores for this reason.[4]

For the younger generation, it is even worse. Born during the first few years of the twenty-first century, the youngest Americans, from high-schoolers on down, have never known a world without mass shootings. More than half of American teenagers worry about a shooting at their school, and a lifetime of active shooter drills, locker searches, and locked school doors has engendered in them an overwhelming fear of imminent death.

The active shooter drills are especially troubling. "This is not a drill," relays the voice over the PA system—despite the fact that it is. Suddenly, faculty and staff receive text messages warning of an active shooter on campus. They lock their classroom doors, pull down the shades, and turn off the lights. They instruct students to quickly, *quietly*, stack chairs and desks, to barricade themselves in. Fearful students then take shelter—in a closet, or on the classroom rug, positioned away from the windows should any bullets fly through. Many of the younger students cry. The older ones will text their last good-byes to their parents, who, in return, will flood the principal and the police with frantic calls. Then, when it's over, it's back to your regularly scheduled programming, like nothing happened.

In some lockdown iterations, a teacher or a police officer will engage in role-play, taking on the part of an active shooter, advancing through the hallways, attempting to open doors as children lie in wait. In the most extreme examples, paid actors covered in prosthetics and fake blood, will also role-play dead, or scream bloody murder.[5] Students may run past them in a zigzag pattern down the hall, so as to evade imaginary bullets; or defend themselves from a shooter by hurling textbooks, flip-flops, and sports equipment. Students in younger grades are primed by singing lockdown-themed adaptations of their favorite nursery rhymes.[6] Some are lied to that they're sheltering in place because a wild animal is loose. At an elementary school in Indiana, "four teachers at a time were taken into a room, told to crouch down and were shot execution style with some sort of projectiles—resulting in injuries to the extent that welts appeared, and blood was drawn."[7]

Resigned to this routine, some schoolchildren now affix a sticker to their ID or cell phone that reads, IN THE EVENT THAT I DIE FROM GUN VIOLENCE, PLEASE PUBLICIZE THE PHOTO OF MY DEATH.[8] Started by students at Columbine High School, the site of the shooting that ushered in the lockdown generation, the My Last Shot campaign was inspired by the graphic posthumous image of Emmett Till, a fourteen-year-old African American lynched in Mississippi in 1955 after being accused of offending a white woman. Till became a civil rights icon when his mother insisted upon leaving his casket open at his funeral: "Let the people see what they did to my boy," she was quoted as saying. Students involved in the My Last Shot campaign hope that a horrific photo of their dead bodies will send a message and lead to an end of mass shootings.

We can't leave our children to wage this struggle alone. And we can't allow mass shootings to continue to be a normal part of our lives. The more we partake in these familiar routines, the more they become part of our identity, and the harder it becomes to break them. But we must break this one.

—

On Valentine's Day 2018, we caught a glimpse of a turning point. Something seemed different in the country's outpouring of grief and outrage after a former student opened fire at Marjory Stoneman Douglas High School in Parkland, Florida, killing fourteen students and three staff. The response was rapid and far-reaching, uniting voices across the country who demanded that leaders take action to create real change instead of offering their, by now, routine "thoughts and prayers." Confronted with an overwhelming and compounding sense of loss, America vowed that Parkland would be the last mass shooting. The public was finally fed up with seeing funerals and candlelight vigils on the evening news; of seeing families and communities shattered beyond repair.

Organized with the support of several Hollywood celebrities, including George Clooney and Oprah Winfrey, more than a million people took to the streets to "March for Our Lives" in the biggest youth-led demonstration in a generation. For a time, lawmakers around the country had seriously discussed gun law restrictions and other comprehensive measures on the legislative floor, and it looked as though things might really be changing.

But for all the activism and attention, protests and political momentum, this horrific shooting generated, we eventually turned our attention elsewhere. Bills got caught up in the partisan gridlock that has gripped Washington in recent years, and mass shootings have remained an almost monthly occurrence, a grim fixture of American life.

This is why we started studying mass shootings four years ago. Frustrated that policy conversations arising out of grief, fear, and "common sense" weren't getting us any closer to the "never again" America kept promising, we decided to start from the bottom up to find solutions that would really work. And the first step to solving a problem is understanding it. We must learn why mass shootings are occurring more and more frequently and figure out who exactly the mass shooters are and what their pathway to violence looks like.

—

This book's two authors have been working closely together for a long time. We're both university professors in criminal justice and cofounders of a nonprofit violence research center, but it wasn't always that way. Jill's first job out of college was as a special investigator on death penalty cases for the New York Public Defense Office, and in many ways it was this experience that set us on the road to writing this book.

At the age of twenty-two, Jill spent her days on Rikers Island, New York City's principal jail complex, talking to men who had committed brutal, bloody murders, trying to reconstruct their journeys into darkness. Her very first client had kidnapped, raped, tortured, and murdered a woman just a few months younger than Jill. After days of digging through records and reviewing crime scene photos, Jill visited the jail for the first time, terrified she was about to meet Hannibal Lecter. Instead, she met a young, broken man with serious mental illness who had lived the saddest story she had ever heard. This became a familiar pattern, so much so that Jill developed a saying: "The worse the crime, the worse the story." It was always true. The stories never excused the crimes or meant the perpetrators were not responsible, but they explained how these individuals gotten to the point of committing such unthinkable violence.

While Jill was frequenting Rikers Island, coauthor James was navigating the prison-like structures of some of New York City's toughest public schools, working as a special education teacher. The experience gave him a deep appreciation for the storm and stress of adolescence, but only after he had moved back home to the United Kingdom did the purpose of his learning become clear. As a PhD student at the University of Oxford, James began studying gangs and serious youth violence. He spent his days and nights interviewing juvenile gang members and hanging out on street corners with drug dealers, watching them work.[9] Through this experience, he discovered, much like Jill, that even the most prolific violent offenders have stories—stories that put their crimes in context.

After being abolished in 1984 and then reinstated in 1995, the death penalty was again abolished in New York State in 2007, so Jill left the big city for the beaches of Irvine, California, and a PhD in psychology and social behavior. Minnesotans usually find their way back home, however, and Jill took an academic post in Saint Paul, at the same university as James, who had married a Minnesotan he met while she was studying abroad. We quickly learned we had similar research interests in violent crime, but, more important, we understood from experience working in the justice system that you can't prevent violence from occurring unless you fully understand its roots. And so it was that the two of us decided to join forces and pivot our research agendas to the topic of mass shootings.

—

It was June 5, 2017, one week before the first anniversary of the Orlando nightclub shooting, the deadliest mass shooting in U.S. history at the time, and there was breaking news of yet another mass shooting, once again in Orlando. A forty-five-year-old factory worker had killed five former colleagues and himself. The pundits, politicians, and "experts" were busy lining up the usual suspects: bullying, drugs, video games, psychopathy, mental illness, guns. It was all conjecture and partisan talking points. Jill said, sincerely, surely, we could do better.

As a psychologist, Jill was driven to understand the pathway that leads a person to the point of mass violence. What separates someone who kills four or forty people from someone who just kills one? What was their childhood and adolescence like? What was going on in their mind and what did they hope to accomplish? Are there fundamental psychological and behavioral differences between offenders who kill family members, partners, or friends first but then go on to kill victims at random, versus perpetrators who target people they have no personal connection to or motive against? What about perpetrators who target their schools or workplaces compared to those who kill at random in other public spaces?

As a sociologist, James thought it was important that we examine how society was affecting trends in mass violence. Was the rise in the number of mass shootings in recent years related to our current economic and political climate? What role did the internet and social media play? Just how allegiant were mass shooters to the ideologies they tapped into? When we focused our policy conversations solely on guns and mental health, were we missing the larger social factors at play that made mass shootings a problem unique to the United States?

We launched the Violence Project in August of that year. The goal was to gather as much information as possible about each and every mass shooter so we could look for patterns in the data and see if profiles emerged that might point us to new ideas for prevention. We made a list of every mass shooter in America from 1966 to the present day who had killed four or more people in a public space—172 of them—and started to interrogate their lives.

Two months into the project, the deadliest mass shooting in history occurred in Las Vegas, Nevada. On October 1, 2017, a gunman perched at the window of a casino hotel opened fire on a crowd of people at an outdoor country music festival, killing sixty and injuring hundreds. The scenes were horrific. They compelled us to immediate action. We worked with a team of undergraduate psychology and criminology students to build a database of mass shooters. Together, we coded each perpetrator based on more than 150 different pieces of life history information, creating the largest and most comprehensive database of mass shooters ever built.

There are basic demographic variables: age, education, gender, sexual orientation, race, religion, military service, immigrant status, and any criminal, gang, or terrorist affiliation. And not so basic: whether they grew up with a single parent; whether any parent had died by suicide; if they'd gone through a recent breakup or employment trouble; whether they had told others about their plans to kill ahead of time (known as "leakage"). A significant proportion of the variables deal with mental health: whether the perpetrator had been hospitalized for mental illness or prescribed antipsychotics; whether there was any evidence of suicidal tendencies or substance abuse. There's also a component on the firearms used: whether they were purchased legally, illegally, or stolen, and the method of purchase, such as private sale, gun show, or store.

We gathered this information from first-person accounts such as diaries, suicide notes, social media and blog posts, audio and video recordings, interview transcripts, and personal correspondence with the perpetrators. We also used secondary sources such as media coverage (television, newspapers, magazines); documentary films; biographies; academic books and journal articles; court transcripts; federal, state, and local law enforcement records; medical records; school records; and autopsy reports. Anything that could be found on the internet or in the occasional Freedom of Information Act request was included. We report on our findings throughout this book.

Public data were valuable in our research, but were far from perfect. After a few months immersed in the darkest corners of the internet researching mass shooters, we started talking about how helpful it would be if we could actually interview some of them directly. "Who do you think you are, Mindhunter?" one of our colleagues retorted, referencing the famed FBI criminal profiler John Douglas. Thinking back to those early conversations from the comfort of our faculty offices, we saw that the idea did sound preposterous. Still, if we could ask the perpetrators of mass shootings questions about why they had done what they had done and what they had been thinking in the days and weeks before their crimes, it might help us understand how they could have been stopped.

Knowing that it was a long shot, we decided to write letters to mass casualty offenders who were still alive—individuals who perpetrated, or attempted to perpetrate, shootings with the intention of killing four or more people. Almost all mass shooters die on the scene—either by killing themselves or being shot by police. But we wrote to all of the living mass shooters in prison, explaining that we were researchers, a psychologist and a sociologist, and that we wanted an interview. The focus of the interview was not the shooting itself but the perpetrator's life story leading up to the shooting. We were clear that they would not be paid or compensated in any way and that we would keep their names anonymous so they would receive no additional media or attention. To our surprise, five perpetrators wrote us back and agreed.

In addition to the shooters themselves, and in the hope of better understanding what had led them to kill, we ended up interviewing dozens of people who knew them and others like them, from their parents to their former grade school teachers. For nearly seventy years, investigators had used such "psychological autopsies," involving extensive in-depth interviews with friends, family members, and colleagues, often to determine motives behind suicides. We adopted a similar approach because the practice can also provide clarity in cases of mass murder.

We also interviewed mass shooting survivors, parents of deceased victims, security experts, first responders, and FBI investigators, because we needed to hear all sides of the story and account for the devastating impact of mass shootings. We reached out to some of these people, while others of them reached out to us. These interviews took place face-to-face, across the country, in offices, coffee shops, restaurants, or in people's homes, and they lasted hours. (A few, however, took place over Zoom during the COVID-19 pandemic.) People spoke to us because they wanted the shootings to stop. They wanted something good to come from their tragedy. They wanted their stories to save lives.

—

We spent one morning in the spotless kitchen of Tom and Caren Teves, loving parents who have experienced unspeakable tragedy. Over a brunch of croissants and fruit, we talked about their twenty-four-year-old son, Alex, whose face looked out at us from a wall of photographs. Caren described Alex as "the light of our family. He had a special gift—whoever he met he made them feel good about themselves. He was fun and funny. He loved to eat and explore. He was the life of the party."

Alex was a wrestler through middle and high school and attended the University of Arizona in Tucson for college. He then moved to Denver, Colorado, to earn a master's degree in psychology. Alex graduated in May 2012 with his whole life ahead of him. Then, in July, during a late-night screening of the new *Batman* movie, he was murdered in an Aurora, Colorado, movie theater. When the first shots rang out, Alex threw himself on top of his girlfriend, shielding her from gunfire. He died protecting her.

In the wake of Alex's death, the Teveses founded the "No Notoriety" movement. Hurt and angry at the amount of media attention the gunman had received after the shooting—his face was on the front page of every newspaper and plastered across newscasts for weeks—the Teveses challenged the media to deprive the perpetrator of the attention he sought. Name the perpetrator as little as possible. Don't show his face. Don't let him inspire others.

Throughout this book, we tell the stories of mass shooters. We do this not to glorify their actions but to understand how we can intervene earlier to prevent mass shootings before they occur. Our goal is to focus not on any one story or perpetrator but on what we can learn from the patterns in the stories over time that can help us prevent more people from dying. We also amplify the voices of the victims, survivors, heroes, and activists whose lives have been changed by these experiences to provide a full picture of this epidemic of violence, how it affects us on a personal level, and what people in communities all over the country are doing to fight it.

In support of No Notoriety, we will not be naming the perpetrators we interviewed, nor any mass shooter, throughout this book. We gave some perpetrators labels, and some minor identifying details have been changed. Great care has been taken to protect the confidentiality of any research participants who requested it, and unless an interviewee gave their express permission for us to use their name, we have anonymized the data to shield them from any unwanted attention.

—

The first letter we received from Perpetrator A was brief. It was written neatly in impeccable cursive on yellow legal paper.

> *Greetings.*
>
> *I received your letter today & would like to thank you for offering me the opportunity to participate in this study. It will be an honor to provide you whatever input/assistance I am able to contribute to your research.*

A few weeks later, Jill answered Perpetrator A's first call from a maximum-security prison. We had no control over when our perpetrator research participants were able to call us, so we had to be ready to answer their collect calls at any moment. If we missed a call, it could be days before they could call again. We set up our research line to run through Jill's cell phone when we weren't at work. This time Jill was at home with her three kids, so she stepped out on the back porch to take the call.

Perpetrator A was polite, formal, nervous—his Southern drawl was a little shaky: "So . . . this is a study about mass shooters?"

"That's right. We're studying the life histories of mass shooters, everything leading up to your crime," Jill began.

"What makes people like me do such awful things?" Perpetrator A asked. "Sounds like a pretty important study. It sure seems like it's happening a lot more often these days, doesn't it?"

Perpetrator A has now spent twenty-five years, more than half his life, locked up for killing four people and wounding seven others in a late-night restaurant shooting rampage, and in that time, mass shootings have only grown in number and severity.

———

Perpetrator B's first letter to us was formal, gracious, written in shaky block letters:

I RECEIVED YOUR LETTER, AND I THANK YOU FOR TAKING THE TIME TO WRITE ME. I HAVE CONSIDERED YOUR REQUEST AND HAVE DECIDED THAT I AM INTERESTED IN BEING A PART OF THE WORK YOU ARE DOING TO PREVENT VIOLENCE FROM HAPPENING IN THE FUTURE. I WISH YOU THE BEST DURING THIS HOLIDAY SEASON AND THANK YOU AGAIN FOR CONTACTING ME. I WILL LOOK FORWARD TO YOUR RESPONSE. GOD BLESS YOU!

Throughout this book, we will show our interactions with mass shooters like Perpetrator A and Perpetrator B in their own words, alongside those of many others throughout this book. Their stories help us question and challenge some common misconceptions about mass shootings and the policies that have followed. As we've synthesized our work, we have found that there *are* patterns in the lives of mass shooters that we see again and again. Understanding these patterns is, we feel, the key to unlocking solutions.

First, many mass shooters experience childhood abuse and exposure to violence at a young age, often at the hands of their parents. Parental suicide is common, as is physical abuse, sexual abuse, domestic violence in the home, and severe bullying by classmates. This early exposure to violence and unaddressed trauma feeds the perpetrator's rage and despair later in life. Mental health concerns such as depression, anxiety, and paranoia commonly develop during adolescence and are rarely identified or treated.

Second, nearly all mass shooters reach an identifiable crisis point in the days, weeks, or months before their violence—something that pushes them over the edge. For some, this is a relationship ending or the loss of a job. For others, it is an interpersonal conflict or mental health crisis. For the Parkland shooter, it was the death of his mother. Mass shooters communicate their crises to others in noticeable ways: in changes in their appearance or behavior, or specific threats of violence against themselves or others. Too often, others notice the crises but don't know how to intervene or to whom to report them.

For many perpetrators, this is a suicidal crisis. The rise in mass shootings in the United States over the past decade maps onto the dramatic rise among white men of "deaths of despair"—deaths by suicide, drug overdose, and alcohol-related conditions. Despite the level of detailed planning that many perpetrators put into their attacks, they rarely have escape plans, because the shootings are meant to be their final acts. But a mass shooting is a unique form of suicide, an angry one, meant to cause as much harm as possible.

Third, homicidal and suicidal ideation is fraught with uncertainty. Prospective mass shooters, looking for guidance, turn to past mass shooters for models of behavior, and the more they identify with them, the more they are influenced by them. They also turn on the news and scroll their social media feeds to watch the same unending coverage of mass shootings as the rest of us. A rise in shootings motivated by fame-seeking has coincided with the ubiquity of twenty-four-hour cable news, the internet, and social media. After studying and heroizing previous shooters, the next generation kills for the notoriety it brings, inspiring others down the line to follow suit.

Mass shooters are angry and lonely, and many of them fixate on specific people or groups they can blame for their own miserable circumstances. School shooters blame their schools. Workplace shooters blame their bosses and coworkers. Others blame racial groups, religious groups, or women. Searching for validation for their hateful beliefs, mass shooters not only research other perpetrators of mass shootings but also spend time in online communities where they become more radicalized toward violence. An increase in ideologically motivated mass shootings has coincided with the emergence of a newly emboldened far right and "involuntary celibates," who've forged national and even international alliances of hate online.

Finally, mass shooters must have the opportunity to carry out the shootings—access to firearms and to the people and places that represent their grievances. Firearms, especially heavy-duty weapons, are readily accessible in the United States at levels much higher than almost any other country. Most perpetrators buy their guns legally. Others lie on their applications or background checks are never run on them. Young shooters take their guns from their family members, most often parents and grandparents who don't have their weapons safely stored.

Childhood trauma, an identifiable crisis point, a script to follow and someone to blame, opportunity—Perpetrator A, Perpetrator B, and many more mass shooters share these four factors. Because mass shootings are extreme and comparatively rare crimes, we cannot say these factors are causal, only that they are highly correlated with mass shootings. There is no one profile of a mass shooter, only multiple pathways to a mass shooting, each filled with missed opportunities for intervention. This new framework acknowledges the complexity of the issue from the individual to the societal level and provides us all with concrete actions we can take to prevent the next shooting—actions that have a broad diffusion of benefits beyond mass shooting prevention.

—

We started this research unsure of what we would find. Maybe there was no rhyme or reason to mass shooters' lives. Maybe they were so set on killing people that there was little we could do to stop them. Maybe mass shooters really were monsters and the best we could do was run, hide, fight.

But talking to mass shooters and the people who knew them has given us reason to hope. We are not helpless. We don't have to accept the unacceptable. As individuals, as institutions, and as a country, we can break the cycle of violence, and this book offers a road map for how—because the power to change lives and the course of history in our schools, workplaces, and communities lies with us.

Mass shootings are not an inevitable fact of American life; they're preventable. Mass shooters are people who can be stopped before they do monstrous things.

CHAPTER 2
AMERICA

Kathy Whitman, a twenty-three-year-old high school biology teacher, was the first. The youngest was Noah Grace Holcombe; she was eighteen months old. Homemaker Louise Vocht De Kler was the oldest, aged ninety-eight. Professor Liviu Librescu, seventy-six, an Israeli born in Romania, survived the Holocaust and died trying to protect his students in Virginia. Sgt. First Class Danny Ferguson, thirty-nine, served in Kuwait, Iraq, and Afghanistan and died shielding his army colleagues in Texas. Lois Oglesby, twenty-seven, a mother of two, was studying to become a nurse. Allison Wyatt, six, wanted to be an artist, and rows of her pictures filled her house. Juan P. Rivera Velazquez, thirty-seven, and Luis Daniel Conde, thirty-nine, were a hairstylist and makeup artist, respectively, who owned a salon together.

More than twelve hundred people have been killed in mass shootings in the United States since 1966. If you subtract their ages at death from their life expectancies at birth, they represent nearly 40,000 years of life lost. They were men (60 percent) and women (40 percent) as diverse as the nation (64 percent white, 10 percent Black, 17 percent Latinx, 7 percent Asian). They were students and teachers, artists and entrepreneurs. Ten percent were still children, bright flames extinguished much too soon.

No other comparable nation has produced a list this long or this tragic. In fact, when you compare mass shooting rates in the United States to rates in other countries, you begin to see American exceptionalism at its worst. One study examined the total number of public mass shooters per country from 1966 to 2012 in 171 countries and concluded that, when controlling for national population size, the United States had six times its share of the world's mass shooters.[1] Notably, all five of the countries with the largest number of guns per capita, of which the United States was number one, ranked among the top countries for public mass shootings, including two countries with reputations for safety, Switzerland and Finland.

At the risk of understatement: Gun rights advocates are uncomfortable with this finding. In 2018, economist John Lott, friend of the National Rifle Association and author of the 1998 book *More Guns, Less Crime*, published a study trying to change the conversation. Drawing on data obtained from the University of Maryland's Global Terrorism Database and additional information from foreign news accounts, Lott said that he found 1,491 mass public shootings worldwide in a shorter time frame—between 1998 and 2012—and that fewer than 3 percent were in the United States. Instead of 31 percent of all mass shooters, Lott calculated that the United States produced only about 1 percent of them.[2]

The only problem was Lott had used a rather liberal definition of *mass shooting* that conflated the subject of this book with "battles over sovereignty," militia or guerrilla attacks, state-sponsored terrorism, and political acts of genocide. He also included a significant number of gang and group attacks, sometimes with twenty or more assailants, which have an entirely different methodology. When consistent definitions were used, Lott's own data confirmed the original finding: The United States had a disproportionate number of public mass shooters who attacked alone.[3] In fact, after merging Lott's data with ours, we found that with 60 mass shooters from 1998 to 2012 and only 132 foreign cases, the United States had about one third (60/192) of all mass shooters—exactly as the original study had said.

With 310 million people, the United States made up about 4.4 percent of the world's population of 7 billion in that same period, which means it had more than *seven times* (31/4.4) its share of the world's mass shooters per capita. In raw numbers, the United States had more mass shooters, respectively, than either Africa, South America, or Oceania—entire continents. More still than Europe, even though Europe has twice as many people. Only Asia had more mass shooters than the United States, but its population was thirteen times as large. And after the United States, the individual countries with the most mass shootings were not peer nations but the Philippines, Russia, and Yemen.

The United States is a lonely island when it comes to mass shootings. The question is: Why? As many people believe, America's gun culture is undoubtedly a major factor, but there is also something about America itself that is to blame.

—

One shooter in our study named his guns. He slept with them. He even simulated sex with them in a video sent to a former classmate a few weeks before his crime. "Look at the size of this thing," he told the camera, euphoric. "Weapons are not like people," he said. "They don't reject you. They need you. I wanted something that could not reject me." As he lay on his bed and caressed the Mossberg 12-gauge shotgun he had bought at Walmart, he added, "I love weapons. I love 'em with all my heart."

This shooter is not alone in loving guns. America's gun manufacturers doubled their annual output during the Obama years, sales fueled in part by fears of a federal crackdown on gun ownership after the 2012 Sandy Hook massacre, a crackdown that never materialized. And in 2020, amid the COVID-19 pandemic and civil unrest in the aftermath of the death of George Floyd, a Black man choked to death on camera by Minneapolis police officers, background checks, a metric for gun sales, hit an all-time high.[4] Since 2006, Americans have acquired an estimated 150 million new or imported firearms on top of the 250 million guns already in circulation. There are now more guns than people in the country—120 guns per 100 civilians. (For comparison, England and Wales have fewer than five.)[5]

Studies have found a correlation between local gun ownership rates and deaths from shootings.[6] There are exceptions to the rule—some Latin American countries with high levels of firearm homicide, like Colombia and Honduras, show low levels of (legal) gun ownership. The rate of gun violence in the United States is not the highest in the world—approximately thirty counties in Central America, Africa, and the Middle East rank much higher. However, those countries with high levels of gun violence, such as El Salvador, the Philippines, and Iraq, are not like the United States in terms of GDP, life expectancy, or education. Americans are ten times more likely to be killed by guns than people in other, similar high-income countries. At 4.5 per 100,000 people, the U.S. gun homicide rate is about eight times higher than the rate in neighboring Canada, eighteen times higher than in the United Kingdom, and twenty to thirty times higher than in Scandinavian Europe.

Americans sometimes see this as an expression of deeper problems with crime. In the 1990s, they blamed "super-predators," young, violent, cold-blooded street criminals who never existed,[7] and gangs, which did and were very much *Made in America*, as the title of Stacy Peralta's 2009 documentary about the Bloods and Crips of Los Angeles implies.[8] But the United States is not actually more prone to crime than other developed countries. A landmark 1999 study by criminologists Franklin E. Zimring and Gordon Hawkins of the University of California, Berkeley, found that American crime is simply more lethal.[9] A New Yorker and a Londoner are equally likely to be robbed, but a New Yorker is fifty times more likely to be killed in the process. After controlling for other possible factors, Zimring and Hawkins found that the discrepancy came down to guns.

America is one of the few countries (including Mexico, Haiti, and Guatemala) where the right to bear arms is constitutionally protected, and much like it contributes to the lethality of American violence, the widespread availability of firearms also contributes to the country's mass shooting problem. However, guns and gun culture alone are not enough to explain why mass shootings happen so much more often here than anywhere else. There are other social forces at work.

First, America was built on violence and has always been tolerant of it.[10] Violence against Native peoples; slavery rationalized a culture of violence against Black people, especially in the old Confederate states, where murder rates are still highest; a bloody Civil War; the revered violence of revolutionaries, frontier outlaws, and Prohibition-era gangsters; violence against women; violence against children; violence against immigrants; police violence; capital punishment; serial killers. America's history is a history of violence.[11]

Mass shootings are not some invasive species that infiltrated our lives from elsewhere. They have been part of the American landscape since at least 1903, when, on August 14, a war veteran deliberately fired into a crowd of people in Winfield, Kansas, killing nine and wounding twenty-five before turning the revolver on himself. Three more mass shootings shocked the country in the 1940s, including an infamous "walk of death" in Camden,

New Jersey, that killed thirteen people and severely wounded at least five others, but it was not until the summer of 1966 that mass shootings truly entered the American consciousness.

On a hot Monday in August, a former Eagle Scout and marine stabbed his wife and mother to death, then shot and killed fourteen people from a twenty-eighth-floor observation deck at the University of Texas campus in Austin. At first, stunned witnesses thought the gunshots were construction noise and the falling bodies were part of a staged protest against the Vietnam War. They quickly learned that the devastation was real. Law enforcement took more than ninety minutes to stop the shooting, eventually reaching the tower using underground maintenance tunnels. Reporters on the scene described the events as they happened, and the American public watched every excruciating minute thanks to the new medium of television. The modern mass shooting was born. Made in America.

Our database starts with this event and shows that American mass shootings are perpetrated by Americans—85 percent of perpetrators were born and raised here. Only 15 percent of mass shooters were immigrants from other nations, people who first came to this land of opportunity in search of a better life. We use this phrase deliberately because, in addition to a culture of guns and mass violence, America has a unique set of values—rugged individualism, the "American Dream," and the "pursuit of happiness." And these, too, may contribute to America's problem with mass shootings. For example, rugged individualism was forged on the frontier, far from civilization and the reach of laws, where gunslingers took justice into their own hands and where people pulled themselves up by their bootstraps. Firearm possession is perhaps its ultimate expression, but individualism assumes that you determine your destiny. It affords people undue credit for personal successes and undue blame for personal failures. By its very nature, therefore, individualism exacerbates the sense of injustice that anyone aggrieved feels. If an American, especially a white man born with all the advantages conferred by race and gender, can't make it here, it's his own fault.

In America, if you work hard, you are entitled to your success. At least, that's the myth. In a landmark 1938 study, sociologist Robert Merton argued that the American Dream guaranteed a level of success that was largely unachievable through hard work and sheer willpower. According to his "strain theory," society had fed people with false promises and had denied them opportunities to succeed in legitimate work. Writing just after the Great Depression, when hard work wasn't paying off, Merton argued that the very structure of American society pressured people to commit crimes.[12] People who failed to achieve what they were socialized to believe was their destiny, who found their aspirations for status and wealth blocked, were forced to adapt.

While millions of Americans feel these strains and never commit a crime, some lower-class men, who feel these strains most, may take what they feel they should have by stealing or being involved in other crimes. Others breed the kind of resentment and rage that can explode into mass violence.[13] In May 1927, in Bath Township, Michigan, a local farmer and school board treasurer was frustrated with what he felt were unfair taxes being levied on town residents to pay for a newly constructed school. He became further disgruntled when he was defeated in the township clerk election. Then his wife fell chronically ill with tuberculosis, a diagnosis that was terminal at the time. Facing foreclosure on his family farm, the farmer decided to take vengeance.

He first murdered his wife at their farmhouse by burning down the building. Next, he detonated several hundred pounds of dynamite and Pyrotol, an incendiary combination used by farmers during the era for excavation, which he had planted underneath the school. After the explosion, he pulled up alongside the gathering crowd in his truck as they frantically searched for their children beneath the rubble of the partially destroyed building. He then exploded the truck, which was loaded with metal debris, killing himself and sending shrapnel flying into those assembled. Forty-five people died that day, including thirty-eight elementary-schoolers, in what still stands as the deadliest mass murder at a school in U.S. history. When police and investigators arrived at the farmer's burning property, they found a wooden sign wired to a fence with the killer's last message stenciled on it: CRIMINALS ARE MADE, NOT BORN.[14]

—

The Bath School disaster wasn't a mass shooting because no firearms were involved, but the perpetrator has much in common with many contemporary mass shooters, including that he took his own life. Merton's strain theory, in fact, stands on the shoulders of a seminal study on suicide. Suicide tends to be viewed as a very individualistic and personal act, but French sociologist Émile Durkheim, widely regarded as the father of the field, offered a different take.[15] He found that the characteristics of communities influenced suicide rates, independent of who was living in those communities. Writing at the height of the Industrial Revolution, Durkheim argued that suicide was related to the amount of social integration and moral regulation one experiences, such that when society undergoes rapid change, the rules become unclear, people's aspirations run wild, and they no longer feel connected or fulfilled, suicide follows.

America's mythical code of self-reliance is implicated in high suicide rates, because there is a point where self-reliance becomes isolation.[16] Our research shows that mass shootings are linked to suicides and may even be a form of them. One in three mass shooters is actively suicidal *prior* to the shooting and 40 percent specifically plan to die in the act. It's rare for a mass shooter to flee the scene in disguise or execute a well-thought-out getaway plan to run for the border. The majority die by suicide after their attacks—around 40 percent by their own hand and another 20 percent by provoking law enforcement into shooting them (known as "suicide by cop").

The 1979 Grover Cleveland Elementary School shooter's infamous explanation of her motive, "I don't like Mondays," inspired Bob Geldof and Johnnie Fingers to write the Boomtown Rats' song. At a 2009 parole hearing, she explained the real motive behind her crime:

"I wanted to die. I was trying to commit suicide," she said.

"Why pick the school across the street?" the commissioner asked.

"Because I knew that if I fired on the school the police would show up, and they would shoot me and kill me. And every time I had tried suicide in the previous year I had screwed it up."

—

A third of shootings in our study occurred in just the last decade. In that same period, the United States has witnessed an equally troubling increase in deaths by suicide, drug overdoses, and alcohol-related conditions, which Princeton economists Anne Case and Nobel Memorial Prize winner Angus Deaton call "deaths of despair."[17] Few other countries have seen a similar explosion in deaths of despair, just as few other countries have seen a similar explosion in mass shootings. Perhaps the two are conceptually linked?

Deaths of despair occur when people fail to find meaning in life. In Case and Deaton's words, "People kill themselves when life no longer seems worth living, when it seems better to die than to stay alive." Deaths of despair have pushed down overall life expectancy in the United States by roughly three years, scientists report.[18] This is a trend not seen since World War I and the Spanish flu pandemic, or in other wealthy nations, which experience continued progress in extending longevity. During the first half of 2020, U.S. life expectancy dropped another year owing to COVID-19, but the disease itself was only part of the cause. Many people lost their jobs due to the pandemic. People in lockdown also were more likely to eat poorly, drink more alcohol, and use drugs. Relatedly, as people stayed home, social isolation and loneliness grew, and people took their own lives. The United States now leads the world in per capita spending on health care yet has the worst midlife mortality rate among high-income countries.

Deaths of despair have risen in nearly every age group over the last decade, but the increase has been especially pronounced for Millennials, anyone born between 1981 and 1996. Millennials are the largest living adult generation and over 40 percent of all mass shooters since 1998 fall within this cohort. Millennials have experienced acute financial stressors stemming from student loan debt, health care, and high housing costs. The oldest ones lived through the 9/11 terrorist attacks and entered the labor market in the recession that hit soon after. They spent their early years struggling to find work during a jobless recovery, only to be hit by the Great Recession in 2008 and another jobless recovery that depressed their lifetime earnings potential. Then, in 2020, just as they were entering their prime working years, Millennials got hit again, by yet another recession, this one triggered by the global pandemic.

Job loss hits especially hard in the United States, which lacks the social programs and support systems more common in other wealthy countries for when working families run into difficult times. Coronavirus laid bare that America remains the only large rich country without universal health care or a robust social safety net. Tying health insurance to employment means that when Americans lose their jobs, they lose their means to live in more ways than one. (During the recession of 2008 and 2009, about 3.9 million American adults lost their health insurance.)[19] The connection between work and happiness is also more intense in the United States, owing to the country's Puritan roots and Protestant work ethic.[20]

Workplace massacres are the most common form of mass shootings, accounting for about 28 percent of the total. They typically are perpetrated by angry employees who were recently fired or reprimanded—like the 2020 Molson Coors shooter, a fifty-one-year-old employee who was fired earlier in the day and then returned to the campus with a gun and killed himself after shooting his fellow employees. The Molson Coors shooter was Black, which surprised many commentators who assumed mass shooters were exclusively white. Part of this stems from biased media reporting, which, studies show, tends to be more sympathetic toward white shooters and inclined to describe them as mentally ill or the victims of society and circumstance.[21]

Only 52 percent of mass shooters are white (compared to 60 percent of the U.S. population), whereas 20 percent are Black (versus 13 percent of the U.S. population), and 8 percent are Latinx (versus 18 percent of the U.S. population). This means Black individuals are overrepresented among mass shooters by about the same proportion that white people were underrepresented, while Latinx are the most underrepresented group. Where we see the most Black mass shooters is in the workplace. Generations removed from slavery, Jim Crow, and "separate but equal," Black Americans still face hiring discrimination, skills-based underemployment, racial harassment and microaggressions for their being Black in a white workplace, fewer job opportunities, lower pay, poorer benefits, and greater job instability.[22]

Years before his crime, the Molson Coors shooter was targeted with racial harassment at work: A colleague placed a noose on his locker.

Workplaces are symbolic of unmet expectations and unrealized goals; by attacking them, shooters seek to exact revenge on the people and institutions they believe have kept them down. Just hours after submitting his resignation in May 2019, a disgruntled city employee fatally shot eleven coworkers and a contractor in a mass shooting at the Virginia Beach Municipal Center in the Commonwealth of Virginia. A public inquiry into events leading up to the shooting revealed that employees had talked about unfair treatment at work for years prior, to the extent that some believed violence in the workplace was almost inevitable. In our data, workplace shootings occurred most often among blue-collar employees without a college degree in small communities where a single company can anchor the local economy and in regions, like the industrial Midwest, that have experienced an acute loss of locally owned industry in recent decades.

While the U.S. economy has been growing ever since the 1970s, growth has increasingly been focused at the top. In their analysis of deaths of despair, Case and Deaton argue that one of the fundamental forces working against less educated Americans is a half century of in-work poverty and low wages. Real wage decline leads to job decline, and this deterioration in job quality and detachment from the labor force bring misery and loss of earnings, along with a loss of pride. At the same time as jobs are being outsourced abroad, or to robots or gig workers, working-class people are experiencing declining marriage rates and declining attachments to organized religion, unions, or employers—which is leaving them more isolated and disconnected.

Murder and violence tend to be higher in nations with the largest income inequality,[23] but as Case and Deaton argue, this "American experience needs an American explanation."[24] It's not just downward mobility that has some men feeling betrayed and contemplating death to themselves and others. In 1980, the population of the United States was 80 percent white. Today, that proportion is more like 60 percent and a handful of Southern states are majority minority. Within this context, sociologist Michael Kimmel argues that the modern push toward greater gender and racial equality in the United States (spearheaded by the Black Lives Matter and

Me Too social movements), which has intentionally challenged traditional white male privilege and power, has left some men feeling bewildered and "tenaciously clinging to an anachronistic ideology of masculinity."[25] Raised to expect unparalleled social and economic privilege, white men are suffering today from what Kimmel calls "aggrieved entitlement," a sense that those benefits that they believed were their due have been snatched away from them.

According to a recent study by the United Nations, men perpetrate 96 percent of all homicides, and this extends to mass shootings—98 percent of mass shooters are male. The reasons men commit ten times more violence than women, both in America and around the world, are many and could fill an additional book. Researchers argue that it's everything from evolution, biology, and hormones; to role models and gender socialization in homes, institutions, and society; to broader cultural norms and expectations. Suffice it to say, for mass shooters in our database, murder was rarely their first violent act—63 percent had a previous violent history. Over a quarter of our sample, 28 percent, had a history of domestic violence, with engaging in physical or sexual violence and coercive control against their wives and families as a precursor to committing a public mass shooting.

Cultural norms, reinforced in movies, sports, and our everyday lives, shape expectations for how aggressively men should react to any sense of status frustration and aggrieved entitlement, and violence is one such adaptation. Michael Kimmel suggests that the relationship between violence and masculinity is particularly acute among the group he labels "angry white men," because they can no longer "do" gender in traditional ways, such as economically providing for their households.[26] When American men lose their jobs, they lose more than their income; they lose their sense of self. It cuts to the core. In America, we admire winners, and winning in America is counted in dollars and social standing. A series of humbling cultural and economic shifts has left some of the long-standing winners in American society feeling humiliated and victimized, unsure of exactly where they fit in, longing to win again.

—

Donald Trump won the White House in 2016 owing in large part to white male resentment. Angry white men were key to Trump carrying Rust Belt states like Wisconsin, Michigan, and Pennsylvania and doing especially well in small cities and towns. Trump appealed to these men by vowing to "take back our country" and "make America great again." These slogans tapped a deep sense that the country was being taken away by immigrants and liberal elites and being betrayed by the big cultural transformations America had experienced over the last few decades, such as the movements for Black Lives and LGBTQIA rights—changes that Hillary Clinton supporters were leaning into and celebrating. A 2016 survey found that a majority of white Americans (56 percent), including three in four white evangelical Protestants (74 percent), believed American society had changed for the worse since the 1950s—it was no longer "winning."[27] "Make America great again" harked back to this mythical golden age of American greatness, a time of strong labor unions and plentiful manufacturing jobs that paid well, an era when white men had more political and cultural power.

This "nostalgic longing for a particular version of America" was also observed by University of Arizona sociologist Jennifer Carlson in her study of American gun owners, the "citizen-protectors."[28] White people are more likely to own guns than are any other racial group—men much more so than women. They are motivated by a desire to protect their wives and children and to defend themselves against people and places they perceive as dangerous, especially those involving racial or ethnic minority men.[29] And white men who have experienced economic setbacks or who experience a great deal of anxiety about their economic futures in general are the group of gun owners most *attached* to their guns.[30] They use firearms to compensate for their losses, as a way of retrieving, restoring, and reclaiming manhood.

And that is what mass shooters do when they take guns one step further and actually use them. A mass shooting is a matter of restoration: Although they are the ones who raise the gun and pull the trigger, mass shooters very often see themselves as the victims; they feel some great injustice has been done to them. Retired senior FBI profiler Mary Ellen O'Toole describes mass shooters as "wound" or "injustice collectors," people who stew in their anger.

They never forget, never forgive, and never let go, nursing resentment over real or perceived injustices until, eventually, they strike back.[31]

As a straight white man, Perpetrator A, the restaurant shooter, talked about feeling personally threatened by President Bill Clinton's "Don't Ask, Don't Tell" policy while he was in the military. "Don't Ask, Don't Tell" modified the military's strict ban on gay soldiers, instituting a policy by which officers would not seek out gays for dismissal from the armed forces. Not long after his shooting, Perpetrator A told a documentary filmmaker, "I don't think there's anywhere in our Constitution that gives anyone the right to be accepted by anyone else. When the Civil Rights Act was passed in 1964, people automatically assumed that they had a right to many different things. Women, Blacks, now carrying into gays. They feel like they have a right to be accepted. Who—who do they need to accept them?" Perpetrator A's sense of injustice was palpable. "They won't even let guys in the barracks hang a flag in their room anymore. It's almost as bad as our public schools—no prayer, no mention of God or Jesus Christ. Same as the military—you are gonna tell these guys that they can't speak out against homosexuals?"

—

If people feel society is unfair, then they are less inclined to play by the rules. In a seminal study, criminologist Gary LaFree found that the murder rate since World War II tracked almost perfectly with the proportion of Americans who said they "trust the government in Washington to do what is right" most of the time and who believed that most public officials are honest.[32] In 2016, Donald Trump courted disaffected and disempowered white voters by tearing up the political rule book and pledging to "drain the swamp." After he took office, his penchant for conspiracy theories (like QAnon, which falsely claimed the president was facing down a secret cabal of Democratic pedophiles) and frequent attacks on the "fake news" media, the federal government, and rival politicians—even fired former administration officials—helped sow seeds of discontent and erode trust in our institutions, from the U.S. Postal Service to the election process.

Writing in the *Washington Post* in 2017, historian Randolph Roth, author of the book *American Homicide*, warned that the growing trust deficit in America could lead to more lethal violence, including mass shootings. "When we lose faith in our government and political leaders, when we lack a sense of kinship with others, when we feel we just can't get a fair shake, it affects the confidence with which we go about our lives," he said. "Small disagreements, indignities and disappointments that we might otherwise brush off may enrage us—generating hostile, defensive and predatory emotions—and in some cases give way to violence."[33]

His words were eerily prophetic. The years 2017, 2018, and 2019 were the worst on record for mass shootings. And in 2021, a violent mob stormed the U.S. Capitol in an attempt to overturn the results of the 2020 presidential election, which Donald Trump baselessly claimed was fraudulent and had been stolen from him.

CHAPTER 3
TRAUMA

Perpetrator A, the mass shooter who killed four people in a restaurant, sent us a long letter about his childhood, written on sheets of yellow legal paper in his neat cursive handwriting. Almost as if he had rewritten it to look perfect. He apologized for how long it took him to write; he had been unable to afford postage stamps after he lost his prison job and was thrown in solitary for fighting. At the top of the first page, he had written and underlined the word *Childhood*. Each page was numbered and headed with his full name and inmate number.

> *I grew up in [city], a small town of 2000 people in [state]. The house I grew up in was a small three bedroom, one bath, home about a mile north of town. My mother was raised on a mid-sized farm (cows, pigs, sheep, chickens, ducks, horses, corn, oats, barley, wheat), one of four children. Her mom & dad were hardworking, catholic, alcoholic & abusive (physically) to each other + their children. She had one child prior to meeting my father (my sister). When she became pregnant with me, her dad wanted to kill my dad, so they took off + ended up in [Southern state] where I was born . . .*
>
> *Mom worked as a care provider at the State mental home in [city]. She worked hard, kept a clean house, cooked two-three meals a day + cared for us 3 kids as well as she knew how. She was quick to punish when we did wrong, cussed + smoked (rarely drank, maybe on her b-day). She had a low self-esteem + a basic education. She loved us + done what she could to provide for our needs + some of our wants. I love my mom, but it's hard not to lay blame at her feet for staying with my dad, who was extremely abusive in several ways. I think her childhood shaped her idea of what was acceptable/ normal in a marriage/family.*

*My father was a bitter, angry, abusive man. He could be gener-
ous to his friends or other family members, but those of us in his
house knew how controlling + violent he could be. He was also
raised on a mid-sized farm in that same rural area. One of four
children in a large farm-house shared by two brothers that married
two sisters with a communal kitchen separating the two sides. His
Aunt + Uncle had four children, also, so twelve people in one house
working one farm. I'm not entirely sure what all took place in that
house, but it wasn't good. I know he was abused physically + I suspect
sexually. He ran away at age 14 if that tells you anything. He was
raised Lutheran + the discipline was swift + severe. So, he brought
his own sense of "normal" behavior to our family.*

*He verbally abused all of us on a daily basis, beat my mom +
I, sexually abused my sister (his step-daughter) from age 11 until
he killed himself when she was 20 + reported the abuse. I lived in
fear of my dad.*

*When I was about 10 years old I heard my dad in my sister's
room one morning. He had to go through my room to get to hers I
woke up hearing her telling him to "stop, it hurts." I had an idea
of what was going on but wasn't sure until when he walked into
my room from her room. I quickly closed my eyes + pretended to
be asleep. He stopped beside my bed + said, "I know you're awake,
you little son of a bitch. If you ever say a word I'll kill all of you!" I
didn't move or make a sound & kept my eyes closed until he walked
out. I believed him & never said a word. My dad terrified me.*

*Dad would beat mom if she made him jealous or if she accused
him of cheating on her (which he was, with several women) . . . I'd
get beat when I really messed up + when I'd try to stop him from
hitting mom. Many times he beat me as if I were a grown man (fists
+ boots). I was yelled and cussed at in addition to slaps, punches,
kicks, and whippings. He forced me to work in the salvage yard
he operated from the time I was old enough to pick up a wrench.
I worked after school, weekends, + summers. He was more of an
abusive over-seer than a father to me. I learned many things from*

him: *carpentry, mechanics, plumbing, roofing, masoning, strong work ethics, what sex was by way of his porn collection, + how not to treat a wife + children. I still resent what he put our family through. He didn't drink alcohol or do drugs + was tough as nails. Just mean!*

My sister is almost 2 years old than I am. We weren't close or loving until we hit our late teens . . . Worked hard to help keep the house clean & would beat me if I didn't help her. Her +mom fought constantly + mom would often beat her with a belt or wire hanger or with slaps + fists. She tried to tell my mom about the sexual abuse but was beated for telling "lies."

At school they told us we could report our parents if they hit us (I was still in elementary school at the time). I got home + told my mom + dad + they said that if I did I had better hope the cops got there before they killed me / I'd be dead before the cops got there.

My little brother was five years younger than me + born with Cystic Fibrosis . . . He spent over half of his life in the hospital for months at a time. Mom would go visit him every night after work + fixing supper. It was a one hour drive to the hospital in [city]. She would take my sister + I alternate nights to visit him + dad would go once a week. [My brother] hated the hospital + would beg + cry for us to take him home every night. When he was home, my sister + I would have to get up at 6 am every week-day so we could perform his lung treatments before we went to school. He didn't like to do those either (Mom + dad would both be gone to work by 5:30 am). He didn't experience any physical or sexual abuse himself, but was exposed to what the rest of us went through. He + I shared a queen sized bed . . . He knew that he probably wouldn't live past his teens. We all knew it. He made it to 19.

Trauma is one of those words that's used so often, it's hard to know exactly what it means. Nick Haslam, a professor of psychology at the University of Melbourne, Australia, argues that the modern tendency of describing every misfortune as trauma, from reading or watching something offensive without a trigger warning to marital infidelity, is perhaps the most egregious example of "concept creep" in psychology.[1] The elasticity of the term, he adds, diminishes the experiences of people who have experienced true trauma.

Perpetrator A's childhood was plenty traumatic. His terrible and tragic circumstances feel qualitatively different from any experience that is merely upsetting or distressing. So, is Perpetrator A traumatized? It seems likely. But to really answer that question, we have to take a step back. Because trauma is an outcome. The input is childhood adversity, a broad concept that captures a wide range of circumstances or events that pose a serious threat to a child's physical or psychological well-being.

Common examples of childhood adversity include child abuse and neglect and family or community violence, but bullying, serious accidents or injuries, and discrimination also qualify. The majority of youth who experience some adversity don't demonstrate any serious clinical symptoms. Of those who do, there are various trajectories, but the majority will recover. For some children, though, these experiences have serious consequences, especially when they occur early in life, are chronic and/or severe, or accumulate over time. Adversity does not predestine children to poor outcomes, but research shows it can become biologically embedded during sensitive periods of development, meaning that without appropriate intervention, it can lead to lifelong physical and mental health problems.

These significant childhood adversities are sometimes referred to as ACEs, for *adverse childhood experiences*. The ACEs concept originated from a seminal study by Kaiser Permanente Health Care.[2] Between 1995 and 1997, researchers asked 13,500 adults in California about childhood adversities in seven categories: experiencing physical abuse, sexual abuse, and/or emotional abuse; having a mother who was treated violently; living with someone who was mentally ill; living with someone who abused alcohol or drugs; and incarceration of a member of the household. They found that the more ACEs an adult reported from their childhood, the worse their physical and mental health outcome.

Subsequent studies have expanded the definition of *ACEs* to include parental divorce and separation and homelessness, but no matter how you slice it, ACEs are linked to increased risk of heart disease, diabetes, substance misuse, and other negative outcomes. Those with the most ACEs, like four or more, also tend to have higher rates of mental illness. It's impossible to say that ACEs *cause* these negative outcomes—some children are more likely to be abused because they have disabilities or because they are being raised by parents with their own mental health problems that lead to abuse, masking the exact role of the trauma in this complex equation. However, the research overwhelmingly shows that ACEs do matter.

ACEs are surprisingly common. According to the Centers for Disease Control and Prevention, about two-thirds of adults report having experienced at least one type of ACEs as a child, and around 13 percent of people, such as Perpetrator A, have experienced four or more.

Which brings us back to trauma. Trauma is one possible outcome of exposure to adversity. According to the National Child Traumatic Stress Network, the American Psychological Association says trauma is "an emotional response to a terrible event," something "frightening, dangerous, or violent" that "poses a threat to someone's life or bodily integrity."

Certain types of childhood adversity are especially likely to cause trauma reactions in children, such as child abuse, the sudden or violent loss of a family member, or refugee and war experience. Witnessing a loved one experience violence, such as domestic assault, can also cause a trauma reaction. Children exposed to extremes of violence and abuse can develop PTSD, meaning they can feel stressed or frightened even when they are no longer in danger, and their experience of violence is played back to them in flashbacks and night terrors.

Our bodies are hardwired to react to adversity. When we experience it, the stress hormones adrenaline and cortisol flood our bodies, dialing up our heart rates and energy levels. Once a threat subsides, our bodies quickly return to normal. But when stressors are always present, and we constantly feel under attack, high alert can itself become normal, and the experiences of violence and abuse will remain in the cells of our bodies like an encoded shock waiting to be unleashed.

When your stress response is routinely activated, it is more likely to be activated in the future. Everyone responds differently, but a stress response can look aggressive, agitated, blunted, or withdrawn. These responses, if not understood, can push people away—teachers, neighbors, peers. When our fight-or-flight reaction stays turned on, it wears down the body and brain over time. This is called "toxic stress." Toxic stress changes how the brain makes connections and processes information, and because of this, children exposed to extreme, long-lasting adversity can have a warped view of the world. For them, the world is a scary, unpredictable, and unsafe place, and the adults in their lives cannot be trusted to care for and protect them.[3] It's enough to make people retreat inward into extreme isolation or lash out violently like Perpetrator A.

In 1989, psychologist Cathy Spatz Widom conducted a pioneering study on nine hundred individuals with experience of abuse prior to the age of eleven. She found a clear link between trauma and violent criminal behavior, showing that abused children were at a greater risk of being arrested later in life.[4] A later, larger study of more than one hundred thousand students in sixth, ninth, and twelfth grade found that each type of childhood trauma increased the risk of both violence against others (delinquency, bullying, physical fighting, dating violence, and weapon carrying on school property) and violence against oneself (self-mutilation, suicidal ideation, and suicide attempts).[5]

Other studies show that girls who experienced childhood trauma were more likely to have internally focused problems such as depression and anxiety, whereas traumatized boys were more likely to project their feelings outward, through aggression, hostility, and delinquency.[6] Childhood sexual abuse, physical abuse, emotional abuse, and neglect are all also strongly associated with suicidal thinking and suicide attempts in teenage boys and girls alike.[7]

———

For many mass shooters, an unpredictable and chaotic upbringing is the first step on their pathway to violence. In our database, we examined childhood trauma histories using publicly available records and sources. For many perpetrators, this was difficult, because little information was out there about their childhoods. For the 60 percent of shooters about whose childhoods we could find enough information, we found significant childhood trauma in over half the cases, or 55 percent; in the general population, that number was more like 15 percent.

Two profiles ended up emerging: those with childhood trauma and those with adult trauma. The shooters who experienced childhood trauma were most likely to be school shooters, college and university shooters, or place-of-worship shooters. In fact, nearly 70 percent of school mass shooters had a known history of childhood trauma. Perpetrators with a history of childhood trauma killed significantly more people than shooters without trauma (an average of ten versus six people). They were more likely to be raised by a single parent and more likely to have been bullied in school. Traumatized perpetrators were also more likely than other mass shooters to have a mental health history, have a problem with alcohol, and have a history of being suicidal. They were also more likely to tell people about their plans to commit a mass shooting before they did it.

Several mass shooters were abused by their mothers in childhood. In 1993, a nineteen-year-old shot and killed four people at a Chuck E Cheese restaurant. The perpetrator, a former employee, was apparently frustrated about being fired five months before and had sought revenge by committing the attack. He fled the scene of the shooting with stolen money and restaurant items. What is less well-known is that he was raised by a mother who had untreated bipolar disorder. She was physically, mentally, and sexually abusive to him throughout his childhood. Also, when he was fifteen, he walked in on his stepfather raping his sister.

Being abused by a father figure was even more common for mass shooters. The San Bernardino shooter, who (along with his wife) left fourteen people dead at a Department of Public Health Christmas party in 2015, was regularly beaten by his violent, alcoholic father, a man who had severe mental illness. The perpetrator and his siblings had to regularly protect their mother from their father's abuse.

Several other perpetrators had a parent die during their childhood. The twenty-one-year-old who killed four people by firing from the balcony of a motel in 1975 lost his father to suicide when he was thirteen. The perpetrator of a 2000 shooting spree at a car wash in Texas witnessed his father murder his mother when he was eight years old. Afterward, he developed a speech impairment that lasted through adulthood; his lawyer described him as "the worst stutterer I've ever seen." The 2018 Pittsburgh Tree of Life synagogue shooter's father died by suicide after being charged with attempted rape when the shooter was just seven.

A few mass shooters spent their childhoods in war-torn countries and came to the United States as refugees. The perpetrator who killed six people on a hunting trip in Wisconsin in 2004 had escaped with his family from the Laotian Civil War, known as the "Secret War in Laos" in the United States. The perpetrator recalled seeing dead children, and his mother reports that the family slept in the jungle, walked until their feet bled, and were afraid of wild animals. The perpetrator of the 2007 shooting at the Trolley Square mall, in Salt Lake City, Utah, was a refugee from the brutal Bosnian War, where he witnessed the murders of women and children, saw the sites of mass graves, and lived in the forest with no food, surviving on wild mushrooms. His brother and sister both died during the war.

Mass shooters often experienced more than one form of trauma throughout their lives, which sometimes could be traced generations back. For example, the perpetrator who killed four people at Lindhurst High School in California in 1992 came from a family with an "incredible amount of trauma," according to the psychiatrist who testified at his trial. The shooter's mother was sexually molested by several family members, his uncle was in prison for murdering three people, his grandmother had died by suicide, and his father had left the family when the perpetrator was a child. The perpetrator had chronic, permanent brain damage, possibly resulting from the spinal meningitis he contracted as a baby, which impacted his logical reasoning. At the age of sixteen, he was molested by one of his high school teachers on three occasions. He became obsessed with the incident, and his IQ dropped from a 95 to 84 the year after the abuse.

Mass shooters without a history of childhood trauma more commonly experienced significant trauma as an adult. They were more likely to commit mass shootings at restaurants, retail establishments, workplaces, and other public locations than at schools or colleges, which equally implies that their will to murder came later in life. Eleven perpetrators had a parent die prior to their crime. A number of other mass shooters lost a baby during childbirth, including the man who murdered five schoolgirls in an Amish schoolhouse in 1993, who had recently experienced the death of his infant twenty minutes after she was born; and the fifty-five-year-old gunman who killed five at Milwaukee's Molson Coors brewery in 2020, who lost a daughter in 2009 after she was born prematurely.

Veterans represent less than 8 percent of the total U.S. adult population, but 27 percent of mass shooters spent time in the military prior to their crimes. Several of them experienced traumatic events while on active duty. A Chicago man who shot and killed two people in an auto parts store in 1988 and then fatally wounded a police officer and a custodian at a nearby school was deeply troubled by his experiences as an army combat infantryman in the Vietnam War. The shooter who killed five travelers at the Fort Lauderdale airport in 2017 had watched two of his friends die in a bomb explosion when he served in Iraq. And the perpetrator of the 2018 shooting at the Borderline Bar and Grill in Thousand Oaks, California, which killed thirteen people, was diagnosed with PTSD after serving in Afghanistan as a marine. He witnessed people dying by IEDs, and many people he knew from the service had died by suicide.

—

Trauma feels like an overwhelming problem to solve. It often goes back generations, and the children may not even recognize what's happening when trauma is their normal. Perhaps the best example of this was in our interviews with Perpetrator B, the school shooter. Despite the abuse he had endured as a child, he was still somewhat protective of his family:

Tell us about your mother; what was she like?
Very loving, kind, and smart. She loved kids and loved being a mother. She was patient and encouraging as well. Faithful wife.

Tell us about your father; what was he like?
He could be strict but had good intentions.

How would you describe your childhood?
It was generally happy, but there were some scary and confusing incidents.

What were the scary and confusing incidents?
My father showed me pornography as a young child, and it disgusted me. My father would sometimes hit or grab my mother.

How often was there violence in your house? Were you afraid as a child?
Violence was not an everyday thing in our house, but more like several times a year. Yes, at times I was afraid as a child. There were good times, too. My father really did love us.

What was it like when you developed mental illness? How old were you?
I started to suffer from some depression during my childhood, although it was not diagnosed at the time, nor did I realize it. I was probably around six or seven. Around age fifteen, I began to suffer from anxiety, and then at seventeen, I developed severe depression and paranoia and suicidal thoughts.

A child who has been abused; who is shy and detached, or impulsive and unable to read others' cues; who elicits certain behaviors and treatment from peers and adults; who has endured trauma—such a child may have trouble making friends because he drives other children away. He may try the patience of adults. How do we as teachers, parents, doctors, and neighbors step in to help these children? How do we identify kids going through trauma, and is it possible to intervene to prevent the negative lifelong impact?

—

We interviewed several people who knew before a mass shooter's crime that they had experienced trauma in childhood but were unsure how to intervene because they lacked training or time or they didn't see it as their role. For example, we spoke to a current college professor who was the former preschool teacher of a mass shooter in the database. We found her name from previous media coverage about the shooting and reached out to her through her university email address. She quickly agreed, and we met over Zoom after canceling our flights to go see her in person.

The professor was previously a special education preschool teacher in a public school, working with about ten students at a time, and the perpetrator was one of her students when he was four years old. She describes him fondly as "withdrawn, quiet, shy, and very sweet." She continues: "He would hide under his mom's skirt. He didn't like playing with other children, and there was a sadness about him. He had some speech and language delays; I think English was his second language."

The perpetrator's mom would always drop him off at preschool each morning, so the professor got to know her pretty well. She remembers one morning when the mother came to the school with the perpetrator and his younger brother; the mother was crying and visibly upset. The professor is calm as she recalls the moment. "Her husband had held a knife to her throat and threatened to kill her and the two boys. I suggested that she go to a nearby shelter for battered women." The professor is quiet for a moment.

"Did she go?" Jill asks.

"She went. I think she actually ended up staying there for a few months, but she eventually went back to him."

Twenty years later, the professor was waiting in an airport, passively watching CNN on a television, when she saw that there'd been a horrific incident at the college where she worked. Someone had gone on a shooting spree, killing six people.

"He even sprayed bullets into a room of the library where students and staff were crouching. Can you imagine the horror?" She describes the moment she made the connection: "I was back at home a day or so later when the news released his name and his picture. I recognized him immediately. I was in shock. He was so quiet. So sweet-tempered. He was adorable. He wouldn't hurt a fly."

With time to reflect, the professor has become more convinced that the schools failed him—and that perhaps she did, too. "I never checked back in with his mom to see how she was doing. He needed a social worker to follow up. The mother did, too. The school needed to really help that family in an aggressive way. That moment was so critical—and she reached out to the school for help. *To me.* She was crying out for help, and we sent her away. I had no training in how to deal with that situation."

"Was there a reporting system? Did you document it anywhere?" Jill wonders.

She shakes her head, "No. I didn't report it to anyone." She feels the weight of the missed opportunity. "The supports are out there, but they are all in their different silos. Yes, the system is broken. But part of me thinks this is simple. Why wasn't this documented? We need one person to gather this information about our kids. One person to keep track of which kids are experiencing toxic stress, so they don't keep falling through the cracks like this. Someone has to be the one to step in."

———

In our current system, it's easy to fall through the cracks. Doctors and teachers aren't uniformly trained in how to recognize trauma or how to step in and help connect a child or parent with the resources they need. Parents may also refuse to consent to treatment owing to their own lack of understanding or fear or even their own trauma and the stigma attached to mental health.[10] According to the National Association of School Psychologists, 60 percent of children don't get the services they need due to access and stigma.

Untreated childhood trauma can cause permanent damage, but even if a traumatic experience itself cannot be undone, early detection can largely resolve its impact, because children are resilient. Safely screening for trauma at the doctor's office or in a school setting is the first step. A model called Safe Environment for Every Kid (SEEK) starts by training doctors and nurses in primary care settings in how to identify traumatic experiences in kids and talk about them with the children. Screening children in the doctor's office and connecting families with needed resources such as housing, crisis centers, and mental health care have shown a number of positive outcomes, like fewer reports to Child Protective Services and fewer reports of harsh physical punishment by parents.[8] They've also been shown to reduce emotional aggression from mothers and reduce domestic violence and parental stress.

However, even if a child is screened, it doesn't mean they can access the services they need. The homes of mass shooters were often chaotic and impoverished in addition to being violent. The idea of bringing a child to a therapist's office several times a week is unrealistic for many families. Then there are other barriers, such as lack of insurance coverage, lack of transportation, financial constraints, lack of treatment providers, and the stigma of seeking out treatment. Home-based intervention is one solution whereby a mental health practitioner visits the child at home to provide assistance. The Nurse-Family Partnership program (NFP) also sends nurses into homes to work with parents of young children. This program has been associated with a 48 percent reduction in rates of child abuse and neglect in families.[9]

Still, when we spoke by phone with school psychologist Eric Rossen, a national expert in trauma screening, he felt that school was the best place for screening to occur because every child is entitled to school-based mental health services, whether or not they have a formal diagnosis or can afford to pay. Unfortunately, there are too many barriers to treatment in clinical or even home settings, Rossen said, and by virtue of their daily proximity to children, school-based mental health providers can also better contextualize trauma and its treatment. The National Alliance on Mental Illness has called to expand school-based mental health services because they are so successful. In the best examples, school-based mental health centers offer a broad range of services, including assessment, treatment, case management, and individual therapy; these centers refer out only for the most severe cases or for ongoing family therapy. And as the Defending Childhood State Policy Initiative argues, trauma screening tools are so quick to administer (taking five to twenty minutes on average) that schools could easily adopt universal screening of *all* children, thus removing the stigma.

We reached out to Professor Katie Eklund, an educational psychologist at the University of Wisconsin–Madison, who specializes in trauma screening. We couldn't visit her in person due to the COVID-19 pandemic, but over the phone she told us, "We do screening for vision and hearing. And for academics. Why don't we do the same for social-emotional and mental health?" She went on: "Screening for trauma gives the data needed [for us] to know where to focus services and support. 'What grade level do we need to think about universal support?' 'About broader social emotional learning systems?'" She added, "If you screen the entire student population, about 10 to 15 percent of children will be identified as at risk. In schools with increased needs, more trauma exposure, lower SES [socioeconomic standing], it may be more like 20 to 25 percent. Schools know about a lot of students, but some of [these kids] aren't known to school staff. Screening data can raise a red flag. What do we need to know about this child? What other information do we need?"

Screening may be easy, but what comes next isn't. Only thirty-one states and the District of Columbia mandate school counselors, and when schools do have counselors on campus, the majority are overburdened. The American School Counselor Association recommends a ratio of 250 students per counselor, but over 90 percent of students attend schools with higher ratios. (The national average is 444:1.) Years of defunding in education have led to chronic shortages of social workers and psychologists in schools. A ratio of 500 students per psychologist is recommended, for instance, but to reach that goal, public schools across America would need to hire more than 50,000 new psychologists—the national average today is 1,500:1. And the numbers don't tell the whole story, because a lack of school personnel in general means that counselors, social workers, and psychologists often are repurposed in schools and tasked with other duties outside their area of focus or expertise.

The term *trauma-informed* refers to how practitioners work with people who have experienced trauma. Trauma-informed practitioners are doctors, nurses, teachers, school aides, administrators, social workers, and psychologists who embrace the idea that a cycle of care can overcome a cycle of violence. Communication is the primary focus of trauma-informed care. Being respectful and nonjudgmental, but also taking steps to make sure everyone feels safe in the space. A trauma-informed approach doesn't just help the trauma victim and their family. Eric Rossen quipped, "It's like seat belts; it's good for everyone."

Most trauma assessments are delivered to all children universally, to benefit all children in school. Responses include universal interventions like safety planning, trauma programming, classroom strategies, prevention programming, and family and community engagement. Then there is targeted trauma-informed programming for the highest-risk kids. However, in order for practitioners to help in trauma recovery, they need to be looked after themselves, by employers who offer adequate support and supervision.

In schools, teachers see children the most, so they need to know the signs of trauma, but in teaching teachers about trauma, "many of them in that moment begin to do some self-reflection and see it in themselves," explains Mona Johnson, executive director of Wellness and Support in the South Kitsap School District, located in Port Orchard, Washington. Johnson is herself a trauma survivor, having grown up around alcohol-fueled domestic violence. She is now a leading voice on the need for trauma-informed schools. Being trauma-informed means "being able to gently tell teachers they have their own issues to work on," she tells us, "because their own struggles can be a barrier to engagement for students."

Once teachers have worked through their own trauma and recognize the signs of exposure, decades of research shows that one of the best things we can do to help mitigate its effect is to teach children how to handle stress, resolve conflicts, and manage their emotions. This is often referred to as "social and emotional learning" (SEL, said as both *cell* and as an acronym), which involves helping children develop their skills in communication, problem-solving, conflict management, empathy, coping, and emotional regulation. SEL is not new, but in the years following the No Child Left Behind Act of 2001, so-called whole-child education took a backseat to high-stakes testing and narrow "common core" academic standards in mathematics and English language arts.

"Thankfully, the pendulum is starting to swing back," Mona Johnson tells us. SEL programs train children to understand the personal coping mechanisms that work for them, such as listening to music, walking outdoors, or playing sports, and to practice understanding what impact their behavior has on the emotions of other people. Reviews of studies looking at social-emotional learning programs constantly find that they reduce violence across ages and demographic groups.

Shortly after her six-year-old son, Jesse, was murdered at Sandy Hook Elementary School in Newtown, Connecticut, in December 2012 while in his first-grade classroom, Scarlett Lewis founded a social-emotional learning program of her own. Speaking to us on the phone, she describes finding a note that Jesse had left written on the fridge the morning he died—"nurturing healing, love"—which she grew to understand as his message to the world. She describes the worst day of her life as also the one that taught her the greatest compassion. "We don't choose what happens to us, but we always have a choice in how we react," she says in her TED Talk. "We can always choose a loving thought over an angry one." Scarlett created the Jesse Lewis Choose Love Movement to deliver social and emotional learning for free to schools, a valuable tool for helping children safely process any adversity in their lives. The program focuses on developing courage, gratitude, and compassion in children so that they might manage their responses to any situation.

—

Childhood trauma does not explain or excuse a mass shooting. Millions of children experience adversity or live with trauma, but only a tiny fraction of them ever goes on to pull a trigger. It's important to identify trauma in children, but its long-term impact is unpredictable. In fact, two children may experience the exact same type of adversity and respond in different ways. So, what separates someone who experiences adversity in childhood and develops heart disease in adulthood from someone who experiences adversity in childhood and grows up to commit mass murder? The characteristics of adverse events (such as their intensity, duration, or whether a caregiver caused the child harm) are important, but individual factors such as the characteristics of the person and their life experiences play a huge role. Gender identity, race, and socioeconomic status create variation. People have different genetic vulnerabilities, different personalities, different relationships with peers and significant others.

The Benevolent Childhood Experiences (BCEs) scale is a new instrument designed to assess *positive* early life experiences in adults that help mitigate the negative impact of adverse childhood experiences (ACEs). It asks: When you were growing up, during the first eighteen years of life . . .

- Did you have at least one caregiver with whom you felt safe?
- Did you have at least one good friend?
- Did you have beliefs that gave you comfort?
- Did you like school?
- Did you have at least one teacher who cared about you?
- Did you have good neighbors?
- Was there an adult (not a parent/caregiver or the person from the first question) who could provide you with support or advice?
- Did you have opportunities to have a good time?
- Did you like yourself or feel comfortable with yourself?
- Did you have a predictable home routine, such as regular meals and a regular bedtime?

People who answer yes to these questions tend to live with less psychological distress despite their high ACE scores and their adverse circumstances.[11] Eric Rossen is clear that context matters: "ACEs are a narrow view. It is ACEs combined with poverty, discrimination, historical trauma, food insecurity, which makes screening an incredibly challenging process. So it's not just 'What happened to you?' You need the context in which it happened and how it was perceived." Rossen explains that you can have a horrific experience, but if you are in a supportive environment or an understanding school, it might not affect you in a long-term way. We can't just look at traumatic experiences in isolation, without other things like family, support systems, and relationships. In doing so, we risk oversimplifying a very complicated picture.

The importance of context becomes clear when you look at the siblings of mass shooters who grew up in the same household and experienced a similarly traumatic upbringing—particularly male siblings, because men tend to engage in crime and violence more. For example, the perpetrator of the 2017 Las Vegas shooting was the son of an infamous bank robber who had spent eight years in the 1970s on the FBI's Ten Most Wanted Fugitives list for robbing three banks in Arizona, running down an FBI special agent with his car during his arrest, and escaping from a federal prison in Texas, where he was sentenced to serve twenty years. He fled to Oregon and was never recaptured. Prior to his life as a fugitive, he had four sons.

Four brothers, each raised by their single mother on her secretary salary. The oldest grew up to become the worst mass shooter in history. Another brother was in constant trouble with the law—vandalism, criminal threats, theft, driving with a suspended license. He was recently homeless and arrested for child pornography. The third brother described all the boys in the family as "bad kids," but the Vegas shooter had supported him growing up, and eventually he retired early thanks to the perpetrator's business ventures. The fourth brother is an engineer in Arizona, living a normal life. Four brothers, each with dramatically different outcomes in life due to genetics, personality, peer groups, and other life circumstances.

This sibling paradox was something Jill experienced firsthand while working as a death penalty mitigation specialist. Her first client, the one who had kidnapped, tortured, and murdered a young woman who was walking home alone, was just nineteen years old. The perpetrator had two older brothers, both of whom were in prison serving long sentences for violent crimes. He also had a younger sister, with no criminal record, who was doing quite well in high school. The four siblings each grew up in the same terrible conditions, removed from their parents' care for abuse and neglect at young ages. But there was one difference with the younger sister. Yes, she was female, but following their mother's death from a drug overdose, the sister was reunited with their aunt, who took a special interest in her. She bought her new backpacks for the school year and made sure she did her homework, checking in with her and providing things she needed. The sister spent a lot of time at the aunt's house; the two had a strong, trusting bond. The sister thrived, while the three boys spent their lives in prison.

According to the Harvard Center for the Developing Child, the single most common factor for children who are resilient in the face of trauma is a stable, committed relationship with a supportive adult in their lives. This adult could be a teacher, coach, extended family member, neighbor, or volunteer. These relationships with positive adults actually buffer against the impact that traumatic experiences have on children. To learn more about this, we sat down with Stefan Van Voorst, executive director of One2One, a nonprofit mentoring program for at-risk youth that is embedded in public schools throughout the Twin Cities. Van Voorst, a musician who years ago performed for audiences in the thousands, knows how to connect. He explains that the role of a mentor, whether formal or informal, is simply to walk alongside someone while they figure out who they really are. Listening is the most important skill. He jokes that "mentoring is an opportunity for mentors to grow ears and for mentees to grow mouths." When it is done right, however, the results can be powerful.

Van Voorst recalled a middle school student who was constantly getting into fights with her peers. One day, she disclosed to her mentor, a community college student only a few years older than she, that her mom and her sister had been arguing a lot. Her sister had once threatened suicide, and their mom had said, "Well, if she's going to do it, you might as well, too."

"The next thing you know, that student's cutting," Van Voorst explains. Knowing that story, the girl's mentor anticipated her behavior escalating, but the opposite happened. The student was now connected to her mentor, meeting with her weekly, opening up to her about her experiences and emotions. Van Voorst adds, "Her response to that event changed because the mentor was with her through that process . . . [The student] stopped getting into fights. So you went from a fight every week to zero fights. There was a mentor there working with her every week, so in the midst of a traumatic experience, she had somebody accompanying her through that. Someone walking with her. That was the difference."

We'll never know if something as simple as a positive relationship with an adult could have turned around the lives of the mass shooters in our study, but we know the majority of them had no one to turn to. As Perpetrator B told us, "People knew I was suffering, but they never knew how bad it was." If only he had had a relationship with an adult who could have asked.

CHAPTER 4

CRISIS

We meet Grace and Larry in their small, sunny West Coast home to talk about the downward spiral their son, Perpetrator C, experienced before committing one of the worst mass shootings in U.S. history. Over cups of tea and coffee, they start out by explaining the culture in their home: "We didn't promulgate a culture of talking. Be stoic, be grateful you have a good house, food on the table. I didn't encourage him to tell me what he was thinking or feeling."

Perpetrator C was attending graduate school, and to Grace and Larry, things appeared to be going well. He had his very first girlfriend, his own apartment near the university, and his parents were feeling hopeful about the future. It was Christmas break when they began to sense things going downhill. Perpetrator C came home sick with mononucleosis and spent the entire two-week vacation sleeping. After he returned to school, his girlfriend broke up with him. He called his parents to say that his classes weren't going well. "We told him that we would send him a ticket if he wanted to come home for Easter. [He] said he couldn't. He had one hundred slides to memorize and a ten-page essay to write," Larry remembers.

Grace and Larry didn't know it at the time, but their son had sought help from a campus social worker after disclosing to his former girlfriend that he was having thoughts about killing people. The social worker said he was "the most anxious person you've ever seen." Perpetrator C also saw a psychiatrist, who prescribed him Zoloft for anxiety and depression.

Grace serves us a lunch of salad and homemade soup. "He was getting sicker and sicker, and [the psychiatrist] kept upping the dose," she told us. You can hear the anger in her voice.

During his oral exams that spring, Perpetrator C mumbled unintelligibly in front of the panel of professors trying to grade him. He started isolating himself, playing violent video games one hundred hours per week.

During this time, Grace answered a call from his psychiatrist. "Did you know your son was dropping out of school?" the psychiatrist asked. "And because of this, I can't provide services anymore." Grace offered to pay out of pocket, but that was against university policy.

Grace immediately called her son to try to understand what was going on. He was more talkative on this call than usual. She offered to come visit him, and she and Larry booked plane tickets for a visit in six weeks.

The shooting took place three weeks after their phone call. Moments before he opened fire, Perpetrator C used his cell phone to call a local behavioral health unit for help. No one answered.

—

Eighty percent of all mass shooters in our database were in a state of crisis in the minutes, hours, days, or weeks prior to committing their shootings. A crisis overwhelms a person's usual coping mechanisms. Someone in crisis is like a balloon full to bursting. When you inflate a balloon, you apply stress, or tension, stretching the body over the air; and the bigger the balloon gets, the more likely it is to pop. A fully inflated balloon becomes so fragile that it must be handled carefully or it will break. A crisis is the same.

Struggling to manage his mental health symptoms, Perpetrator C was ready to burst, and failing out of graduate school was the final puff of air into the balloon. Our data show that mass shooters don't just snap, acting violently out of the blue. There's a slow build over time, with air being added to the balloon little by little. Small failures and indignations add up, so the crisis is more than the sum of its parts. For some mass shooters, the final blow is a major loss, such as having their wives leave them, or being kicked out of school or the military. For others, it's something smaller, like failing a class, being rejected by peers or coworkers, or experiencing paranoia that eventually becomes unbearable. For mass shooters, no matter the cause, reaching this crisis point makes them violently angry and hopeless that things will ever change.

Half of all mass shooters in our database had been reprimanded, suspended, or fired from work shortly before committing their crimes. Many were workplace shooters who killed their coworkers and supervisors. One, who in 1986 murdered fourteen people at the Oklahoma post office where he worked, had been rebuked for his tardiness and for misdirecting mail. The shooter who, in 1997, killed four people at the maintenance yard in Orange County where he worked had been fired for stealing scrap metal. And the man who went on a shooting spree in 2019 in the West Texas cities of Midland and Odessa had been fired from his job just hours before he killed eight people.

About one in four mass shooters had a relationship end right before they committed their crime, especially those who murdered people at restaurants and retail establishments. The shooter who killed six people at an Oregon restaurant in 1977 had just attempted suicide after his wife left him. In 2018, the man who killed four people at a car wash in Pennsylvania had been stalking a woman who had just broken up with him.

A number of mass shooters faced financial ruin prior to their crimes, which seemed to push them over the edge. The man who killed eight people during a shooting spree in San Francisco in 1993 had recently filed for bankruptcy. The perpetrator who murdered seven coworkers at a technology company in Massachusetts in 2000 had recently had his paychecks reduced owing to an IRS tax lien, which triggered a psychotic episode. And the perpetrator of the worst mass shooting in U.S. history, who killed sixty people in 2017, was a high-stakes gambler who was reportedly depressed after losing large in the Las Vegas casinos.

A true crisis is communicated through a change in behavior *from baseline*—something different or unusual from that person's norm, something noticeable. Parents, spouses, friends, coworkers, neighbors, pastors, mental health professionals, and even law enforcement report observing significant behavioral change in a majority of mass shooters.

For example, the perpetrator who killed four people at a Texas church in 2005 had previously gotten into an argument at church service and was asked to leave. He started screaming obscenities at neighbors and firing a gun while in his yard. He also left rambling, nonsensical notes on parishioners' cars and would yell at them as they left the service.

The Newtown, Connecticut, shooter, who murdered twenty-seven people, including twenty first graders, in 2012, had become a recluse, writing about violent and graphic things in his journal. He would spend hours dancing maniacally at a video game console in the lobby of a local theater.

One of the only female mass shooters in our research, who killed seven people at the post office in California where she worked as a carrier, had started shouting to herself not long before her crime. She ordered food at restaurants and then bolted out the door before eating. She would kneel in prayer at the roadside and even undressed in public parking lots prior to the shooting. This behavior was visible to the people who knew her, but there was no intervention; she was never connected to mental health resources.

—

Perpetrator A's second letter to us was focused on his "Adolescence." In it, he disclosed the following:

> I realize now that I was frequently depressed, although at the time I thought everyone felt like I did. I didn't know I needed help and probably wouldn't have admitted it if I had. Only "crazy" people needed mental help, right? I wasn't crazy and wouldn't have admitted to being so "weak" that I needed help.
>
> I thought about suicide many times. Even stuck the barrel of a loaded gun in my mouth a couple of times. I'd say fear and lack of commitment were the biggest reasons I didn't pull the trigger.

He sent us a follow-up letter titled "Adulthood." He labeled the pages 8–10, so we could connect the letter to his previous seven pages of correspondence. He described feeling completely "overwhelmed" at the time of his shooting:

> In addition to my military duties + studying for military courses I helped [my fiancée] study for nursing school sometimes until 1–2 am . . .

The signs that mass shooters were in crisis prior to their shooting

Increased agitation	67%
Abusive behavior	42%
Isolation	40%
Losing touch with reality	33%
Depressed mood	30%
Mood swings	27%
Inability to perform daily tasks	24%
Paranoia	24%
One to four signs of a crisis	43%
Five or more signs of a crisis	38%

Duration of crisis before shooting

Days before shooting	14%
Weeks before shooting	16%
Months before shooting	30%
Years before shooting	40%

I was a functional alcoholic + drank nearly every day. At lunch time, I would go to my room in the barracks + slam a pint of MD 20/20 Orange Jubilee + then eat orange flavored cough drops to cover it up. I normally kept 1/2 pint or pint of Jack Daniels in my trunk + would take a few swallows on the way home to my fiancée's house. Once home or off duty I would continue drinking mixed drinks or beer, especially if I was going out with friends. There were many times I drank alone, also.

In his next letter, titled "Prior to the crime" (labeled pages 11–15), he described the buildup to his crime:

There were quite a few things going on in my life right before my crime. I had just been informed that I would possibly be transferring to another military base, which I did not wish to do. . . . Fighting to maintain a semi-decent level of sobriety + not doing well with it. Adjusting to my promotion in rank and the role/duties expected of me. Adjusting from being single to engaged with two children. The constant worry of my little brother's battle with Cystic Fibrosis. Slight concern about finances/bills. I had a good bit on my plate + was doing my best to try + handle it all. With the mental/emotional trauma from my childhood still unresolved I can see now that it was only a matter of time before my juggling act collapsed.

The night before the shooting, Perpetrator A went out drinking with friends. He got so drunk that he slept at the army barracks that night. He didn't get up to go on a planned beach trip the next morning, and he didn't show up for his dress uniform inspection, either. Instead, he rented movies on his way home. When he got home, he crashed. His fiancée and kids were gone for the weekend.

I got up around 2 pm, got something to eat + started watching movies (the porn first, then "Sometimes They Come Back," more porn, etc. . . .)+ drinking. I had a fifth of Wild Turkey 101 + a 12-pack of

Coor's [sic]. Sometime that evening, I made a call to my mom + we
talked about my little brother, both of us getting pretty emotional.
I love my brother + was worried about him. I got so upset/crying
that my mom even offered to drive up from Florida to make sure
I was okay.

His mom never made it up to see him, because he committed the
shooting that night.

—

Much of our public policy debates have centered on the role of mental illness
in mass shootings. "Mental illness and hatred pull the trigger. Not the gun,"
President Trump said after the mass shootings in El Paso and Dayton that
killed thirty-one during the summer of 2019.[1] It's true that about six in ten
mass shooters have a history of mental health diagnoses or treatment, but that
fact conceals more than it reveals. The vast majority of people with serious
mental illness living in the community are not violent, and people with serious mental illness are more likely to be victims than perpetrators of crime.[2]

Just because someone has a mental illness, it doesn't mean their every
action is related to that diagnosis or that their mental health symptoms
directly cause all their behavior. Symptoms of mental illness wax and wane
over time, depending on factors such as treatment and stress.[3] In order to
understand if mental illness played a direct role in a mass shooting, we need
to know more than whether the perpetrator had a history of treatment or a
formal diagnosis. We need to know if they were actually experiencing symptoms when planning and committing the shooting and if those symptoms
influenced their decision to act.

It is difficult to assess the role of symptoms of certain serious mental illnesses in motivating mass shootings because some symptoms are
traits that motivate violence for individuals both with and without serious
mental illness. For example, irritability and hopelessness are symptoms of
depression, and impulsivity is a symptom of bipolar disorder, all traits that
potentially could contribute to mass shootings regardless of one's mental
health diagnosis.

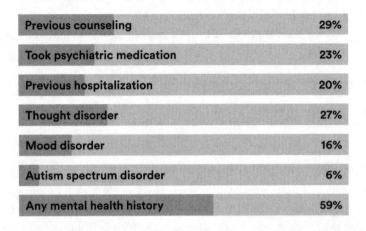

The mental health of mass shooters

Previous counseling	29%
Took psychiatric medication	23%
Previous hospitalization	20%
Thought disorder	27%
Mood disorder	16%
Autism spectrum disorder	6%
Any mental health history	59%

It's easiest to examine the role of mental illness in mass shootings when looking at symptoms of psychosis, namely delusions, and hallucinations. This is because delusions and hallucinations tend to be specific to a serious mental illness, and because they are not based in reality, they are easier to conceptualize as directly motivating violence, even if the vast majority of people experiencing them are never violent. Hallucinations can occur in any of the five senses—touch, sight, hearing, smell, and taste. Visual hallucinations, for example, include seeing shapes, colors, objects, or people who aren't physically there. Hearing voices is the most common form of auditory hallucination and is commonly associated with certain mental illnesses such as schizophrenia. Delusions, by contrast, revolve around concepts, ideas, and beliefs that are strongly held in the mind, such as paranoia, grandeur, or somatic delusions related to the body and its functions.

Our research finds that in 11 percent of cases, psychosis may have played a *minor* role in the shooting, meaning the perpetrator had experienced delusions or hallucinations when planning or carrying out the shooting that may have influenced their thinking or decision-making, but these were not the main motivating factor. For these shooters, psychosis may have reduced their ability to cope with other life stressors, contributing to their crisis point—as with the 2019 Midland-Odessa shooter who had been fired from work shortly before his shooting spree: He had been repeatedly hospitalized throughout his life for delusional beliefs about government conspiracies, which likely contributed to his actions.

In 9 percent of mass shootings, psychosis played a *moderate* role in the crime—meaning the perpetrator experienced psychosis prior to or during the crime, but they also had another motive. For example, the 2012 Oikos University shooter was failing out of school and, on the day of the shooting, planned to request a $6,000 tuition refund for the semester. After a university administrator did not meet with him, the shooter got angry and shot his fellow students at Oikos, a Korean Christian college in Oakland, California. However, the shooter was also diagnosed with paranoid schizophrenia and believed that the staff at the university were conspiring against him, alienating him from classmates, and surveilling him. He had started living in his car when he thought the university was wiretapping his home, then had abandoned the car because he believed the university had put a GPS tracker on it. A psychiatrist who examined the shooter before trial said he had auditory and visual hallucinations as well as delusions.

For another 10 percent of shootings, psychotic symptoms appear to have played a *major* role in the shooting, meaning the shooter experienced psychosis both prior to and during the crime, was responding to delusions or hallucinations in planning and committing the crime, and had no other discernible motive. For these shooters, a psychotic episode was their crisis point. For example, the perpetrator of the 2018 Waffle House shooting in Nashville, Tennessee, had been experiencing psychotic symptoms for years prior to the shooting. He believed that pop star Taylor Swift was stalking him, that they had met at a Dairy Queen, that she had scaled a building to get away, and that she and the police were hacking into his phone and bank accounts. A year before the shooting, he was arrested while trying to break into the White House to meet with President Trump. After his arrest for the shooting, forensic psychologists diagnosed him with severe untreated schizophrenia and found him incompetent to stand trial.

This all means that 70 percent of the time psychosis played no role in a mass shooting, meaning the shooter had no history of experiencing delusions or hallucinations either before or during the shooting. In other words, the data do not support blaming mass shootings *exclusively* on serious mental illness, as President Trump did. Doing so not only risks stigmatizing the millions of Americans who are affected by serious mental illness each year; it also misses other explanations and motivating factors.

Such stigma exists, in part, because the term *psychotic* is used frequently and interchangeably with *psychopathic* to explain mass violence in popular culture. They are, in fact, two distinct concepts. The latter is a personality disorder distinguished by grandiosity, a lack of empathy, limited emotional range, and manipulation. There is a vast academic literature on the exact nature of psychopathy, but colloquially, psychopaths are often described as narcissists with little conscience, which is a natural description for people who kill instinctively without remorse—people such as the character Dexter or Hannibal Lecter, the "psychopaths" we know and love from TV. Some experts argue that mass shooters *must* be psychopaths.[4] Why would anyone perpetrate a mass shooting if they had the capacity to truly understand its consequences? "Law-and-order" politicians, who favor individualized explanations for aberrant behavior over critiques of social structure, also like the label because it magically explains away mass shootings in their communities—the psychopath is the natural ally of the "monster."

People get labeled psychopaths largely based on the results of a psychological evaluation tool called the Hare Psychopathy Checklist—Revised, named for Canadian psychologist Robert Hare, who developed it in the 1970s. After years of research, however, expert psychiatrists and psychologists have concluded that the test cannot precisely or accurately predict an individual's risk for committing serious violence.[5] Psychiatrist Hervey M. Cleckley, who originally conceptualized psychopaths in his 1941 book *The Mask of Sanity*,[6] describes psychopaths as charming and glib, without empathy or the ability to experience the full range of human emotion. In his framework, Cleckley describes psychopaths as calm individuals, distinctly not anxious, which makes them immune to suicide. However, our research has found that mass shooters are neither charming nor calm, and they are certainly not resistant to suicide. Take the teenager who repeatedly texted his ex-girlfriend about killing himself the week before he killed four people at his Washington State high school in 2015. For most mass shooters, the psychopath label doesn't fit.

—

Molly reached out to us after hearing about the Violence Project on social media. Her initial email was a bit cryptic—she said she had a story to tell—so we didn't know what to expect when we met via Zoom. Turns out her story is about an incredible moment of crisis intervention.

Molly is engaging, with a loud, friendly voice and a bright smile. She's clearly an amazing middle school counselor. "I need to start at the beginning and then go straight through," she starts out. "That's the only way I can tell this."

She explains that she was a counselor overseeing seventh and eighth grades in a rural middle school in the South with around seven hundred students. One morning, a student approached her in the hallway and said she was worried about someone in her class; she had noticed cut marks under his watch band. Molly thanked the student for reporting and called the student in question into her office. "He opened up to me," she explains, "He seemed to have some delusional thinking; he believed he was part of the online music industry and some sort of pyramid scheme for others to advance in. I learned that his mother had passed away, apparently from a drug overdose."

The next morning, the same young man sought her out in the common area and asked to see her again. Molly was having breakfast with a colleague and hadn't started her day yet, so she told the student to go wait for her in her office. When Molly entered her office, she knew something was wrong. The student didn't make eye contact. He was wearing a gray Dickies jacket zipped all the way up, as high as it would go. He was sweating and fidgeting.

"As we started talking, I felt dizzy, like I was going to faint," Molly tells us. "Something just didn't feel right. He asked a number of strange questions, like 'Are there any drugs here? Where is the police officer's office in the school? What would you do if I pulled all the phone cords? Do you have any scissors?'"

Molly asked him what was going on.

He replied, "I need to tell you something, but I don't know if I can."

Molly's voice intensifies, and as she tells this part of the story, we feel like we're in the room with her and the student. "Immediately, I thought, *He has a gun. I'm going to have to talk my way out of this.*"

The student unzipped his coat and reached inside. "I bet no one has told you they have a loaded gun before?" he said and pulled out a 9mm. He also stood a magazine up on the desk and pulled out a holster from his ankle.

Molly got down on her knees beside him. She remembered some of the hostage negotiation training she had been through years before. She didn't know it at the time, but she now believes she had been trained for this moment.

"I needed to relinquish power to lower the emotion," she whispers to us. "I put my hand on his shoulder and interlaced my fingers with his."

The student told Molly that an entity had called him on the phone and told him that if he didn't kill everybody in the school, they would kill his family.

Molly started silently praying, *Lord, give me the words.*

"I came to you because I think you're the only person who can talk me out of it," the student told her, and then he asked, "Do you believe in God?"

She responded, "I do, but I can see that maybe you don't."

He was quiet for a while, then told her, "Do you know how many times I prayed for help and He never helped me?"

So Molly started praying out loud, the most heartfelt prayer she'd ever prayed. She prayed to remove the student's pain. They were both in tears. He raised the gun up at one point, and she truly thought he was going to shoot himself in the head, but all he did was scratch the top of his skull with his finger. They stayed there, kneeling on the floor and praying, for one hour and fifteen minutes.

"I'm going to stay here until you give me the gun," Molly told him.

He put the weapon's safety on and handed the gun to her. He put both arms around her. They hugged and sobbed for several minutes. She told him "I love you" and "I'm proud of you; doing what is right is hard."

She finishes her story, and we all take a deep breath. Molly believes she was meant to be there that morning, for that moment, to save all the kids at that school. We're all lucky she was.

———

A majority of mass shooters had a significant life stressor in the days, weeks, and months prior to their attacks, and they often made threatening communications, provoking concern from others, during this same period. The problem was, most people didn't know what to do with that concern.

Like CPR, crisis intervention is a skill anyone can learn—you don't have to be a doctor or psychologist. And, like CPR, crisis intervention can save people's lives. If a person in crisis is a balloon ready to pop, think of crisis intervention as the art of letting a little bit of the air out. It's not completely deflating the balloon, or figuring out then and there how and why it got so full, or making sure it doesn't ever get inflated again. It's not a long-term mental health treatment. Crisis intervention is nothing more than recognizing when someone is in a crisis and stepping in to help them through that moment. A crisis is a time-limited event. Crisis intervention is helping to take someone out of the danger zone and bring them back closer to equilibrium, to a place where the moment feels manageable again. This can be done for our coworkers, our neighbors, our families, or anyone in our community.

Crisis intervention is teachable. We know this because we've taught it to thousands of people over the last few years: police officers, teachers, journalists, church volunteers, college professors, and office workers. We started down this road by researching what protocols for crisis intervention various professions used, from policing to psychiatric nursing to special education. We went through hours and hours of existing training in various professional fields, looking for commonalities among the techniques. Jill spent forty hours in Crisis Intervention Team (CIT) training for police officers. We saw some questionable techniques that we knew couldn't be working ("Clap your hands in someone's face and scream their name"). We also reviewed published studies of crisis intervention strategies, looking for evidence of effectiveness.

The result of our research is a simple, effective four-step model:

- **Step 1: De-escalate yourself.** We can't help someone else in crisis when we are escalated ourselves. In psychology, this phenomenon is called emotional contagion—other people unconsciously pick up on our internal state. Have you ever been in a bad mood at home, and then, all of a sudden, *everyone* in your house is in a bad mood? If we're angry or panicked, it's impossible for us to calm down someone else who is also angry or panicked. The best way to de-escalate oneself is to take a few deep breaths, which literally stops our biological fight-or-flight response. De-escalating oneself also requires acknowledging when we are not the right person to do this because of our own stress and limits. A crisis is not personal. Although someone in crisis may hurl insults our way, crisis intervention involves knowing that the crisis is not about us and being able to brush off any negativity directed at us.
- **Step 2: De-escalate the space around you.** Having an audience is escalating. Someone in crisis should be in a private space, without others watching. When a student is in crisis in one of our college classrooms, we first ask them to leave the room with us. If that doesn't work, we send the other students in the class into the hallway, so we can talk to the student alone. Lowering the lighting and reducing noise and distractions also de-escalates. Helping someone through a crisis takes a bit of time, which often means pausing what was previously scheduled in order to be truly present.
- **Step 3: Use nonverbal communication.** When someone is in crisis, what we do with our bodies is significantly more important than what we say. Having an open body position, a soft tone of voice, leaning into the person, and sitting down are all helpful. Place yourself at eye level or lower than the person in crisis; looking down at someone can be escalating. Sitting down to talk, or even

kneeling next to them, is effective. Mirroring is something we all unconsciously do: We mimic the body position and posture of the person we're talking to. So, if we want someone in crisis to sit down and open up, we must do so first.

- **Step 4: Actively listen.** The final step is what we say, but rather than saying anything in particular, it's most important to listen. Active listening involves deeply and authentically listening to another person, with respect and without judgment or advice. A crisis is not logical. Although a person in crisis may be upset about something specific, trying to reason through the details of the situation is not helpful. The important part is focusing on their feelings. When someone is in crisis, naming what they are feeling—whether it is fear, anger, or hurt—is the most proven de-escalating strategy we have. For example, "It sounds like you're feeling really upset right now." When we understand what someone is feeling, they feel seen and heard.

Another component to verbal de-escalation is to provide two options to the person in crisis, so they are allowed to make a choice about what happens next. When Jill recently had a student in crisis in her classroom, she got her into the hallway, they sat down, and the student immediately began to sob and shake. Jill gave her two options, "Would you like to go into the classroom and get your backpack, and then we walk to the counseling office? Or would you like me to go get your backpack, and then we can walk to the counseling office?" Either way, the student was going to the counseling office. The student chose to have Jill get her backpack.

When someone chooses an action, they feel more in control, and they are more likely to comply. Being told what to do is escalating; providing agency and choice is calming. However, more than two options can feel overwhelming. Knowing what two options you have is part of preparing and training.

Many of these same principles apply when trying to de-escalate someone experiencing a psychotic episode, says Professor Diane Reis, a psychiatrist and innovator in behavioral health care. That is because a psychotic episode is itself a crisis. "The definition of a delusion is a fixed false belief," Professor Reis told us. "That means they can't be talked out of it. I don't argue with someone over the delusional nature of their belief. Instead, the goal is, again, to focus on their feelings: 'Wow, that sounds like a really scary thing to be experiencing. That must be really hard. What's that been like for you?' You don't negate or affirm the perception. If someone is delusional, we won't agree on the nature of the distress, but someone is in crisis, discomfort—we can agree on that, join with them in their distress. Acknowledge and witness it."

These principles also apply when talking to children and young adults in the aftermath of a mass shooting. It's only natural that young people would want to process the terrible events they have been exposed to by the media, social media, and overheard conversations about the shooting, but doing so as a parent or teacher can be tricky.

First, do not focus on the shooter, or the "bad man," because this will only increase the child's fear and threat perception. Focus instead on the needs of that young person and of the family, classroom, school, or community.

Similarly, do not say "Everything will be okay" or focus on "resilience" and how to recover, because this could come across as you not listening to the child's worries and fears. Instead, using language they can understand, calmly talk about your own feelings and thoughts about the shooting and about the positive coping strategies you have used that have been helpful during past stressful times. The goal is to avoid lecturing. Just try listening. Wait for the child to volunteer a question or thought, idea or fear, and then go from there.

Similar rules apply for someone in a suicidal crisis. When Jill trained to work on a suicide hotline in New York City in her early twenties, she was surprised by how simple and effective the training was. First, you have to specifically and directly ask the question "Are you thinking of hurting yourself? Are you thinking of suicide?" This can be a hard question to get out of our mouths to a neighbor, friend, student, or coworker. It can feel awkward. We're afraid that if we bring up suicide, we might put the idea in that person's head, but experience and evidence tell us that's a myth—you can't plant what was already there.

If someone says no when you ask the question the first time, explain why you asked: "Sometimes people going through what you are going through think about suicide." Then ask again, because you may get a different answer the second time. And you have to truly *want* to hear the answer. Sometimes we word the question like we don't want to know: "You aren't thinking about suicide, are you?" We have to be unafraid of hearing "yes."

If someone says they are thinking about suicide, there's no need to panic. We don't have to try to talk them out of it. We don't have to try to solve it. We need only remain calm and listen. Truly, deeply listen. Ask what's going on, and keep the person talking. Pose open-ended questions—questions that cannot be answered with a simple "yes" or "no"—and speak without judgment, again focusing on feelings. Unless it's an acute emergency—e.g., the person has already swallowed a handful of pills—you just need to be present for them and witness the pain they're experiencing. Let some air out of their full-to-bursting balloon.

Anyone can do these things for someone in crisis. The right person to reach out is the one to whom the person in crisis has revealed their crisis or who has noticed the other's crisis. It doesn't have to be the person with the right letters after their name. We have a tendency to think crisis intervention can be done only in a counselor's office. But the right person to step in often has a previous relationship with the person in crisis—a teacher, coworker, neighbor, pastor. In one averted school shooting we studied, it was the janitor who stepped in to de-escalate the student.

In his viral TED Talk,[7] Aaron Stark describes almost becoming a school shooter. He wanted to do a shooting at his high school, he planned to do the shooting, and he was suicidal and wanted to take others with him. But one night, a friend invited him over, and the friend's mother had baked a blueberry-peach pie in his honor. She had no idea what he was going through or contemplating doing, but they all sat together and ate the pie.

And that human connection and act of thoughtfulness were enough to get him through the crisis. The problems in the lives of mass shooters feel so massive and overwhelming, but sometimes it's the smallest act that can get someone through a moment, let enough air out of the balloon so they can breathe again.

CHAPTER 5

RELATIONSHIPS

Perpetrator B, a school shooter, began suffering from anxiety around the time he entered high school. By age seventeen, he had developed severe depression and paranoia. "Toward the last years of my adolescence, I was determined to commit suicide," he tells us. "I tried to kill myself when I was fifteen, seventeen, and eighteen."

However, a bright spot in his high school experience was meeting Lacy, a kind student who made it her goal not to let anyone sit alone at lunch or be bullied in the hallways.

We meet Lacy at a loud coffee shop in a Southern state; the place is full of twenty-somethings eating avocado toast and bowls of popcorn. We sit with Lacy at a small table and drink overpriced iced tea. Lacy is confident, engaging, and genuine. She speaks slowly, choosing each word carefully and never breaking eye contact.

She and her friends, "a strange group of people . . . nerdy, weird kids," by her own admission, let Perpetrator B sit with them at lunch so he wouldn't have to eat alone every day. "There were twenty of us or so who would gather kids who were being bullied. We were a protective place for kids who were treated poorly, like garbage, by the jocks," she tells us. "We offered to let [him] sit with us so he wouldn't get picked on."

Lacy worries, though, that this group could have contributed to Perpetrator B's problems. Some of those friends were "troubled teenagers spiraling down," "anarchists" who joked about school shootings. Others "tried to be edgy" by talking about Adolf Hitler and checking out as many library books about him as possible. "We had a lot of fire and bomb threats," she remembers, "a record number in eleventh and twelfth grade. Kids figured out that if you called in a threat, it killed at least thirty minutes of the school day."

She recalls Perpetrator B back then: "He seemed young and smaller than other boys his age. He didn't drive or have a car." She notes that she only ever hung out with him at school, "never outside of school." She explains: "I chose never to be alone with him. He asked me to prom. I said no, then asked someone else to cover for me." Lacy just had a bad feeling about Perpetrator B. "He wasn't a safe person. He didn't understand his own emotions or boundaries. He couldn't feel when people were trying to connect with him. He didn't understand when someone was trying to help," she tells us.

Lacy was probably the "first girl he'd ever talked to or he knew," and Perpetrator B quickly became infatuated with her, she thought, although he kept his feelings to himself until after graduation. After high school, he enlisted in the army, where he served for a year before being deemed unfit to serve.

"I began to suffer from depression and suicidal thoughts," Perpetrator B told us. "Then I tried to kill myself with a shotgun and spent a week in the psychiatric unit. I did not receive mental health treatment in the army. I felt relieved when I was asked to leave."

After his discharge, his mental health continued to unravel. He is brief in his letters; it's like pulling teeth to get him to elaborate. So we exchanged letters with him for months, to tease out more information:

How was your mental health prior to the crime?
Not good. I was paranoid, depressed, anxious, obsessive, homicidal, and suicidal.

You said you developed paranoia. What types of paranoid thoughts did you have?
Pictures were staring back at me and that there were cameras or recording devices in the air vents.

Did anyone know how bad your mental health was prior to this crime? Did family or friends notice?
No. My family knew I had begun to suffer from mental health problems but not how bad they were.

What did you think would happen to you after the crime?
I would either be killed by the police or myself. Or I would
be executed.

During this time, Perpetrator B became obsessed with studying other high school shooters and thought that God wanted him to commit this crime to "send others to heaven" and "end their pain and suffering." At a retail chain store, he bought himself a gun, which his mother eventually found. His parents agreed that he could keep the gun if he gave them the ammunition to hold.

Perpetrator B began sending Lacy letters telling her he loved her. She was a college student now, so her mother received the letters at their home. Eventually, Perpetrator B sent Lacy a VHS tape of himself holding his gun, saying he was going to kill himself because she didn't return his love. Lacy remembers that her little brother, who was thirteen at the time, called her that day "dying laughing"; he had the video playing in the background. But as the video went on, her brother's demeanor changed, and his laughter turned to tears. "He's saying he's going to kill himself. There's a gun in the background." Lacy was scared. She stayed with a friend overnight, thinking that Perpetrator B might try to find her. Her mother reported the incident to the police, and Perpetrator B was taken to a state psychiatric hospital.

The police told Lacy and her family not to worry, giving the impression that Perpetrator B would be hospitalized for a long time, that he would be cured of his problems. But as it works in our mental health care system, once Perpetrator B was stabilized and no longer deemed a threat to himself or others, he was released. He was far from "cured." A month later, Lacy was visiting home from college and bumped into him at the local movie theater. "He walked up to me and said he was sorry. His lip was bleeding, like he'd bit down on [it]." After an awkward exchange, Lacy went back to the police and asked for help. I was "super freaked out," she tells us, because he "knew my address and where my sister and mom lived. My mom even thought about moving." The police told Lacy that there was nothing they could do. Perpetrator B had committed no crime, and the hospital had released him.

"They told me to stop worrying. I asked if I should get a restraining order, and they said no," she recalls. "I told them he had access to guns, but they were brushing it off."

Around the same time, Perpetrator B went to see a social worker at a local outpatient treatment center, which was part of his discharge after-care plan from his hospital stay. We found the social worker through trial transcripts, and she invited us to fly down for an interview.

We meet her first thing in the morning, before her other clients, in her small private-practice office within a larger multiuse office building in an industrial part of town. We're seated on a comfy couch, as though we were patients, while she sits across from us in an office chair. She's friendly but guarded. This story is a difficult one for her to revisit.

She was only two years out of graduate school, working at a local community clinic, when Perpetrator B came in for a discharge appointment, scheduled as part of his release. He was suicidal and depressed, and the social worker noted that he had been in the hospital longer than a usual stay. "These are typically thirty-minute 'screening' appointments," she explains, "but this one lasted about seventy-five to eighty minutes. Off the bat, something was off. It was in the air, it was palpable, that something was really, really wrong with this guy and his world."

"What was it, exactly?" James probes. "Can you describe what you noticed?"

The social worker remembers what Perpetrator B told her—his obsession with the Columbine shooting, his anger at his father for being controlling, his perception of his mother as a victim. He talked about how the military had been an abusive situation for him. He also talked about a picture of a woman in a bathroom that moved when he looked at it. The social worker wondered if he was psychotic, but it was more than that: "He scared me. But . . . he didn't seem like a bad boy. He was a rule follower. He felt like a boy, a vulnerable kid who was fragile. I couldn't hospitalize him because there was nothing to hospitalize him on. He wasn't suicidal."

She made a follow-up appointment with him and then went immediately to a psychiatrist colleague for advice and assistance. She decided to contact an inpatient treatment program for psychosis, but they wouldn't take Perpetrator B on because they didn't think he was truly psychotic.

When Perpetrator B didn't show up for his scheduled follow-up appointment, the social worker tried calling him multiple times, but she couldn't get him on the phone. She even wrote him a letter. "There was nothing legally I could do. . . . I was a very small cog in a very big wheel," she laments.

A couple of weeks after his meeting with the social worker, Perpetrator B woke up and tried to die by strangling himself with a seat belt. When that didn't work, he decided it was time to commit the school shooting he'd been fantasizing about for so long.

The day of the shooting, Lacy got a text from her younger sister, who was hiding in the basement of the high school. "As soon as she told me there was a shooting on campus, I knew," Lacy says. The next day, another letter arrived. Perpetrator B had mailed it to her right before going to shoot up the school. "Don't worry, I'm not going to try to shoot your sister," he'd written. Lacy describes the letter as self-loathing. He also sent another video, but she didn't watch it. When she handed it over to the police, their response was "There's no way we could have known," she says angrily. So many opportunities to intervene had been missed.

Lacy's experience with Perpetrator B was "super traumatic." She spent years in therapy and is still "fearful of men in general." She thinks about the experience all the time—mostly, of all the opportunities for intervention that were missed. The experience certainly shaped Lacy's life trajectory: She now works as a special education teacher for children afflicted with emotional and behavioral disorders. She runs groups for high school kids who feel lonely and disconnected. She often thinks of the irony in Perpetrator B meeting all the criteria to be in the programs she now leads. She wonders what diagnosis he might have had, with his cyclical thinking and false impressions. Obsessive-compulsive personality disorder? Borderline personality disorder?

There is a calm about Lacy as she describes her current work—a sense of strength and resiliency: "I use the experience every day in my teaching practice. I'm intensely passionate about unstoppably advocating for students. What can we do to reconnect the disconnected to our community? We can't brush off brokenness."

———

The first time we meet Missy is at a small local coffee shop on a chilly November afternoon. She heard Jill talking on a local news station about our project, which had just begun, and reached out by email. Missy is in town for Thanksgiving, staying with her parents, who are watching her kids this afternoon. She arrived early and is sitting at a table with a large cup of coffee, a huge smile, and a pile of handwritten notes in front of her. She recognizes Jill instantly and jumps to her feet.

Missy is originally from Arkansas and has retained her country charm and Southern wit. She is warm and funny and easy to connect with. She taught high school math in her home state for two years before moving up to Minnesota because of her husband's job. She took a high school math teacher's position on the Red Lake Indian Reservation near where they moved. In her Upper South accent, she describes the community as small and close-knit: "Everyone knows each other," but "it's like a third world country; there's so much poverty."

Missy met the 2005 Red Lake school shooter during one of her first years teaching ninth-grade math. She still struggles to talk about him, her anger and pain cutting through her cheery and upbeat demeanor.

"He was not reactive. He was very difficult to bond with. He never made eye contact, and he didn't want to be touched," she says, though it's hard to imagine her unable to bond with someone. "He dressed goth; lots of kids did," but he liked to style his hair into devil's horns, she says. "He didn't really try in school; he just sat there; just took up space. He wasn't scary, just quiet. I just had a teacher gut feeling about him. I knew enough to leave him alone. There were kids that I would push; I would get in their face if they didn't do their homework. But I knew enough not to push him."

"Teacher gut"—that's what Missy calls it: that sixth sense that teachers sometimes have about their students that something just isn't right.

"Were there any warning signs?" Jill asks softly. "Anything you saw beforehand? When you had him as a student?"

Missy pauses; this story is difficult for her to tell. "One day in class, he said to me, 'Did you know Hitler liked math?'" The Hitler reference caught her attention. "Then he quietly slid up his sleeves to reveal the cut marks running down his arms. I sat down and told him that I was a mandated reporter," Missy says. "Then he said that he wanted to see [another teacher in the school]. I can't remember if the other teacher wrote it up or if I did.

"I realize now that he was asking for help," Missy goes on. "I can't remember if he ever came back to class after that day. But that was not abnormal there," for students to cut themselves, she says. Just a few months before, another student had died by suicide, so the faculty had been told to watch for cutting and to report what they noticed. But they had never been coached or trained in what to do in these situations, what to say or how to help.

What Missy didn't know was that the cutting incident was, in fact, just one piece of a much larger jigsaw puzzle of information. For example, she wasn't the only teacher who had trouble bonding with this student, about whom she had a "teacher gut" bad feeling. Other teachers felt it, too, but there was no forum or mechanism for them to share these concerns with one another.

Some of them suspected that the student had called in a bomb threat that once forced the school into lockdown. Others were alarmed that the student was writing admiringly about Nazis and Hitler in class, and drawing pictures of guns and death, but when one of them escalated it to the school counselor, they were told not to worry. Perhaps that's because the counselor didn't know that the student's father had died by suicide in a standoff with police; or that the student's mother was physically abusive and an alcoholic and had been permanently consigned to a care home owing to life-changing injuries sustained during a car accident; or that the student's grandfather had instructed his grandson to kill himself outside so he wouldn't make a mess on the floor; or that the student was being bullied and was failing classes; or that he had previously been treated for depression and suicidal ideation and on social media was posting stuff like the following: "16 years of accumulated rage suppressed by nothing more than brief glimpses of hope, which have all but faded to black. I can feel the urges within slipping through the cracks, the leash I can no longer hold." In a blog post, he had written that his "favorite thing" was "moments when control becomes completely unattainable . . . times when madden [sic] psychopaths briefly open the gates to hell and let chaos flood through."

The FBI investigation into the Red Lake massacre states that at least *thirty-nine* people knew the student was thinking about shooting up the school. Some students who suspected his plan even notified school authorities, but no one believed he would really do it.

Even though he had obtained a map of the school.

Even though he was obsessed with school shootings, so much so that he screened a movie about one in class and checked out from the school library a young adult novel centered on one, called *Give a Boy a Gun*.

Even though he loved firearms, had access to them, and used to "target practice" in the woods.

Even though his last online journal entry read:

So fucking naive man, so fucking naive. Always expecting change when I know nothing ever changes. I've seen mothers choose their man over their own flesh and blood, I've seen others chose [sic] alcohol over friendship. I sacrifice no more for others, part of me has fucking died and I hate this shit. I'm living every mans [sic] nightmare and that single fact alone is kicking my ass. I really must be fucking worthless. This place never changes, it never will. Fuck it all.

All Missy knew was that a student was cutting himself and that she had to report him to the counselor. She wishes only that someone had put all those little puzzle pieces together to see the bigger picture before he entered the school three years later and killed five students in her classroom.

—

The vast majority of mass shooters signal their intentions in advance, which is easy to see with hindsight but difficult to appreciate at the time. In fact, nearly half of all mass shooters tell someone that they are thinking about violence before they do it—again, something that threat assessment experts call "leakage."

Eighty-six percent of mass shooters aged twenty and under leak their plans in advance. Relatedly, K–12 school shooters are most likely to leak their plans and do so most often to their peers, increasingly online, in chat rooms or on social media—which makes sense when you think about how children and young people communicate. Shooters who leak their plans are more likely to be suicidal and to have been in previous counseling than shooters who do not, which suggests, importantly, that by leaking their plans, prospective mass shooters are in fact crying for help. Still, their mass shooting events show a high degree of planning, and the shooter is more likely to have studied past mass shootings. Shooters who leak are also more likely to include in their crimes an element of performance, such as a costume or a live video stream, which suggests leakage might even be a part of the act.

How do mass shooters leak their plans?

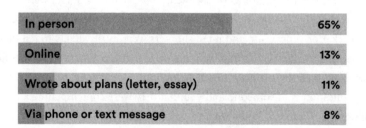

In person	65%
Online	13%
Wrote about plans (letter, essay)	11%
Via phone or text message	8%

Who do mass shooters leak their plans to?

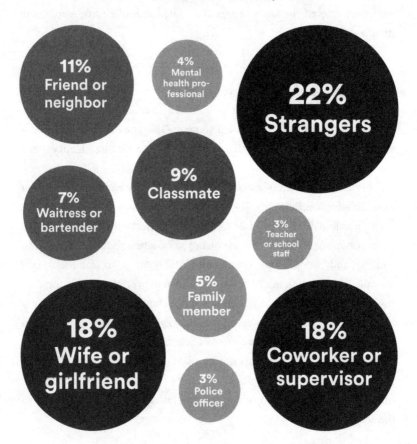

Of the perpetrators who leak their plans, school shooters were most likely to tell a classmate, workplace shooters were most likely to tell a coworker or supervisor, and retail shooters were mostly likely to tell their wives or girlfriends. The implication here is that most mass shooters told *someone*, and the majority told someone they knew on a personal level. The question is: If someone told you that they were contemplating a mass shooting, would you know what to do and who to tell?

—

The former principal of a rural high school that very nearly suffered a mass shooting spoke to us about the scariest day of his life. He recalled that it was a crisp fall morning when a six-foot-five-inch, 350-pound seventeen-year-old brought his father's 12-gauge shotgun to school in a duffel bag and assembled it in a boys' restroom. The student then changed into black clothes and a ski mask. When another student entered the bathroom and said the gun did not look real, the perpetrator fired a shot into the ceiling. No one was hurt, but the sound and recoil of the shot reverberating around the small tiled bathroom caused panic. The scared student ran out of the bathroom and to the principal, who happened to be nearby, doing his morning rounds.

Without thinking, the principal entered the bathroom alone. Standing outside the stall where the perpetrator had hidden, he convinced the shooter to put the gun down and then restrained him until police arrived some eight minutes later. "I just kept saying [his name], you're not going to do this today. We're not going to do this today," the principal tells us.

This was a school that routinely ran lockdown drills. It even had an active shooter response plan. But on that day, nothing went according to plan. The shot was fired at around 7:30 A.M. School hadn't even started yet. Students and teachers were still filing in and congregating in the cafeteria and hallways. No one had taken attendance. The marching band was practicing on the football field. Nothing was like what they had rehearsed in the lockdown drills they'd run for years. Teachers had no advanced warning, so no one was in their position. Also, the school resource officer was absent that day because he was visiting the nearby elementary school to talk about his career in law enforcement.

"You can't practice for the unknowable," the principal tells us. "There are too many variables."

We ask him what he thinks actually works. How can schools really prepare for mass shootings?

His answer is one word: "Relationships."

Relationships are key. Relationships enable someone to notice when one of their students, friends, colleagues, or coworkers is in crisis and on the path to violence. Relationships empower people to say something if they see or hear something. A common theme in our research was that people often did see or hear something indicative of violent intent, but there was a reluctance to report because they did not want to be seen as a "snitch"—or, in the case of school shooters, adults did not see threats made by children as viable. People were especially hesitant to call the police, who naturally are front of mind for this, because the police have limited tools in their toolbelt and a criminal justice response has the potential to do more harm than good.

In order for students to report their peers, they need to trust that the adults in the school will handle the situation well. A positive culture and climate, both of which provide time and space for teachers to connect with their students one-on-one and establish meaningful relationships, are critical to this endeavor. Students must feel they have access to at least one trusted adult in the building. Equally important is a centralized reporting mechanism with anonymous reporting options. Students must feel confident they will be protected if they say something, and if they *do* say something, someone will actually do something.

The FBI receives upward of twenty thousand tips from the public every week, and in the week following the 2019 mass shooting in El Paso, where a gunman shot and killed twenty-three people and injured twenty-three others in a Walmart, the Bureau's National Threat Operations Center received close to forty thousand.[1] Just four days after the massacre at Walmart, a thirteen-year-old boy was arrested in Weslaco, Texas, after making a comment on Instagram targeting another Walmart. A few days after that, a man was arrested in New Haven, Connecticut, after making a comment on Facebook about needing "30 round magazines" for a local Puerto Rican festival. Another man, in Tallahassee, Florida, was arrested after posting on Facebook that he was going to be off probation soon and would get his AR-15 back: "Don't go to Walmart next week," he wrote. A high school student in California made threats on Snapchat, sharing a photo of a gun case with the caption "Don't come to school tomorrow." And a fifteen-year-old boy in Florida was arrested because he had threatened online to kill several people at his high school.

We'll never know whether these threats would have been followed by shootings had the police or FBI not acted, or whether the subsequent arrests and criminal charges were an overreaction. The FBI has missed opportunities to prevent violence by not taking seriously past social media missives that promised violence. For example, the Bureau admits that it mistakenly chose not to investigate a credible and specific tip about the 2018 Parkland shooter, even after he posted a number of disturbing items online, including this comment on a YouTube video: "Im [sic] going to be a professional school shooter."

But we must not lose sight of the fact that in the vast majority of cases, any threat is really just a cry for help, evidence of an underlying personal crisis, so unless violence to self or others is credible and imminent, reporting options that can triage cases and adjudicate the best course of action from a menu of options may be better than reporting directly to law enforcement and funneling people into the criminal justice system. For example, "P3 Campus" is an anonymous reporting system designed for schools that students, teachers, staff, and parents can access as an app on their phones to register a wide range of concerns, from violent threats to signs of a mental health crisis.

P3 Campus is used by the Sandy Hook Promise crisis center, which launched in 2018. Based in Florida, the center handles tips from over a thousand school buildings across the country. It is staffed 24/7, 365 days a year, by ten counselors, all of whom are trained in crisis intervention and suicide prevention. On a daily basis, the center intervenes in dozens of threats of suicide and school violence that are reported through the app. The director of the center, Kenji Okuma, tells us, "The rate is alarming. The public really needs to see the frequency of which these calls are coming in."

Okuma put us in contact with his colleague Alexis, and we spoke on the one-year anniversary of her working as a counselor at the crisis center. Like Okuma, Alexis had previously worked in law enforcement, first as a beat cop and then as a crisis negotiator for the Bureau of Alcohol, Tobacco, Firearms and Explosives. When we met, she had just recently defended her PhD dissertation, a study of the inadequacy of trauma training in counseling master's degree programs.

Alexis walks us through how the center operates. First, Sandy Hook

Promise, a national nonprofit founded and led by several family members whose loved ones were killed during the Sandy Hook Elementary School shooting in 2012, trains all students, teachers, and staff in a school to use the P3 app. Then, if someone has a concern about a student, that person can pull the app up on their smartphone or go directly to the website to enter a "tip." Each tip includes basic information—who, what, where—and the school or district in question; the school is notified every time the app is used. Users also check a box to indicate if the concern is suicidal ideation, threat of violence, weapons, or mental health. Once the tip is sent, a crisis counselor is notified and has one minute to respond using the app's chat function. Typical starter questions are: Where are you right now? Are you safe? Is this incident happening now or later, or did it already happen? The goal is to gather enough information to assess how immediate the threat is.

Alexis stresses that she's not working a counseling line: "The goal is resolution of one form or another. Does this incident need law enforcement? Does the school need to be notified? Is there someone at school the student is comfortable talking to? Or a family member? We aren't going to let it go. We are going to make a plan for the next step."

The counselors work in three shifts: 7:30 A.M.–4:30 P.M.; 4 P.M.–1 A.M.; and midnight–8 A.M. The day shift is busiest, especially over the lunch hour or right after school. A couple of counselors work the evening shift because "as our boss says, teenagers get existential at night," Alexis laughs. The midnight shift is quietest, but calls that come in then can be more serious. Everyone works together as a team—one counselor may call the school in question while another keeps chatting with the student in crisis. Counselors are trained to handle four to five tips at one time, which Alexis says is stressful. But typically they are working with only one to three tips at once.

It is not a perfect system. There are hoax calls and times when the app is used to bully someone. A bunch of students will report a kid all at once, targeting them as a school shooter when they are not. It's awful for the targeted student, but rare, and the counselor can usually figure out the truth pretty quickly. The pros of teaching people to "say something" and safely report any warning signs and potential threats still outweigh the cons, Alexis says.

The test of the crisis center's efficiency is the absence of something, a nonevent, which really is the paradox of prevention. As a researcher herself, Alexis is mindful of this, but when she looks back on her first year on the job, she is satisfied with the results: "There have been times where we've intervened to avert a shooting. Or times when a student reports that someone has a gun in their backpack, and we are able to tell someone at the school, who goes and finds it. There is a lot of success with suicidal kids, where law enforcement is able to transport a kid to the hospital before anything happens."

"What's the hardest part of the job?" James asks.

She answers quickly: "It's not always knowing the outcome. You chat with these kids, and you always want to know; you'd like to hear that they got help. We don't always know how much we're averting. That's impossible to measure."

Anonymous reporting in schools has been shown to increase students' willingness to report weapons in school settings.[2] With anonymity, students feel insulated from possible retaliation or social consequences. Okuma says that, ideally, any crisis center would send potential threats to crisis response teams to handle, but most communities don't have such teams in place. Instead, they often end up relying on local law enforcement, especially if there are weapons involved. "We try to make sure we leverage all of the resources responsibly and effectively," he tells us. "We don't want to cause additional harm by traumatizing them." Okuma, who became the director of the crisis center after a long career in law enforcement, reflects, "I think I've done more in the last two years of my career than I did in the first twenty-four."

—

Whether the mechanism is an anonymous app, an online form, an email address, or even a jar with paper and pencils, reporting someone in crisis is only the beginning of the intervention process. The next step is to refer them to the right resources. To do this well, schools need in-house teams that can assess students' risks and needs and provide necessary follow-up. A team approach is critical. And because no one person feels responsible for the ongoing well-being of a student in crisis—because that's a heavy cross to bear—no student gets lost in the shuffle.

The first step to building a crisis response team is deciding who should serve on it. The team can be dynamic, with individuals joining it on a case-by-case basis depending on the student under question. The core team will likely comprise the principal, a counselor or nurse, a teacher, a school resource officer or local law enforcement representative, a community mental health provider, and parents or peers who can advocate for the student under question. The team has to determine how often, when, and where they will meet and how they will communicate. Its members must also determine what level of behavior or crisis would initiate an immediate meeting beyond regularly scheduled check-ins. Specific threats of harm against self or others should be handled by the team immediately, for instance.

The second step in initiating a crisis response team involves identifying what resources are available, both within the school and in the surrounding community, for students who are in crisis and in need of services. Resources should be identified in each of the following areas: mental health (school-based or community-based); substance abuse treatment; social services; housing; education, employment and training; community crisis response teams; peer support; parent and family resources; and local law enforcement. Any missing resources need to be identified. The team should establish contact with each resource, asking the necessary questions in order to connect each student in crisis:

Who is the point of contact?
Exactly what services are provided?
Are you taking new clients/patients?
Is there a wait list?
Is there a fee associated with the service?
Do you take insurance?
How are referrals made?
What is your location? Your hours?
Do you have emergency appointments?

A crisis will look different for each person. For some students, signs of a crisis may be loud and disruptive, while for others, signs of a crisis may look quiet and withdrawn. The third step for the crisis team is to define what types of behaviors or concerns need reporting to them. Over 90 percent of K–12 school mass shooters end up being current or former students of the school they shot up; therefore, it's critical for schools to investigate any threats made *while that child is under their care*. However, any marked changes in behavior from baseline or "normal" should be treated just as seriously, because each crisis is a unique and fluid situation. Small signs of a crisis for one person may signal significant concern.

What are those signs? At the Violence Project, we focus on "the four *Ds*":

1. **Disruptive behaviors:** behaviors that interfere with the environment, such as unruly or abrasive behavior, a low tolerance for frustration, or being unusually argumentative;
2. **Distressed behaviors:** behaviors that cause concern for the person's well-being, such as marked changes in performance, appearance, or behavior; unusual or exaggerated emotional responses; or signs of hopelessness, despair, or suicidality;
3. **Dysregulated behaviors:** behaviors that cause others to feel uncomfortable or scared, such as a withdrawn, isolated, or depressed mood; agitation; an inability to complete daily tasks; suspicious or paranoid thoughts; or writing or drawing with unusual or concerning themes; and
4. **Dangerous behaviors:** behaviors that threaten safety or well-being, such as harassment, stalking, intimidation, procuring weapons, threats of harm to self or others, or planning or rehearsing violence.

This is not a complete list of signs to look for, but it offers some initial guidance. In each area, concern would be related to a *marked change*—something noticeable that feels different—from a student's usual behavior.

Some behaviors obviously require immediate law enforcement action, but unless they are absolutely necessary, punitive measures that may contribute to or exacerbate the crisis, such as school exclusions or criminal charges, should be avoided. The 2018 Parkland shooter had been recently expelled for disciplinary reasons, proving that simply removing a student from school does not eliminate the threat of violence. Expulsions may in fact cause a student in crisis to escalate quickly. Step four in building a crisis response team thus is establishing criteria for times and situations when law enforcement will be asked to support or take over an assessment and, similarly, when community resources should be called in.

The next step in the process is training all school community members (teachers, students, coaches, volunteers, etc.) to recognize the warning signs of a crisis and respond to them appropriately using crisis intervention, de-escalation, and suicide prevention techniques. Everyone needs to know what types of behaviors to report to the team and exactly how to report them, ideally through a central reporting mechanism. Tied to this, the team should create a communications plan and host information sessions explaining who they are and what they do to parents and other community stakeholders.

When responding to a report of a student in crisis, the team should create an individualized action plan that is guided by answers to the following questions:

Who has a previous relationship with the student?
Who is in the best position to make an assessment?
How will that person reach out?
When and where will the assessment take place?
Who else needs to be interviewed (e.g., parents, teachers, school staff, or peers)?

Once someone connects with a student in crisis, ask them what they meant by their comment or action:

What did they think would happen next?
What resources do they need?

How quickly do they need them?

Are there others who should be contacted to support them?

The action plan should identify what resources will be used, how the student will be connected to those resources, when follow-up conversations will take place and with whom, and whom the student can reach out to in case of an emergency.

We spoke with Chris, the education director at a charter high school in the Midwest, who had attended our mass shooter prevention training the year before and embraced the crisis response team model. His high school is a drop-in recovery school for around 350 students who have lived through significant trauma. The school has crisis teams made up of advisors, teachers, social workers, therapists, and administrators. The teams meet frequently, at least twice a week and sometimes more, to discuss the well-being of their students and to exchange information.

Chris is passionate about this system-wide approach, explaining, "If you are being mean and hostile in class, but I don't know that your dad died last week, that becomes a self-fulfilling prophecy. Now you are punished, you are excluded, it's criminalized. We have to figure out what's going on with students before we punish them."

The advisors are full-time staff, many recruited from the local community, and each is responsible for twenty to twenty-five students. Their goal is to get to know each student and their family and to be their advocate. Chris describes how advisors check in with each student daily by email, phone, or text: "It's a daily reminder that 'I *see* you and I *value* you. I acknowledge your existence.' It's critically important to do that daily wellness check." A central focus of Chris's school is wraparound services: "Showing care. Getting to know young people. That's the path toward success. It's about trust. And strong relationships."

Crisis response teams should be universally mandated in all districts and schools, and if they're mandated, they should be funded. Money is available for school safety; it's just a question of how we spend it. In 2019, Fruitport, Michigan—a town of just over a thousand people—announced that it was spending $48 million to redesign its high school campus to minimize casualties in the event of a mass shooting. The plan included curved hallways to shorten a shooter's line of sight, hidden wing walls to give students more places to hide, and an alarm and lockdown system to isolate a threat at the touch of a button.

Across the United States, a $3 billion school safety industry trades in Kevlar backpack inserts, bulletproof whiteboards, impact-resistant film for classroom windows, "ballistic attack–resistant" door shields, armored safe rooms, surveillance cameras, facial recognition systems, software to monitor potential threats, gunshot and "aggression-detector" microphones,[3] and even smoke cannons to disrupt an active shooter in progress.

There's no evidence that any of this "hardening" works.[4] The fact that school shooters are nearly always schoolchildren, well versed and practiced in how to access the school and move through any security upgrades, forces us to rethink this school security theater. Classical deterrence measures designed to keep the bad guys out are really just locking them in.

We spoke with a retired FBI special agent who responded to practically every school shooting over a twenty-five-year career and who now consults on active shooter responses. He stresses caution in relying too heavily on hard security measures to stop a shooting. He says every shooting is "dynamic," because mass shooters are always adapting, trying to circumvent the obstacles, learning from precedent. If the only thing that stands between a shooter and a shooting is a reinforced door or a pane of bulletproof glass, then we've missed a lot on the front end, he says.

"[Shooters] are not averted from the security," the special agent tells us. "They are averted from someone saying something, someone reacting to spillage from the perpetrator" when they leak their plans.

School shooters are schoolchildren. In addition to *preparing* for a mass shooting, teachers, staff, and students are well placed to start *preventing* them. They do this by building warm and trusting environments that encourage reporting and by instituting crisis teams that can respond quickly and appropriately to a student at risk with care and compassion rather than punishment. This takes a shift in our thinking about what school violence prevention and public safety look like. It's not metal detectors and bulletproof doors. It's noticing when children and young people are struggling and then giving them what they need to thrive.

—

We meet Tim at a fancy café overlooking a pristine lake filled with yachts in a wealthy suburban neighborhood. He is sitting in the corner booth, drinking a cup of coffee. Tim is a scientist and manager at a medium-size Midwest company where Perpetrator D, a workplace shooter, worked as a machine operator for the past decade.

"He was fairly talented at his job—but also difficult and introverted," Tim tells us. "He was hard to communicate with and give feedback to. He had no friends. But he wasn't obnoxious. He had strange eyes."

"What do you mean, strange eyes?" Jill probes.

"Almost like he had no soul."

Perpetrator D had never missed a day of work . . . until he started arriving late almost every day—sometimes ten minutes, other times an entire hour. When his line manager confronted him about it, Perpetrator D just hung his head in silence and gave no response.

"Afterward the media said he had schizophrenia, but we didn't know that at the time," says Tim. "I had no idea he was mentally ill."

While Tim was on a business trip in Europe, the owner and line manager made the decision to fire Perpetrator D. They had sent a formal letter to him a week earlier with a final warning, but his tardiness had continued. When Tim returned to the office, he was greeted by the human resources director, who told him that everything was prepped for Perpetrator D's termination. Tim didn't agree with the decision, "but I wasn't going to argue," he tells us. Then the HR director had to take Friday off for personal reasons, and she asked Tim if he'd fire Perpetrator D in her absence.

The next day, Friday, Tim called Perpetrator D into his office late in the afternoon, along with his line manager. Word had already gotten out that Perpetrator D was being terminated. Tim had a large manila envelope with Perpetrator D's name on it sitting on his desk. He told Perpetrator D that the company was letting him go. He handed him the envelope and went to open the door of his office. When he looked back over his shoulder, he saw that Perpetrator D was holding a gun.

Without warning or speaking a word, Perpetrator D shot Tim twice in his right side. He then shot his line manager several times, including once in the head. He left Tim's office and entered the owner's office next door, where he fatally shot him. He then calmly walked past two secretaries outside their offices, one in the process of dialing 911, and down to the machine floor, where he shot two more employees and one of his supervisors. He then went down to the basement, sat on a chair, and shot himself in the head.

Tim was lucky to work close to a level-one trauma center. The first responders and doctors saved his life. It's taken many years, but he's finally starting to feel okay physically again.

People are buzzing around the café, but Tim's story has left the air heavy at our table. "How has it changed you?" Jill asks.

Tim's response is flat, controlled: "I don't laugh as much, I don't tolerate as much, I trust people less."

———

Like Tim, Jon Harris has experienced significant trauma in the workplace. About ten years ago, one of his colleagues, someone he knew was struggling in life, died by suicide in the office parking lot the morning after he was laid off. The man used one of ten rounds of ammunition on himself. Jon has always wondered whether the other nine rounds were meant for him and everyone else in the building.

James meets Jon at a local chapter meeting of the American Society for Industrial Security (ASIS), a professional organization for security professionals like him. Jon doesn't scream "security professional" when you see him—he's not an ex-military, ex-cop, take-no-prisoners type of guy—and it is clear from sidebar conversations between agenda items that he has a bigger story to share. Later, over coffee on a cold Minnesota morning, we talk over the specifics of creating a system of identifying and managing data that point to someone in crisis—something Jon has been working on for years.

After the shooting at his workplace, Jon helped train staff there in crisis intervention and de-escalation skills, following a model similar to what we outlined in the previous chapter. But more important, he encouraged them to take an active interest in the lives of their colleagues so that they could spot what he calls "yellow flags," or early warning signs that someone is in distress, and refer them to management. These are not the "red flags" of imminent threat to life, Jon clarifies, but rather, often subtler, which is why they can go unnoticed: things like someone suddenly showing up late for work or appearing more tired and stressed than usual—changes from their baseline.

Management, in turn, tried to integrate themselves more and have a greater presence with staff. Management tends to see employees on their "best and worst days, when they're hired and fired," Jon says, but it's everything in between that's illustrative of what's really going on in people's lives. Human resources then sought to mitigate disgruntled employees by checking in with them early and often and offering support even for problems that originated outside the workplace, such as a messy breakup or a divorce.

Jon is now a workplace violence consultant, and he firmly believes that each and every member of a company (employers, managers, workers, and HR professionals) can help prevent violence, provided that the right structures and supports are in place. For example, a workplace could assemble or outsource a multidisciplinary, collaborative effort among its security team (which may be aware of some incident involving the person), the HR department (which may be privy to something in the person's personnel file), and the legal department (which may know of an outside lawsuit or protective order) to identify, assess, and manage people in crisis.

Some places call these "threat assessment" or "threat management" teams, and they can include senior leaders, local law enforcement, personal advocates or labor unions, and other experts. Who sits on the team will be context specific, but in order for the team to be successful, it needs to establish when and where it will meet, how its members will communicate, and what types of behaviors will trigger a meeting outside its normal routine.

The idea of threat assessment was first developed by the U.S. Secret Service after several high-profile attacks on public officials and other public figures. Its "protective intelligence model" was later adapted for other sectors—workplaces, K–12 schools, and colleges and universities—in many cases following high-profile attacks at these locations. For example, it was in the wake of several post office shootings in the 1980s and early 1990s that the U.S. Postal Service implemented a workplace threat assessment program, using district-level threat assessment teams as part of its broader workplace violence prevention initiative.

Jon cautions that the "threat" concept could unduly narrow the scope of the team if the term is taken literally and if someone's behavior is concerning but not inherently threatening. "You don't help troubled people just to prevent a mass shooting. You help troubled people because they need help," Jon notes. He advises broadening the definition of *threat* or adopting a name that avoids the term entirely. He liked our idea of "crisis response teams" in schools and felt that this would apply in workplaces, too.

Much like in schools, crisis response teams in the workplace are the first step toward establishing more than a zero-tolerance policy for workplace misconduct. Part of their role is to educate employees on warning signs that could potentially lead to violence if left unchecked, such as a marked change in behavior, sudden withdrawal, depression, or disgruntlement. Employees don't need to memorize long lists of warning signs or flags; "that's what the team is for," Jon says. They simply need to speak up if they see any behavior that makes them worry about their own or someone else's safety.

Workplace teams have a lot in common with school teams. They are part of creating an open and transparent work culture and keeping an eye out for people in crisis, but not in a way that erodes trust among coworkers or fosters a hostile, fearful environment. There may be times when employers react with termination, suspension, or some sort of law enforcement intervention after learning about a threat or incident, but that shouldn't be the default reaction, because employees will be less likely to speak up if they fear the company will overreact or punish the person they're reporting. If an organization's response is always punitive, Jon explained, then people will feel they can report only if they're 100 percent certain their concerns are valid, for fear they, too, will be thrown under the bus for wasting someone's time. But if the response is not punitive—if it's thoughtful and measured and helpful—then it doesn't matter if someone overreacted when reporting to the team. After all, this is not a whistleblowing exercise. "You're not trying to get your coworker or an outsider in trouble, but rather, [to] ensure the safety of all involved," Jon says.

The team must show compassion rather than fear or recrimination. Treating a person in crisis disrespectfully or adding humiliation by failing to keep matters confidential could increase their risk for violence. Instead, establish mental health support and policies and be open about them. Adopt a beneficent response aimed at helping the person, not hurting them. This might involve referring them to an employee assistance program, arranging for them to receive mental health care, transitioning them to a role that better suits them, facilitating additional training, or mediating a dispute. Even if the employee needs to be terminated, consider benevolent severance or outplacement assistance.

In the end, the team is responsible for identifying resources available for people under their duty of care and making connections for appropriate intervention.

CHAPTER 6
PROOF

Perpetrator B was persistent. He had spent months trying to convince his mom to take this vacation, and finally she had caved, hoping it might "just cure his obsession." From the second they arrived at the hotel, Perpetrator B's excitement was palpable. He used his new camcorder to capture every moment, every detail, so that the memories would last a lifetime. He filmed the parking lot, the queen-size beds, the bathroom; he even filmed his acne-ridden face in the mirror.

It had been a long travel day already, and his mom was tired, but Perpetrator B was impatient to hit all the attractions. So they quickly unpacked, then immediately got back in the car to drive some more. Perpetrator B kept the camera rolling from the passenger seat, admiring the open mountains against the vivid blue sky. The sun was shining brightly, and to him the scene was like something out of a movie. Awed by so much natural beauty, Perpetrator B gave a running commentary of his emotions while his mom kept her eyes on the road ahead, smiling because her son was finally happy.

Perpetrator B was a planner, and he had a list of things he wanted to see and do that day: visit the pizza shop. Buy a jacket. Tour a couple of neighborhoods. Visit the school. This may not sound like much, but for Perpetrator B, it was everything. For him, this was the vacation of a lifetime. Perpetrator B was in Littleton, Colorado, making his pilgrimage to Columbine High School.

—

On April 20, 1999, two high school seniors dressed in trench coats murdered twelve students and one teacher before killing themselves in what, at the time, was the worst high school shooting in U.S. history. Local news stations and CNN began broadcasting the scene live to viewers around the country about forty minutes into the attack. The coverage continued unbroken for hours. This was the heyday of twenty-four-hour cable news, but also "the year of the

Net."[1] Google was founded in September 1998, one month after the release of the iMac, a sleek all-in-one desktop designed primarily "to get on the internet, simply and fast."[2] Columbine was the first mass shooting of the internet age and is now widely considered a defining moment for the Millennial generation, like the assassination of President John F. Kennedy was for the Baby Boomers.

Columbine frightened everyone, and at times the conversation about it bordered on hysteria. It was not only the scale of the slaughter that terrorized Americans but also the fact that the perpetrators were themselves children. THE MONSTERS NEXT DOOR: WHAT MADE THEM DO IT? was the headline when the shooters graced the cover of *Time*. The boys became household names. They were misfits, loners, targets of bullying by more popular students, we were told, part of a "trench coat mafia," goths obsessed with Satanism and Nazism. Once these untruths were out there and spread across the globe, they were impossible to reel back in.

After the shootings at Columbine, a fandom for the shooters emerged on a fledgling internet, and it has only grown in the decades since. This subculture of "Columbiners" dresses like the shooters for Halloween or cosplay and creates memes, fan art, and fan fiction about their crime.[3] Many divulge Columbine fantasies online in Tumblr blog posts, but never carry them out.

However, some do. Columbine has been the blueprint for no fewer than twenty school shooters in the last twenty years, not to mention all the people who compiled hit lists, phoned in threats, or brought guns to school but never went through with the shooting.[4] Each was fascinated with Columbine and researched the massacre before their own. This includes a fourteen-year-old who aspired to be "the youngest mass murderer" and a fifteen-year-old who shot at his teacher after she refused to praise Marilyn Manson, the rock singer who was erroneously blamed for inspiring the Columbine killers.[5]

Past school shooters have talked of how they were going to "pull a Columbine." Others discussed Columbine with classmates, even joked about it. The Sandy Hook Elementary School shooter, who shot and killed twenty first-graders and six adult staff members in 2012, idolized the Columbine killers and curated a Tumblr account paying homage to them, alongside a graphic collage of their victims. The sixteen-year-old student who killed nine inside a high school on the Red Lake Nation Native American reservation in northern Minnesota in 2005 scoured the internet for information on the Columbine killers. After he was kicked out of school and placed on homebound services, he spent more and more time online watching their homemade movies and reading their writings. He also studied the 2003 movie *Elephant*, by Gus Van Sant, which chronicles the events surrounding a school shooting, based in part on Columbine.

Multiple shooters, including one fifteen-year-old in Oregon and another in Washington State, were similarly inspired by a 2004 documentary about Columbine, *Zero Hour*, which included detailed re-creations of what happened. A Wisconsin teenager held his classroom hostage after reading a book about Columbine. An October 2018 shooting at Kerch Polytechnic College, in Crimea, and a March 2019 copycat shooting in Brazil that killed eight show that the shooting's influence is global.

It's ironic that Columbine became a euphemism for school shooting, and so readily copied, because it was never intended to be a shooting and because it, too, was a copycat crime. On April 19, 1995, two years to the day after law enforcement officials raided a compound near Waco, Texas, precipitating a lengthy standoff and eighty-six fatalities, a truck packed with explosives was detonated outside the Alfred P. Murrah Federal Building in Oklahoma City in protest of Waco, killing 168 people and leaving hundreds more injured. The Columbine attackers, who felt that Timothy McVeigh never fully reached his potential for destruction, intended to emulate the Oklahoma City Bombing with a more spectacular and deadly explosion, one that would level the entire school building; they picked April 19 for their deed—postponed by an unknown reason to April 20, Adolf Hitler's birthday, which only adds to the conspiracy around the incident. Only after the attackers' crude improvised explosives failed to detonate did they resort to plan B: a shooting.

This chain of copycat crimes explains why the most common date of a month for a school shooting is the twentieth and why mass shooting anniversaries give us pause. Just three days ahead of the twentieth anniversary of the Columbine shooting in 2019, authorities closed schools across Colorado owing to a credible threat from a teenage girl armed with a shotgun who was "infatuated with Columbine" and who was an active contributor to related online chat rooms. The eighteen-year-old Floridian flew from Miami to Colorado, bought a pump-action shotgun and ammunition upon arrival, and then disappeared, prompting a massive manhunt. The FBI later found her dead from an apparent self-inflicted gunshot wound.

Less than three weeks later, on May 7, 2019, there was a fatal shooting at the STEM School Highlands Ranch, just seven miles from Columbine High School. Two students went into the school carrying handguns and other weapons hidden in guitar cases. They killed one student and injured eight others.

—

This trend is not new. The idea that imitation can play a role in the genesis of crime goes back to the work of Gabriel Tarde, *The Laws of Imitation*, published in French in 1890. Tarde argued that the media were the primary source of all crime ideas. "Epidemics of crime follow the line of the telegraph," he quipped.[6] Tarde assumed a natural tendency to imitate, but there is psychology behind why criminals (and non-criminals, for that matter) copy one another, something called "social proof."

Social proof, a term coined by Robert Cialdini in his 1984 book *Influence,* is like "safety in numbers" or "the wisdom of crowds."[7] When we don't know what to do, we look to others for social cues that validate our own actions. So, for example, if a colleague is working late, then we may feel we should also work late. Or if we see that a restaurant is full of people, then we may be more likely to eat at that restaurant. To quote Cialdini: "The principle of social proof states that one important means that people use to decide what to believe, or how to act in a situation, is to look at what other people are believing or doing there." As they say, when in Rome, do as the Romans do.

Perpetrator B never visited Rome, but he did travel to Columbine. So, we asked him, "How did you feel when you made this visit?"

In a written reply, he said:

I admit that I was very excited and happy to see the high school and the town that I had read about for almost a year. It was overwhelming. I was amazed at the town.

When and how did you first hear about the Columbine shooting?
When it occurred on April 20, 1999. I was 11 and I remember that my parents were talking about it. I also saw the *Time* magazine cover that showed the two shooters in the cafeteria and I believe I read the article.

What initially piqued your interest in the shooting?
When I was 17 I watched the documentary *Bowling for Columbine* by Michael Moore. I remembered about the event when I was 11 and wanted to learn more because it was a historical event, though a tragedy. Also because of the firearms and the high school.

What other massacres did you study?
Columbine massacre, Jonesboro massacre, Thurston High School shooting, Red Lake High School massacre.

What interested you about these other shootings?
I heard about some of these shooters either in movies or news articles and I wanted to know what they had done. . . . I was curious. After researching the Columbine massacre, I found a link to other school shootings and decided to read on them. A few I had already heard about when they happened. And I wanted to be better informed. I related a lot to [the Columbine shooter] and [the Thurston High School shooter]. [The Columbine shooter] was about my age and suffered from depression like I was [*sic*]. He committed suicide and I also longed for suicide at times.

Perpetrator B was struggling to find himself, and mass shooters were the only people he saw that he recognized himself in. Many people experience social and psychological strain. How they deal with that strain is often contingent on how others just like them have chosen to deal with it. Who is more similar to an angry young man in crisis than another angry young man in crisis? Eventual mass shooters may have already wanted to kill people, but seeing someone else do it provides them with an incentive. When people are isolated and uncertain how to act, social proof binds them to models of behavior. It resolves uncertainty, reduces the cost of trial and error, and speeds up learning.

We came to realize this after an averted school shooter, Jacob, reached out to us to tell us his story. He'd read about our research and contacted us because he felt a study that focused only on completed mass shootings was incomplete. Jacob could offer a different "useful perspective," and after years of silence he was finally ready to offer it.

Jacob had been abandoned by his parents as a child, raised by his grandparents, and violently assaulted whenever his drug-addicted father came back to visit. "If you ever tell anyone what I do to you again, I'm going to kill you," his father once said after a school counselor suspected child abuse and called a meeting. "I can kill you because you belong to me," he clarified.

As a Black kid, Jacob also experienced intense racial bullying at his nearly all-white high school and faced daily violent harassment. One of his classmates, "a cowboy guy [who] lived on a ranch, [made it] his hobby to see how many times he could call me a [N-word] before it pissed me off," Jacob said.

Jacob became angry, depressed, and anxious, and was actively suicidal. He started cutting himself but said his teachers turned a blind eye.

His grandpa was a hunter who owned a lot of guns. They were behind a lock, in a cabinet, but Jacob knew where to find the key, and the ammunition was stored with the weapons. Jacob reported sitting in his living room sometimes, putting his grandpa's shotgun in his mouth or under his chin to "dry-run" his death.

He was certainly traumatized, and he was in crisis; he also had the opportunity to commit a shooting and easy access to guns. Jacob didn't just hate himself; he hated the people in his life who had made him feel the way he did. He decided that there was "only one way to take care of this," so one morning he put one of his grandpa's guns in his backpack and went to school with the intent to kill his classmates.

Jacob had spent his whole life feeling powerless, and to overcome the accompanying shame and frustration, he was strongly motivated to exploit whatever power opportunities he could lay his hands on. A gun and the will to murder are two of the purest forms of temporary, situational power. All he ever wanted was "to feel better, to feel safe," and in choosing such a high-profile crime, he was reaching for one final chance to give his life meaning.

"It was like, the best day. It didn't matter what anyone said or did. I held power over life and death in my backpack," he told us. But as the day wore on, things weren't living up to Jacob's high expectations. Something was missing. There was no precedent, to his knowledge, for the type of violence he wanted to inflict, nowhere to look for models. It was 1998, and school shootings were still in the realm of far-fetched fantasy. The closest thing in Jacob's mind was "Jeremy," a Pearl Jam song about a real-life fifteen-year-old Texas boy who shot himself in front of his teacher and classmates in 1991.

Like Jeremy, Jacob expected to die that day, "maybe [in] a shootout with cops. Maybe shoot myself." Unlike Jeremy, he wanted to kill his classmates first. But he was stuck on how to communicate his motive to the world. His goal was to "get people to stop hurting me or [to] acknowledge that I was being hurt." But he knew that if he went through with the shooting, he'd be "just another Black kid who shot some white kids"—his message would be lost in translation. "I never even thought of writing a manifesto!" he exclaimed when we asked him. Of course he hadn't—because no one had shown him how to do that yet.

Just a few months later, they did. The Columbine killers wrote the playbook for all future mass shooters by leaving behind legacy tokens of their act—multiple and detailed diaries filled with drawings, personal reflections, poems, violent rants, and kill lists, as well as "basement tapes" of their preparations for others to consume. They offered social proof of concept, sources for others to cite. And crucially, because of the timing of the internet, these items weren't just filed away in court documents. They circulated. This is why Columbine is the one mass shooting against which all others are measured, and why Jacob never fired his gun.

—

If you look carefully at school shootings today, you will certainly see a pattern of ritual among them. School mass shooters tend to fit the mold of the Columbine shooters. They are either current or former students of the school, and, like the Columbine killers, they are young (fifteen and sixteen being the most common ages) white (76 percent) males (98 percent) with a disciplinary record or violent history who target suburban public high schools.

Curiously, college and university shootings look different. Like K–12 school shooters, they are insiders (78 percent are current or former students), but unlike their younger counterparts they are more similar to the image of the most high-profile shooter in this category, the 2007 Virginia Tech shooter, who was a nonwhite immigrant motivated at least in part by psychosis. The nine college and university shooters in our database tended to be nonwhite (11 percent Black, 45 percent Asian, 33 percent white) males who targeted large, urban, public universities. A majority were immigrants, and psychosis played a role in 45 percent of their crimes.

Is this social proof at play? Hard to say, but what both K–12 shooters and college shooters shared was an interest in other mass shootings, notably Columbine, and a tendency either to leave behind messages about their crimes, such as videos or "manifestos," or to incorporate an element of performance in their shootings, like a costume.

Like genre conventions in movies and pop culture, many mass shooters conform to expectations of *what mass shooters do*, mimicking those who came before, then adding their own flourishes. One mass shooting creates social proof for the next mass shooting and so on until, eventually, there is a generalized knowledge about mass shootings that resides in all of us. This script guides behavior and also tells participants what to expect—a mass shooting isn't a mass shooting until it looks like a mass shooting. Social proof thus explains the preponderance of long black trench coats and even

AR-15s in these events—the same props and weapons other shooters have used, thus giving them meaning beyond any intrinsic use.

You obviously can't copy a previously unthinkable thing unless you see or hear about it first. Columbine was one of the most covered news events of the 1990s, receiving higher ratings on CNN than the fall of the Berlin Wall, the 1993 World Trade Center bombing, the 1992 and 1996 presidential elections, and the death of Princess Diana, according to Nielsen. Columbine also left an indelible mark on pop culture. The shooting inspired Michael Moore's 2002 documentary, *Bowling for Columbine*, and countless true crime shows and podcasts; it was even made into a 2005 video game titled *Super Columbine Massacre RPG!* Artists ranging from rapper Eminem to indie pop band Foster the People have referenced Columbine in their songs, music videos, and lyrics.

Before Columbine, there was no accessible script for how mass shooters should behave, dress, and speak—no common knowledge.[8] This is why many assume the Columbine shooters turned to fiction for inspiration. *The Matrix* was released in theaters exactly three weeks before Columbine, and there was a lot of speculation at the time that the shooters had evoked Neo, Keanu Reeves's character, when they donned their trench coats and packed duffel bags full of weapons. The fact that the Columbine shooters referred to April 20, the day they murdered twelve students and one teacher, as "the holy morning of NBK"—a reference to *Natural Born Killers*, Oliver Stone's 1994 satire on the media's obsession with and inadvertent glorification of violence—only added to the intrigue surrounding their crime.

Some pundits in search of easy causation blamed Columbine on violent video games, namely, because the shooters had enjoyed the popular first-person shooter game *Doom*. Today still, politicians and the media cite violent video games as an inducement to mass shootings. After a spate of shootings in August 2019, President Donald Trump called for an end to "gruesome and grisly video games." However, according to our data, only about 14 percent of all mass shooters played violent video games, and in those cases, what they played had little bearing on their decision to pull the trigger. For every scientific study that has found an association between violent video game use and real-world aggression,[9] there is a better study that has found no relationship whatsoever.[10] Playing violent video games may well desensitize people to the horror of violence. Soldiers do train on first-person shooter games to overcome the natural aversion they have to blood and gore in a virtual environment before they confront it in real life. But, as the Supreme Court ruled in 2011, there is no evidence that violent video games *cause* real-life violence.

Perhaps the best way to think about the role of violent video games in mass shootings is as an accelerant. In 1977, master of horror Stephen King wrote a psychological thriller novel titled *Rage* under the pseudonym Richard Bachman. The novel describes a high school shooting in which a young man kills his algebra teacher and holds his class hostage. At least four high school shootings between 1988 and 1997 came to vaguely resemble events in the book. After the book was found in possession of one of those shooters, King instructed his publishers to pull the book from publication. (It is now out of print.) The author explains that *Rage* "did not break" those boys or "turn them into killers." Instead, "they found something in my book that spoke to them because they were already broken."[11] *Rage* was an accelerant. After each of the four shooters had reached an identifiable crisis point, the book offered someone—albeit someone fictional—with whom they could identify and an imaginative framework for the idea of a shooting. Video games do the same, nothing more.

During the COVID-19 pandemic, elderly people were more susceptible to the disease because their immune systems were weaker. They were also more vulnerable to exposure by virtue of communal living. For mass shooters today, exposure comes from spending time on the Internet immersed in the lives of past mass shooters. Susceptibility comes from past trauma and personal crises. The Columbine shooters were clearly susceptible, but the fact that they did what they did without the same exposure tells us that they were somewhat different from those who followed in their footsteps later; their barrier to entry was higher. The principle of social proof tells us that the greater the number of people who find an action correct, the more the action will seem to be correct to us. With each new person we see jumping on the bandwagon, our threshold for it drops, until eventually we reach the tipping point, and the pace of mass shootings starts to accelerate.[12]

—

Another legacy of Columbine is the active shooter drill, which is fast becoming its own form of social proof. The self-declared "gold standard" in active shooter response is ALICE, which stands for "Alert, Lockdown, Inform, Counter, Evacuate." Its full two-day certification training costs about $700, but its creators also offer a forty-minute online introductory course for $99. It starts with an ominous mash-up of archival news footage from Columbine and other school shootings, with the message "This course will help you participate in your own survival." One of the exercises involves hearing loud banging sounds and seeing if you can identify which ones are gunshots. (It's a trick; they all are.) The training recommends having a five-gallon "go bucket" in the classroom filled with duct tape, food and water, toilet paper, and a space blanket. Cartoon children in a cafeteria throw food at a kid dressed in black to "force him to flinch." And you watch child actors throw themselves on top of a large man armed with an assault weapon, piling their small bodies on top of his in an effort to "overpower a shooter using strength in numbers." The video is both tragedy and comedy.

One study found that one in ten fourth- through twelfth-grade students experienced a negative psychological outcome after ALICE training.[13] Students otherwise fearful of crisis/emergency preparedness practices were worst affected. One parent we interviewed described the impact of these protocols on her young son. "In kindergarten, every time there was a lockdown drill—I think there are four a year—that day, he'd come home and wouldn't talk," she said. "His extremely extroverted self would hide inside a shell, and not knowing what had happened, as parents, we'd attribute it to a bad day. Sometimes that day he wouldn't listen, and we'd automatically have one of those days that things are just off and [that] ends up in some manifestation of tears or time-outs."

This parent started to notice a pattern. "Like clockwork, he'd admit at night in bed that he had [had] a lockdown drill, or some other parent would alert me that their kids [had] admitted it, and we'd sigh in a 'aaaand *that* is why' way." Her son's response to the drills became so routine that this parent would preemptively ask, "Was there a lockdown drill today?" when he was off, "because it was so correlative."

But then, in first grade, her son came home from school one day and again he was "off." After some probing, he admitted that there had been another lockdown drill. He explained that he had been "very quiet" during the exercise "but felt like coughing and tried his hardest to not cough. But underneath the hiding corner, he involuntarily coughed, I think the teacher reminded him to be quiet, and then he let out crying, because according to him, 'I let the bad people know where we were, and because of me we could have gotten hurt.'" She added, "No kid should carry that load."

According to the National Center for Education Statistics, about 95 percent of America's schools conduct lockdown drills meant to protect students from active shooters. Some drills are obviously better than others, but an investigation by the *Washington Post* found that during the 2017–18 school year, more than 4.1 million students experienced at least one lockdown or lockdown drill, including some 220,000 students in kindergarten or preschool. These drills are required by state or local law in most cases with little guidance for how to run them humanely. Our home state of Minnesota mandates at least five lockdown drills per year, meaning that our children will experience seventy drills from pre-K through twelfth grade.

This would make sense if lockdown drills genuinely made students safer, but there is no evidence that they do. Deterred shootings (nonevents) are impossible to measure, but our data on 133 completed and attempted school mass shootings over the past forty years show that there were no differences in the number of people killed or injured between schools that regularly ran lockdown drills and those that didn't. The number of casualties in school mass shootings has remained relatively steady over the past forty years, while our attempts at security have become more time-consuming, costly, and elaborate.

In fact, evidence suggests that active shooter drills may do more harm than good. Jill conducted one of the first and only rigorous studies on active shooter training with community college students.[14] She found that although watching a mass shooting training video increased students' feelings of preparedness compared to a control group shown a different video, it also increased levels of fear and anxiety (particularly among women). A more recent study of a large district in New York State found similar findings: The drills increased feelings of preparedness but decreased feelings of safety at school.[15]

According to Melissa Reeves, former president of the National Association of School Psychologists, "What these drills can really do is potentially trigger either past trauma or trigger such a significant physiological reaction that it actually ends up scaring the individuals instead of better preparing them to respond in these kinds of situations." Dr. Laurel Williams, chief of psychiatry at Texas Children's Hospital in Houston, argued something similar: "It's psychologically distressing for a young child to practice active shooters coming into your area. It's not clear to them that the drill is not real. The younger the child, the less likely they are to understand that an act of violence is not occurring during a drill." The sense of dread these drills can evoke can be quite pervasive, Williams says. "If you're constantly given the viewpoint that the world is scary and [that] unpreventable things happen, it pervasively makes us less secure as a society. We see everyone as suspicious, and it changes the way we act around people."[16]

While it's important for *adults* in the school to be trained in how to respond to a shooting, regularly running *children* through active shooter drills may essentially be writing and disseminating the script for mass violence at a very young age, drilling into young children's heads that school is a scary and dangerous place and that the best they can do is hide quietly under their desks. It normalizes this form of violence by having children rehearse for it over and over and over again—which can create a fascination among vulnerable kids. It's critical to remember that the majority of school shooters are current and former students of the school. This means that potential shooters are running through the drills along with everyone else, learning the school's exact response, rehearsing for the act.

—

In March 1996, a forty-three-year-old killed sixteen children and one teacher at Dunblane Primary School in Scotland, in what remains the deadliest mass shooting in British history. One month later, a lone gunman committed another mass shooting ten thousand miles away, in Port Arthur, Tasmania, killing thirty-five people and injuring twenty-three—allegedly motivated in large part by media coverage of the Dunblane massacre, particularly the attention given to the perpetrator.

Mass shootings tend to cluster. In August 2019, there were three high-profile shootings in a week, first in Gilroy, California, then back-to-back shootings in El Paso, Texas, and then Dayton, Ohio. One 2015 study led by Sherry Towers, a mathematician at Arizona State University, found that a mass shooting was "contagious for an average of 13 days" and every one of them inspired 0.3 more, meaning that after three shootings, a fourth was imminent.[17] In August 2019, that fourth shooting was twenty-seven days later, in Midland-Odessa, Texas, where a thirty-six-year-old went on a shooting spree from his vehicle, killing seven and injuring twenty-three.

Towers's study compared three data sets to a mathematical model of a contagion: (1) mass killings where four or more people were killed; (2) school shootings; and (3) mass shootings where three or more people were shot but fewer than four people were killed. For mass killings and school shootings, the contagion model explained the data better than simply assuming the events were random. The third set of data, events in which fewer than four people were killed, showed no signs of triggering other incidents. The reason? Shootings with fewer than four people killed, while obviously troubling, are less well publicized and usually do not generate national news coverage.[18]

An analysis of data from an independent company that collects information from more than one hundred thousand news sources revealed that perpetrators of seven mass killings from 2013 to 2017 received media coverage equivalent to that of A-list movie stars.[19] This model of heavy, transparent circulation inspires some people to take up arms and commit atrocities of their own. It also provides them with information they can use to plan their own shootings, potentially giving them clues as to how to cause more damage or evade capture for longer. Presumably, this is why the student suspected of killing three people at Naval Air Station Pensacola in late 2019 hosted a dinner party the week of his crime where he and his friends watched videos of mass shootings—to find proof of concept.

—

Sometime after he murdered two people in a university dormitory, but before he murdered thirty more in a classroom building, the Virginia Tech shooter mailed NBC News a carefully produced multimedia package that included a twenty-three-page written statement celebrating "martyrs like [the Columbine shooters]," twenty-eight video clips, and forty-three photos. The material had little investigative value, but NBC broadcast the videos anyway and published the shooter's writings on MSNBC.com. After NBC first broadcast the tapes, all major broadcast and cable newscasts and channels followed suit, airing portions of the tapes. Newspapers and magazines then put the photos on front pages worldwide, just as the shooter had intended.

In 2015, five days after a gunman shot and killed two television journalists in Virginia and posted footage of the shootings on Facebook and Twitter, the man who went on to shoot and kill nine people at an Oregon community college posted the following message to his personal blog:

> On an interesting note, I have noticed that so many people like him are all alone and unknown, yet when they spill a little blood, the whole world knows who they are. A man who was known by no one, is now known by everyone. His face splashed across every screen, his name across the lips of every person on the planet, all in the course of one day. Seems the more people you kill, the more your're [sic] in the limelight.

The message is chilling in hindsight, in part because after his own attack, the Oregon shooter's social media profiles started to go viral, especially a photo of him posing with a rifle on his Myspace page. The shooter handed papers and a flash drive to one victim, demanding they give it to the police, and left a series of inconsequential "clues" lying around his apartment, in what can only be described as a trolling attempt to bait the public into interrogating his actions, magnifying the attention paid to him and his deadly act.

We've been down this road before. Forty years ago, serial murder (the unlawful killing of two or more victims by the same offender in separate events) exploded onto the scene. Horror stories of sadistic killers like Jeffrey

Dahmer, who kept decapitated heads in his freezer, and John Wayne Gacy, who dressed as a birthday clown and stored bodies in his basement crawl space, tapped our fears and captured our imaginations like nothing else. The notorious BTK Killer studied other killers; he even sent letters, drawings, and poems to the news media, taunting the police.[20]

For the networks, serial killers were the gift that kept on giving. Ted Bundy participated in the first criminal trial to be televised nationally in the United States. Leslie Allen Williams had local Detroit media compete for an exclusive interview and the "privilege" of printing his twenty-four-page open letter to the public. David Berkowitz reveled in his own celebrity to the extent that the State of New York passed "Son of Sam" laws to prevent criminals from profiting from the publicity created by their crimes. After extrapolating from unsolved crime rates that there might be upward of five thousand serial murder victims every year—an erroneous statistic at best and an outright lie at worst—newscasters shaped the perception that serial killers were everywhere.[21] And the FBI didn't correct them, because the inflated serial killer threat funded its Behavioral Science Unit.

The term *serial killer* was coined only in 1981,[22] but—spurred on by the media and law enforcement—copycats began killing in the name of fame. By 1989, there were about two hundred separate serial killers in operation across the United States. The media's obsession with serial killers had created a minor snowball effect: People inspired by the violence reported by the media acted out violence in a similar pattern. By the end of the twentieth century, however, the number of active serial killers had halved. In the current decade, it has halved again, to fewer than fifty.[23] As quickly as they came, the serial killers were gone.

Where did all the serial killers go? Perhaps the better question is where did they come from in the first place? The rise of the serial killer correlated with improvements in data collection and police record keeping, which made it easier to connect the dots between criminal cases, especially across state lines, and identify examples of serial murder. Eventually, smart policing, advances in DNA evidence and forensic science, the proliferation of security cameras, and even social media and cell phone location data made catching serial killers easier. Longer prison sentences and tighter use of parole also meant that serial killers who once had killed, gone to prison, and then were released to kill again were a thing of the past. Potential victims also became harder to target: We changed our behaviors and stopped hitchhiking to San Francisco or letting our children play outdoors unsupervised.

But another reason there are fewer serial murderers today than in the 1980s is because serial killing does not provide the same level of celebrity as it did in the past. It's not that such killers have disappeared entirely—about fifty people are killed by serial killers every year in the United States, according to best estimates, comparable to the number killed by mass shooters. The big difference is serial killers just aren't the sensation they used to be; none of the recent perpetrators have made national headlines. Serial killers tried to live in their infamy. Once the media stopped giving them what they wanted, their crimes moved from prime-time television to reruns of *Forensic Files* and episodes of *Mindhunter*, and some of the motivation for serial murder faded away.

Sadly, the same cannot be said about mass shootings. Thanks to continued media reporting, mass shootings have evolved into a sort of cultural "meme"—an idea or practice transmitted like a virus from person to person, often via the media, that takes on a life of its own as it propagates. The term *meme*, a neologism, is derived from the Greek word *mimeme*, meaning "something imitated," and was first coined by the famed evolutionary biologist Richard Dawkins in his 1976 book, *The Selfish Gene*. Dawkins defined memes as ideas that spread from brain to brain—a cultural analogue to genes that replicate and spread. The concept is mostly used now to describe funny or irreverent images that go viral online and then are altered to keep the joke or idea alive as it ricochets around the internet. But in a digital age, when attackers can upload their own words and deeds to social media rather than relying on TV to achieve notoriety, it has a darker connotation.

—

There is a tragic and recent history of mass shooters producing their own clickbait for public consumption. During the 2017 attacks at Pulse, a nightclub in Orlando, Florida, which killed forty-nine, the shooter checked Facebook and Twitter to make sure his massacre was going viral. It was.

The extremist who killed fifty-one people at two mosques in Christchurch, New Zealand, in 2019 even livestreamed his rampage to Facebook from a head-mounted GoPro camera. In the highly disturbing video, the gunman drives to the first mosque, walks inside, and shoots multiple people before leaving the scene in his car and narrating his journey to the next mosque. The video was taken down within twenty minutes by Facebook, but anything posted online leaves a digital fingerprint, so versions of it stayed online for a worrying amount of time. Within twenty-four hours, Facebook banned 1.5 million versions of the video footage—1.2 million of which the company stopped from being uploaded at all.[24] But one copy of the video lingered on its platform for six hours, and another on YouTube for three.[25] The quick and seemingly unstoppable spread of this video typifies how social media has changed mass shootings: They now go viral and are viewed unedited.

There is something uniquely modern about the quest for celebrity status. The adage that "there is no such thing as bad publicity" has long been part of the American cultural landscape, but we now live in a society in which self-promotion is constant. Platforms like Facebook, Instagram, and YouTube are powered by a framework that encourages, rewards, and creates performance. They are driven in large part by spectacle, and they have, in turn, made it much easier for someone both to create the spectacle of gruesome violence and to distribute it widely by themselves.

Mass shootings made for social media are a form of what criminologist Ray Surette calls violent "performance crime."[26] That is, the posting and video streaming are integral to the violence itself; they're not incidental to the crime or some horrible personal trophy for the perpetrator to relive later. Performance crime is predicated on a kind of exhibitionism and desire to be publicly identified as the performer of the violence.[27] Its perpetrators are inspired by the attention that will inevitably result from the online archive they create leading up to and during the event. Mass shooters are unique only in that they don't want to live in the glory of their newly achieved social status and visibility. They want notoriety, to become legends in their deaths.[28]

Among young people especially, becoming famous (that is, as measured by the number of likes and followers on Instagram and Twitter) and being imitated (as on Tik Tok) is considered the ultimate form of success. One 2011 study found that a desire for fame solely for the sake of being famous was the most popular future goal among American preadolescents, overshadowing hopes for financial success, achievement, or a sense of community.[29] A recent survey found that one-fourth of Millennials would quit their jobs to become famous. One in twelve would detach themselves from their families for fame. One in ten would rather be famous than go to college.[30]

The desire to be seen or valued is often the biggest perceived appeal of fame. A mass shooting is certainly an extreme means of pursuing it. However, according to our data, the past decade has seen a rise in shootings motivated by fame-seeking, and the idolization of fame drives nearly one in ten of all mass shooters. When news organizations report casualty figures in boldface, or index the deadliest mass shooters in video game–style scoreboards, they tempt angry, anonymous, and alienated men with the tantalizing promise of infamy and immortality—especially if the body count is high enough. After all, bigger body counts mean bigger headlines. One 2016 study found that mass killers who expressed a celebrity-seeking motive killed twice as many people as those who did not.[31] One recently thwarted mass shooter posted online that "a good 100 kills would be nice." Another wanted to "break a world record." This suggests that fame-seeking could foster one-upmanship among shooters.

The motivations of mass shooters

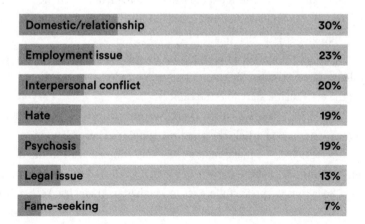

Domestic/relationship	30%
Employment issue	23%
Interpersonal conflict	20%
Hate	19%
Psychosis	19%
Legal issue	13%
Fame-seeking	7%

—

It was every parent's worst nightmare. On July 20, 2012, Tom Teves's phone rang in the middle of the night. It was his son's girlfriend, Amanda. She was hysterical.

"There's been a shooting," she said through sobs. "They dragged me out of the theater . . . I wanted to stay . . ."

"Are you okay?" Tom asked.

"Yes, Alex saved me."

"Where's Alex?"

"I don't know. We can't find him. They dragged me out of the theater. They made me leave. . . . He was shot. I tried to wake him up, but I couldn't wake him up, he wouldn't get up."

"I knew then he was gone," Tom tells us as he relives the moment over breakfast in the family home. Tom Teves's story is well-known. He has shared it in a powerful TEDx Talk that has racked well over a million views.[32] His son Alex was killed along with eleven other people at a midnight screening of *The Dark Knight Rises* at a movie theater in Aurora, Colorado. In the twilight hours, Tom called all the local hospitals, to no avail. Then he did what most people would do and turned on the television in search of answers. The shooting was breaking news. But instead of details about his son's whereabouts, all Tom kept hearing was the name of the shooter—again and again and again. And then, after flying home from where he and his wife, Caren, were on vacation in Hawaii, all they saw on the front page of every newspaper was "that image."

"That image" was the now-infamous mugshot of the shooter released by the Arapahoe County Sheriff's Office in Colorado. The mop of hair dyed red. The eerie, blank stare into the camera.

"All we could see was him. There was no mention of Alex, but we counted, and in one article they had the shooter's name forty-one times in six paragraphs." To make matters worse, a rumor began in the hours after the shooting that the shooter had actually referred to himself as "the Joker." Speaking at a press conference in Manhattan, then New York police commissioner Ray Kelly said that the shooter "had his hair painted red, he said he was 'the Joker,' obviously the 'enemy' of Batman."

The shooter never actually said this. But like the myths associated with the Columbine shooting, the idea that the shooter had fashioned himself after a comic book villain, the "Clown Prince of Crime" no less, spread like wildfire and remains one of the most persistent "zombie ideas" (falsehoods that should have been killed by contrary evidence) associated with any mass shooting in recent memory.[33]

The more the rumor spread, the more the "media was acting like PR for the shooter," Tom Teves said. It was then that he and Caren decided to channel their grief into action.

To honor their son, the Teveses initiated the No Notoriety campaign, introduced in the opening chapter of this book. It's not a blanket ban on reporting. The No Notoriety protocol asks the media to minimize use of a perpetrator's name, especially in headlines, to a few constrained circumstances and to avoid gratuitous details about the killer's biography and belief system—"Don't Name Them, Don't Show Them, but Report Everything Else," as the title of one academic article explains.[34] Still, critics argue that No Notoriety undermines "the public's right to know" and to be fully informed about critical incidents. At the extreme end, they say No Notoriety is a call to limit First Amendment protections. Absent every last detail, they say, researchers can't profile mass shooters and make sound policy suggestions.

We'd be lying if we said we could have built the Violence Project Database without all the media reporting on mass shooters. We learned where shooters got their weapons, how they planned their attacks, and how the police responded. However, a lot of what was published had no research value whatsoever, such as shooters' yearbook photos and favorite vacation spots.

Take, for example, reporting on the 2017 Las Vegas shooter, which highlighted "his enjoyment of karaoke, his favorite casino games, and even what he ordered from room service prior to the shooting."[35] These excessive, irrelevant details have no bearing on the shooter's motivation or inspiration, which by our calculation was experiential and, ironically, fame-seeking.

No Notoriety implores the media to report on the perpetrator with dispassionate language and to show them in the most unflattering light possible, perhaps on an autopsy table or incarcerated. And never to print the full text or video of a mass shooter's propaganda or "manifesto" when a simple summary will do. Better still, don't characterize their ugly rants and justifications for murder as a "manifesto," because the term implies it deserves to be read. Instead, the word should be reserved, as intended, for characterizing an important political statement crafted by a public official or a person of prominence. The media should similarly avoid reposting posed photographs or action shots that might be seen as glorifying the killer. Instead, they should report responsibly and use any photos sparingly.

These guidelines are similar to existing policies against showing fans who run out on fields during televised sporting events or publishing the names of juvenile offenders and sexual assault victims. "It's like a kid throwing a tantrum," Tom explains. "Don't give them negative attention." They are also consistent with best practices for media reporting on suicide: The American Foundation to Prevent Suicide and the World Health Organization both caution the media to avoid sensationalizing or normalizing suicide and to avoid an explicit description of the method used or of photographs or videos that might inspire copycats. They've called for the inclusion of protective factors, like helplines and information on how to get help for suicidal impulses, when publishing stories on such events.

Despite some pushback from media professionals, Tom adds, "reporters start to get it when you ask them if they can name any of the victims." The point here is that while many mass shooters are now household names, shooting victims, by comparison, remain anonymous. No Notoriety seeks to shine a spotlight on the real heroes: the victims and survivors, communities and first responders. Place emphasis on the effect of the crimes on the victims and their loved ones. Focus on stories of bravery, strength, and resiliency instead of reveling in scenes of carnage and chaos.

"News media local to where these events happened, they get it," Caren Teves says, because they're living it, too. It's the national outlets, who are detached from the tragedy, who need constant reminding.

One of the barriers to adoption of the No Notoriety protocol lies in the economics of news media. Media put information out there in part to put a face and a name to a crime, but mostly to increase views . . . and clicks. That's because the media are in the competitive business of human attention and engagement. More engagement means higher ratings and market share, greater page views and unique visitors, all key performance indicators that attract advertisers and keep shareholders happy. And media outlets know that the spectacular, the stirring, and the controversial keep people watching. There is something especially captivating about violence. "If it bleeds, it leads," said journalist Eric Pooley in his 1989 critique of mass media sensationalism. Hence the drip feed of information, the crawl, or scrolling headline ticker that appears at the bottom of the TV screen, communicating BREAKING NEWS to keep us watching.

Free expression is necessary for a peaceful society, but when we create spectacles out of tragic situations, we inadvertently signal that mass murder is an effective means of communication. We the public have the power to change this. "It doesn't take an act of Congress; it takes an act of conscience," Caren explains. We just have to "hit them in the wallet."

Remember, Fox News fired ratings king Bill O'Reilly in 2018 not because of allegations of sexual harassment but because more than sixty companies, ranging from Angie's List to Mercedes-Benz, in solidarity with victims of sexual harassment, pulled advertisements from O'Reilly's show, seriously affecting its revenue. And it's not like news consumers will stop watching cable news once it stops sharing frivolous details about mass shooters. Recent experimental research suggests that focusing on the heroic bystander of a mass shooting generates just as much, if not more, interest from readers as the stories about the perpetrators.[36]

No Notoriety is starting to catch on. CNN anchor Anderson Cooper is a supporter. A similar proposal, the "Don't Name Them" campaign, was recently put forward by the FBI. And in an open letter to the media, 147 experts on mass shootings (coauthor James included)[37] pledged support for not naming the shooters or showing their photographs and for avoiding in-depth descriptions of the shooters' rationales. We can also reduce the duration of news coverage after a shooting; avoid live press conferences, which increase the level of "excitement" around an event; eliminate the perpetuation of clichés and stereotypes about criminals and the causes of their behavior; and lessen detailed accounts of their actions before, during, and after, which can prompt imitation.[38]

According to new research, the unprecedented reluctance by the New Zealand media to feature the Christchurch mosque shooter as a protagonist or even to publish his name—as modeled by political leaders, notably Prime Minister Jacinda Ardern—helped promote a sense of collective responsibility for change.[39] With media concentrating instead on victims and societal issues, within weeks there was a groundswell of bipartisan support for new gun control laws in New Zealand. It's amazing what can happen when the media choose to focus on solutions, especially solutions ordinary people can apply, not just the terror and tragedy of every shooting.

On the topic of social proof, media education and literacy in homes, schools, and workplaces are key to promoting awareness of media influence and to creating an active stance toward both consuming and creating media. In a socially mediated world, Big Tech must also do more to flag violent content before it is even uploaded or to prevent it from ever being reposted. A bit like how we can time-delay the Oscars to mute celebrities' profanity, platforms could immediately "hash" (techspeak for "scramble") any livestreamed violence to silence the persuasion of mass shooters, or introduce temporary quarantines so that content is flagged for immediate removal but then reexamined at a later date. There will always be false negatives (i.e., content allowed online even though it incites violence) and false positives (i.e., bits of content that are blocked even though they are benign), but at the very least, the tech giants could adjust the sensitivity of their algorithms so that people are allowed to share content but also so that platforms catch a lot more of the nasty stuff quicker.

Social media platforms could also limit the number of times that violent content can be shared and potentially ban shares between sites. This seems unlikely, given that sharing is a fundamental part of social media and that platforms actively encourage it, but easy sharing is the reason dark matters go mainstream and spread to large audiences. Under a new French law, for example, content judged to be inciting violence (or hatred, racism, or sexual harassment) has to be taken down within twenty-four hours of notification.

Failure to remove such content could attract a fine of up to €1.25 million. Also, France's regulator, the Superior Audiovisual Council, will have the power to impose fines of up to 4 percent of global turnover for companies in continuous and repeated violation.[40]

—

Collectively, we all need to be more alert, more compassionate, and in some cases more restrained in order to stop the mass shooting contagion. With hundreds of hours of material uploaded every minute on platforms like YouTube, the internet still relies on us, the users, to flag content and to hold social media platforms accountable for how they shape us. The foundations of our society now rest, on some level, on our social media system. Yet, this is a system that to date has failed to protect us. As users, we must demand more of social media companies and educate ourselves on how to be better consumers of online content as well as recognize that our own need to process mass shootings by posting about them on Facebook and Twitter can inadvertently feed the "disaster narrative,"[41] because any interaction with such content, whether it's by sharing it or only by "liking" it, can send that content up to the top of the Facebook News Feed.

Performances close their curtains when people stop buying tickets. We must starve mass shooters of the oxygen of publicity they desire. In the end, our attention is our power.

CHAPTER 7

HATE

We arrive at Tyler's trailer home on a sultry South Carolina summer morning. The home is set back on a wooded plot of land, behind a long dirt driveway punctuated by a handwritten FOR SALE BY OWNER sign.

We walk up the sun-bleached wooden steps and past a neat row of thirty or more empty Bud Light cans lined up in silent vigil along the deck. The front door is wide-open because the air-conditioning is broken, and Tyler is sitting shirtless on the couch, watching the History Channel. Behind him, high on the wall, sits a crossbow and a large deer shoulder-mount taxidermy with a baseball bat perched between its antlers. The trailer is hot and humid. The acrid smell of cigarettes hangs in the air. Flies buzz in and out, and a cockroach or two scurries about a full ashtray and an assortment of tools lying on the coffee table.

Tyler invites us to take a seat next to him. He claims his story is "the only true one" about why, in 2015, his twenty-one-year-old nephew walked into a Bible study at "Mother Emanuel" African Methodist Episcopal Church in Charleston and shot and killed nine people, all African Americans. Tyler is brash like that, a storyteller, crass at times, but charismatic. Between long drags on a cigarette, he has lots of unsavory things to say about his sister, the shooter's mom, and his niece, her daughter, but it's clear that he cares deeply for his nephew, who was sentenced to die in prison.

Tyler describes the Charleston church shooter as "smart"—which is true; he has a high IQ—but always lacking the ability to bond and connect with people. He "couldn't have a conversation" and would "never talk to other people," Tyler says. He gestures at the three of us sitting down together and indicates that the current situation is one his nephew would not have been able to handle. Tyler recalls a surprise birthday party one year at which his nephew locked himself in his bedroom, refusing to come out until everybody had left. Official records show he has a developmental disorder, autism spectrum disorder, a symptom of which is "polarized" or black-and-white thinking, where people see the world in absolutes and find it difficult to distinguish truth from lies, making them potentially vulnerable to manipulation and indoctrination.[1] Tyler doesn't know anything about that, only that his nephew became increasingly isolated during adolescence, using internet research as the source for his ideas, which eventually became fixed and unchecked by reality.

That part of the story is well-known. After hearing about the 2012 death of seventeen-year-old Trayvon Martin on the news, the shooter searched for the case on Wikipedia and determined that George Zimmerman, the Neighborhood Watch coordinator on trial for Martin's murder, was "in the right" to see Martin as a threat. The Charleston shooter then googled "black on white" crime, and the search sent him tumbling down the rabbit hole.

The Charleston shooter became "fixated on Negro history," Tyler says. According to prosecutors, he "self-radicalized" online and engaged in a "self-learning process."[2] For people veering toward the fringes, the internet can do that—because you can find almost anything there, you can always find someone or something to affirm your worst instincts. Top hits sent Tyler's nephew to the website for the Council of Conservative Citizens, a group that sounds official but that once called Black people a "retrograde species of humanity."[3]

Next, Tyler's nephew became a reader and commenter on Stormfront and the Daily Stormer, two white nationalist websites known for fake news conspiracies. Tyler says of the shooter, "He wanted to be a Nazi. He loved Hitler." The shooter then downloaded Ku Klux Klan propaganda. He made his own website, the Last Rhodesian, a reference to the former white supremacist state in Africa. In the site, he posted a 2,500-word rant degrading Black people and glorifying slavery. He also posted photographs of himself posing with guns, the Rhodesian flag, the Confederate flag, and the number 1488, which has numerological significance for white supremacists ("14" refers to the fourteen words of American white supremacist David Lane, "We must secure the existence of our people and a future for white children"; "88" stands for "Heil Hitler," H being the eighth letter of the alphabet). "He wishes Hitler was his father" is Tyler's take on it all.

Tyler wipes sweat from his brow and neck with a folded green T-shirt as he remembers the time his nephew asked his mom for gas money because he was going to Charleston to visit a museum. "Did you know they have an all-Negro church?" he told her. That should have been a red flag. The shooter didn't have a job, he'd only just gotten a driver's license, and he otherwise stayed in his room a lot of the time. "Why has he been going to Charleston every weekend for the last two months?" Tyler asks us rhetorically, implying that the shooting was "well planned."

At this point in the interview, a car pulls into the driveway. A Latinx couple appears in the doorway and asks to meet the homeowner. "How much do you want for the house?"

"I'm the gringo," Tyler replies. They negotiate for a minute, and Tyler drops a few Spanish words he knows—*pesos*, *ocho*, *cinco*. The woman seems genuinely interested in the trailer, but the man is skeptical. They leave to think it over, and Tyler turns to us and smiles. "These fucking foreigners, man."

We ask Tyler if he is close to his nephew. He replies, "For a moment in time," and says that his nephew used to describe him as his favorite uncle. "I used to tell him stories about the real world," Tyler recalls, laughing. They bonded over their interest in history, Tyler says, pointing to the World War II documentary still playing in the background.

The last time they saw each other, about six months before the shooting, his nephew asked, "Have you ever thought about what it would be like to be with a man?" Tyler says he screamed, "Hell no. It's an abomination. That's a fucking faggot." He reenacts for us how he threw his Bible at his nephew and cited Scripture: "You shall not lie with a male as with a woman; it is an abomination." His nephew allegedly retorted, "How can you say that if you never tried?" Tyler grew angry: "Now I need to talk to your mother because you're a fucking queer. Now I see why you couldn't get a girlfriend." His nephew then walked out.

Tyler has no regrets about that conversation, except that the next time he saw his nephew, it was on the evening news. He recognized him instantly from the security camera footage. "I was in a state of shock," he says.

We ask if that last argument may have pushed his nephew over the edge, but Tyler is unwilling to go there. So we ask if he ever thought his nephew was capable of such violence.

Tyler shouts, "Fuck no, he was smart!" And with that, he gets up off the couch to urinate off his front deck. The interview is over.

—

Mass shootings in places of worship became more frequent starting in the mid-2000s, and the number of shootings motivated by religious hate have increased most dramatically in the last five years since the Charleston church shooting. Some of the deadliest worship mass shootings also occurred within this time frame, including Charleston, and the shooting inside Pittsburgh's Tree of Life synagogue in 2018, in which a gunman killed eleven people. Before opening fire, the Tree of Life gunman had vented on the far-right social network Gab about Honduran migrants traveling toward the U.S. border and about the alleged Jewish conspiracy behind it. "I can't sit by and watch my people get slaughtered. Screw your optics, I'm going in," he had declared.[4]

Twenty nineteen was an especially deadly year for attacks on religious groups and places of worship. In April of that year, on the last day of Passover, four people were shot, one fatally, at the Chabad of Poway synagogue in Poway, California. In December 2019, a shooting at a church in White Settlement, Texas, left two dead and one critically wounded. This followed a mass stabbing that injured at least five people at a rabbi's house in New York State a week earlier and a mass shooting at a kosher grocery store in Jersey City, New Jersey, two weeks before that, which killed three.

More than a third of all mass shootings at places of worship have occurred in Texas, including the first mass shooting in a church that we know of. That one took place in 1980, in Daingerfield, where a former high school teacher killed five and wounded ten after members of the church refused to appear as character witnesses during his incest trial. Texas was also the site of the deadliest church mass shooting ever: In 2017, twenty-six people were killed when a gunman opened fire at a Baptist church in Sutherland Springs during a Sunday service. (Because there was no gun involved, our

database doesn't include the 1963 bombing of a Baptist church in Birming-
ham, Alabama, by Ku Klux Klan members, in which four children were
killed and twenty-two other congregants were injured.)

In all, seven of the worship mass shootings in our database (64 percent)
occurred in Southern states—four in Texas, two in Louisiana, and one in
South Carolina. Wisconsin is the only other state with more than one mass
shooting at a place of worship, with one at the Living Church of God in
Brookfield in 2005 and another at the Sikh temple in Oak Creek in 2012.

There are two distinct groups of worship mass shooters. The first is
motivated by domestic issues: The church is the setting simply because a
girlfriend, spouse, or other family member happens to be worshipping there.
They typically had criminal records and histories of violence and substance
abuse. The second, more predictably, aims to intimidate a specific subgroup
and is motivated by ethno-religious hate, including anti-Semitism, Islamo-
phobia, or anti-Christian sentiment. The perpetrators of these killings tend
not to be members of the congregation. Their attack is born out of some
grievance, namely a perceived sense of injustice, a threat or loss, and the
need for revenge against the specific group of people they blame for their
disappointments. Interesting, three-quarters of all worship mass shooters
had recently lost or changed jobs, with most of them having been fired.

—

Georgetown psychology professor Fathali Moghaddam argues that the pathway to violence is like a narrowing staircase: Anger and frustration instigate
a search for a target to blame that results in an us-versus-them mentality.[5]
A violent denial of diversity is something many violent extremists share.
They want everyone to have the same values and lifestyle. This means that
when they encounter people who are different, they distance themselves
from those people and dehumanize them. The higher someone moves up
the staircase, the fewer alternatives to violent action they see. What ideology
does is help mass shooters neutralize, or "switch off," the moral voice within
them that would normally prohibit them from perpetrating lethal violence.

Central to the contemporary white nationalist narrative is the belief that
whiteness is under attack and that anyone who is nonwhite or left-leaning

politically is conspiring to undermine or "replace" the white race "through means as varied as interracial marriage, immigration, 'cultural Marxism' and criticism of straight white men."[6] People who feel powerless or vulnerable are more likely to seek solace in conspiracy theories like the "white genocide." And it's especially hard to change a conspiracy theorist's mind, because their theories are "self-sealing,"[7] in that even absence of evidence for the theory becomes evidence for the theory. That is, the reason there's no proof of the conspiracy, the thinking goes, is because the conspirators did such a good job of covering it up.

White nationalism appeals to some of the same working-class white men, particularly younger working-class white men, described in chapter 2, because they are the last generation of Americans born when white births outnumbered those of nonwhites. Demographic change, increasing racial and ethnic diversity coupled with rising numbers of refugees and asylum seekers, has created a sense of threat for these men. White nationalists are reminiscent of American philosopher Eric Hoffer's "new poor"—they recall their former wealth with resentment and blame the "other" for their current misfortune.[8] What separates this strain of white nationalism from prior iterations is that it doesn't simply dislike the "other"; it views the other's very existence as part of a zero-sum game.[9]

Hate actually looks a lot like fear—unfounded allegations of Hispanic "invaders," rising Black-on-white crime, and "Jewish" plans to sabotage American sovereignty. Just hours before he opened fire at Walmart, the 2019 El Paso shooter published a short screed disparaging immigrants and warning of an "invasion" of Hispanics. That word is one that President Trump himself used to describe migrants seeking entry to the United States from Mexico and other "shithole countries." The president's angry rhetoric and his failure to shame white supremacy throughout his tenure, including on the 2020 election debate stage and immediately after his supporters, dressed in far-right hate symbols, stormed the U.S. Capitol carrying Confederate flags, was responsible for fomenting a rise in hate and, in rare but an increasing number of cases, violence. In May 2019, someone at a Trump rally in Florida responded to the president's rhetorical question about how the arrival of migrants could be stopped by saying they should be shot.

Trump replied, "That's only in the Panhandle you can get away with that statement."

—

The Charleston shooter has been described as "a most American terrorist."[10] The description seems fitting—the shooter's motive was "retaliation for perceived offenses" against the white race, and the shooter hoped above all that his attack would worsen racial tensions and incite a "race war."[11] The shooter chose Black congregants because killing a Black drug dealer would not have garnered the same attention, he said. In other words, his violence was a deliberate political act meant to be exemplary to others and to serve as a catalyst for revolution—or what terrorism scholars call "propaganda of the deed."

After the Charleston shooting, President Obama said the target of the shootings, Mother Emanuel, was especially troubling not only because it was a place of worship with a rich, lengthy history but because it held "a sacred place in the history of Charleston and in the history of America." Mother Emanuel is the oldest African Methodist Episcopal church in the Southern United States and was a sanctuary for some of the most influential figures in Black history, from Booker T. Washington to Martin Luther King Jr. At trial, lead prosecutor Jay Richardson called the crime "a modern-day lynching." Cornell William Brooks, NAACP national president in 2015, labeled it an "act of racial terrorism."

Acts of terrorism are performances of power by people who typically have very little. The Charleston shooter absolutely incited terror, and by attacking such a sacred space, he did more than put on a display; he also deliberately tried to change the social order.[12] By most measures, this is terrorism, and for a while the Department of Justice considered terrorism charges against the perpetrator. In the end, however, those charges never came—instead, out of thirty-three felony counts, twelve of them were considered hate crimes. The reason? No specific federal statute covers acts of terrorism inside the United States that are not connected to Al Qaeda, ISIS, or other officially designated global terrorist groups and their sympathizers. Even though "domestic terrorism" was defined in the Patriot Act of 2001, and even though, under federal law, anyone who provides so-called material support to a designated terrorist organization can be prosecuted, suspected domestic terrorists are investigated by the FBI's Civil Rights Program under the rubric of hate crimes.[13]

U.S. intelligence agencies maintain databases of suspected terrorists and work hard to map connections among extremists. After a man plowed his car into a crowd of protesters during a white supremacist rally in Charlottesville, Virginia, in 2017, killing one and injuring twenty-eight—and, more recently, after the riot at the U.S. Capitol in 2021, which killed five, including a police officer—America revisited the question of whether home-grown extremists should be labeled terrorists. Doing so would authorize the Department of Justice to redirect its vast resources at the domestic terrorism problem. The FBI would then have greater latitude in monitoring what the perpetrators did before they acted and in directing more investigative resources to follow up on any suspicious behavior.

Prosecuting hate-motivated mass shooters as terrorists would also send the message that the threat of extremism is just as serious when it is rooted in domestic issues as it is when based on international ideologies. The problem is these measures carry serious civil liberties concerns. Separating racism from potential domestic terrorism is not always easy, especially when even the most contemptible hate speech is protected by the U.S. Constitution. Social media platforms are overflowing with heated and hateful rhetoric, making it difficult to separate tense debates from actual threats, and many words and deeds posted online aren't illegal in and of themselves, however sinister or prophetic they might appear to be in hindsight.

There's also something the terrorist label misses. The designation doesn't really explain anything—in fact, it just explains things away. It's another variation on the "monster." For a crime to be classified as terrorism, the Department of Homeland Security says, there has to be a "discernable political, ideological, or religious motivation."[14] However, even some of the most hardened extremists are neither learned scholars nor subject matter experts in politics, ideology, or religion. Their understanding of the causes said to motivate their actions is often very shallow, contradictory—convenient, even.[15]

This is because, like the Charleston shooter, their ideology often is sourced from the internet. In the internet age, even "lone wolves" are never truly alone, and it is ideology that helps them feel part of the pack. In fact, extremism is less an ideological movement and more a social one. It offers people with shared individual deficits a sense of collective identity and belonging that previously did not exist.

Research with online hate groups suggests that there are "high-intensity" posters, who post infrequent but powerful messages of hate; "high-frequency" posters, who post a lot but mostly just noise; and "high-duration" posters, who have posted hate online the longest and appear the most committed to the cause.[16] Some clearly are more invested in hate than others, but what they all have in common is they are searching for something to make sense of their lives. Their ideologies have necessary companions in their lives' trajectories, and it's the quest for personal significance that leads them to ideologies that justify violence. No one living a happy and fulfilled life goes searching for answers in the darkest corners of the internet. And not everyone finds who or what lives there equally compelling. The internet helps facilitate violence for some and enhance it for others, but either way, we have to remember why people opt into extremism in the first place. As we've argued throughout this book, the story of mass shooters extends well beyond their online search histories.

—

In a letter to us about the motive for his shooting, Perpetrator A, the restaurant shooter, wrote:

> At the time of the shooting I'd have to say there was a good amount of hate, anger, and rage taking place. I have no memory of it, but descriptions of my words and actions tell me I was not a happy individual to say the least.

Perpetrator A's shooting has long been considered a hate crime because, at the time, he was upset about President Clinton's "Don't Ask, Don't Tell" position on gay people in the military, and when he opened fired in a crowded restaurant, he "made statements along the lines of 'I'll show you

Clinton-loving faggots [for] letting gays in my military!'" he tells us. Perpetrator A admits, "I was not happy at all with President Clinton's 'Don't Ask, Don't Tell' policy (felt it made all of our military look bad in the eyes of the world)," and he is even on public record as saying, "I needed to voice my opinion on it. . . . I'm not going to apologize for my views that I hold against gays or homosexuals." However, in a letter to us about this issue, he wrote:

> I don't think that I went in with the intention of singling out any group of people, be it black, white, male, female, gay or straight. I was just angry at the world, I guess, at the time. I was taking out my aggression on whoever was there. . . .
>
> I didn't "decide" to commit my crime. . . . I don't believe I planned it at all. I had all of my military gear there at the house to include a bullet proof vest, Kevlar helmet, fatigues, boots, etc. I had all of that available and yet what was I wearing during my crime?—No shoes, tan Levi Docker shorts, a peach colored "Montego Bay" tank top and a blaze orange hunting vest full of shotgun shells. Common sense says I might have been just a little better prepared had I "planned" to go on a shooting rampage. I don't know what I was thinking.

He added, "As far as I know, I had no 'goal.'" And when asked how well informed he was on the object of his supposed hate, he joked, "You'd had to have beat me to read a book! The only books I remember reading were: 'Where the red fern grows,' [sic] one on reptiles, and an adult sex novel I found in a junk car."

It is clear that whatever hateful ideas or ideology motivated Perpetrator A's crime, they were ancillary to whatever struggles he was facing at the time. And it is these struggles that propel somebody to violent extremism in the first place, making them especially vulnerable to indoctrination and exploitation, whether from famous politicians or anonymous extremists.

The Charleston shooter had many personal issues that made him susceptible to extremist propaganda. He grew up with parental discord. He was "angsty all the time" in elementary school, one of the shooter's child-hood friends—coincidently, his one and only Black friend—tells us over iced coffee at a bohemian café. He was "uncomfortable" around people and "didn't fit in" even then, his friend says. "He was always gullible," he adds, and "never really accomplished anything." He was a "quiet fellow" who "flew under the radar," the shooter's elementary school principal confirms during a meeting at home, where he shared yearbook photographs of the shooter and stories of a once-thriving middle-class community that fell on hard times, a community where it was now not uncommon to "hear discouraging things about Black people" being uttered by white residents.

The shooter dropped out of high school after repeating ninth grade and then dropped out of an online alternative school before later earning his GED. He abused alcohol and drugs. He also had many obsessive-compulsive behaviors and was preoccupied with various somatic beliefs, some of which were delusional. He hated his "feminine" and "lopsided" appearance, for instance.[17] And if his uncle Tyler is to be believed, he was questioning his sexuality in a family where that wasn't acceptable.

Four months before the murders, the shooter anonymously posted an ad on Craigslist that he was seeking a companion to join him on a tour of historic Charleston. "Jews, queers, or [N-word]" need not apply, he wrote. The tone of the ad troubled a retired child psychologist, Dr. Thomas Hiers, who responded to the post and struck up a correspondence, hoping to help. In response to continued racist and anti-Semitic comments, Dr. Hiers even offered to pay the shooter to watch online TED Talks as a way of expand-ing his view of the world. The shooter politely declined. "I am in bed, so depressed I cannot get out of bed," he wrote. "My life is wasted. I have no friends even though I am cool. I am going back to sleep." Hiers didn't give up. He tried to get the shooter to meet with one of his professional colleagues for lunch, but the shooter never replied.

———

A seventeen-year-old boy accused of fatally stabbing a woman in Febru-ary 2020 recently became the first person ever charged with carrying out an "incel" terrorist attack. The suspect had already been charged with murder when Toronto Police and the Royal Canadian Mounted Police announced the terrorism charges.

An incel is someone who is "involuntarily celibate." Journalist Naama Kates, host of the *The Incel Project*, a podcast devoted to the personal stories of people who identify as incels, worries about labeling them as "terrorists" because even though some incels are violent, violence is not integral to their group identity.

Kates reached out after hearing James talk about incels on television and being pleasantly surprised by his opening acknowledgment that the incels who make national news for their acts of violence were the exception, not the rule. Over Zoom, we chatted for nearly two hours about Kates's forays into incel life.

Kates explains that the term *incel* was originally created by a Canadian woman who in 1997 created a website for people struggling to find love, called Alana's Involuntary Celibacy Project.[18] It was a platform for men and women in similar situations to express feelings of loneliness and process their inability to find romantic or sexual partners. But over time, *incel* evolved into shorthand for online groups of men who blame feminism in general and women in particular for any and all grievances. The attitudes of men who visit the online message boards vary widely, but these men frequently vent anger against sexually prolific men ("Chads") and women ("Stacys"). Like teenagers on the subject of sex, incels talk about doing harm to these people far more than they actually engage in violence, but all that talk dials up the expectation that "everyone is doing it," which can mobilize some people to action.

Kates thinks incels are a by-product of a patriarchal culture obsessed with sex and body image. "Women are idealized and overly sexualized," Kates says, something she experienced firsthand as a Hollywood actor. Social media have made matters worse. "Everyone's their own mini-publicist now," she jokes. People post only their best and most curated selves on Facebook and Instagram, thus creating a hyperreal image of life and beauty. Apps like Tinder, which invite people to "swipe right" to approve of someone based on only a few pictures, a short bio, and subjective or superficial dating criteria such as good looks. And internet pornography creates distorted expectations in the bedroom, which hinders healthy sexual development and lowers levels of sexual self-esteem.

Incels tend to be young white men, but Kates stresses that they are not a monolithic group. Some are "LARPers" (live-action role players), pretending to be someone or something they are not in order to infiltrate the subculture. Others are "Edgelords," the online equivalent of shock jocks, who, in an effort to appear cool or edgy, talk about offensive or taboo subjects to get a rise from other users. Still others are "number crunchers," shy Silicon Valley types who use their STEM skills to quantify and analyze topics incels care about, such as Darwinian sexual selection and the "science" of physical attractiveness. Then there are those with the biggest profiles, the influencers and content creators, who post video confessions online that attract huge followings. Kates says that while many incels are quirky, with their own unique lexicon,[19] and socially awkward, even fatalistic about life, most are perfectly benign.

The term *incel* is most synonymous, however, with the twenty-two-year-old who in 2014 shot and killed six people in Isla Vista, an area that is part of the University of California, Santa Barbara, campus. Kates explains that the Isla Vista shooter was not the first incel killer—that honor belongs to a twenty-five-year-old Canadian who murdered fourteen women and wounded ten others in a 1989 shooting in Montreal—but the Isla Vista shooter has become the "charismatic father of the movement." As his rage spiraled out of control, he began to blame the "wicked hearts" of women for his years of pain and suffering. In his sprawling 141-page autobiography, he wrote that "women's rejection of me was a declaration of war" and that he would "punish all females for the crime of depriving me of sex."

However, much like how the Charleston church shooter was radicalized online, these ideas were not his own. We spoke to two people who knew the Isla Vista shooter well but asked not to be named. Over a series of joint conversations, both in person and over the telephone, we learned that there was more to this person than meets the eye.

"There's a different voice in the manifesto" that went viral, because by then "he had a plan," one of our interviewees explains. In fact, our interviewees now consider the shooter's autobiography to be his public "suicide note," written with an audience in mind. They remember hearing that the shooter was writing the document. They first thought it was a positive thing, because it seemed to keep him engaged and occupied. They realize now that this was a mistake. "Being alone changes you. You start hearing this voice that you think is yours, but it's not."

Our interviewees told us about a boy who grew up in privilege, the son of a successful Hollywood producer and someone who was largely very happy until puberty. From that point on, "he couldn't talk to girls. Other boys have charm, but he didn't," one of them says. "He tried so hard for so long," they add, before channeling his perspective: "I have the clothes. The BMW. I am better than everyone else, but they [girls] don't like me." That was how he felt.

Then, suddenly, "there was a switch. He went from '*I'm* the loser' to '*They* are the losers.'" But "these ideas didn't just come from him." It's well documented that the shooter visited websites like Pick Up Artist Hate, which opposed the industry of teaching men the art of attracting women, and other misogynistic forums. One of our interviewees is clear: "We also need to talk about the toxic environment of those online forums. . . . I don't want to make excuses for him, but he didn't come up with all this stuff. He was encouraged. He was emboldened. And now he's idolized."

"Idolized" is a fitting description. Having already stabbed his two housemates and another man to death, the Isla Vista shooter filmed himself from behind the wheel of his black BMW coupe, bathed in golden hour lighting, and uploaded to YouTube his intent to exact "retribution" on a world he believed had deeply wronged him. The video went viral. In his autobiography, the shooter wrote, "Infamy is better than total obscurity." Some incels now call the Isla Vista shooter their patron "saint" and share memes of him superimposed onto paintings of Christian icons. The 2015 Umpqua Community College shooter described the Isla Vista shooter as being among "people who stand with the gods." The 2018 Parkland shooter, who killed seventeen people at a Florida high school, posted online that the Isla Vista shooter "will not be forgotten."

But when he was still alive, the Isla Vista shooter was just another incel who frequented a number of misogynistic chat rooms and communicated with other incels online. More than a means to perform socially deviant roles collectively, the internet also offers a platform to do it anonymously. And this is important if you don't want to be held accountable for your abhorrent, sexist views. "People were on his side. They understood him. It was the only place he felt accepted, after being ostracized his entire life," one of our interviewees says. "They thought the exact same way as him," they add, but the problem with that was the chat rooms and message boards became an echo chamber, and the shooter increasingly encountered only beliefs and opinions that coincided with his own, reinforcing his existing views. "There's no responsibility on these sites. You just type words. Without consequence," they say.

As his time online became less cathartic and more confirming, the Isla Vista shooter developed a form of "hostile attribution bias" that is common among mass shooters, meaning he began to infer hostile intent not just from obviously hostile actions but also from ambiguous ones. When he saw people dating or kissing in public, he began to assume they were doing it to spite him. Years before his crime, he threw coffee on a couple he was jealous of and on two girls for not smiling at him. He also got into a fight at a party.

In the end, the Isla Vista massacre was revenge for perceived injustices, bullying, female rejection, and public humiliation. "After I picked up the handgun," the shooter said, "I brought it back to my room and felt a new sense of power. I was now armed. *Who's the alpha male now, bitches?* I thought to myself, regarding all of the girls who've looked down on me in the past." His actions quickly inspired copycats. In 2017, a twenty-one-year-old walked into his former New Mexico high school and shot and killed two students. In online forums, he had used the name of the Isla Vista shooter as his pseudonym, as well as "Future Mass Shooter." In 2020, a self-described incel targeted romantic couples at Westgate Entertainment District, a mixed-use development in Glendale, Arizona. He shot and injured two people in front of a restaurant, fired additional shots, and then shot a third person in a parking lot.

Most notably, in 2018, a twenty-five-year-old drove a van onto a busy commercial street in Toronto, killing ten people and wounding sixteen. He later told police the attack was retribution for years of rejection by women and that he identified as a member of the incel movement. In a message he posted on Facebook just before his rampage, the man cited the "Supreme Gentleman," a term the Isla Vista shooter had used to describe himself, as his inspiration: "The Incel Rebellion has already begun! We will overthrow all the Chads and Stacys! All hail the Supreme Gentleman . . ."

—

Tackling the hate that underlies some mass shootings is tricky. In a classic experiment, a team of psychologists asked people to read a series of studies that seemed either to support or to reject the idea that capital punishment deters crime.[20] They found that people readily accepted any data that supported their initial beliefs, but rejected any information that opposed them, thus leaving participants even more convinced of their opinions and even more polarized. In other words, trying to correct misperceptions can actually reinforce them.

Researchers call this a "backfire effect," whereby individuals hold fast to their perceptions, whether true or false, even when presented with evidence to the contrary, becoming increasingly intransigent the more they are presented with countervailing evidence.[21] They do this because they have already invested so much of themselves into a particular position, such as racism, misogyny, or homophobia, that any evidence to suggest they invested in the wrong position threatens their very identities. When people hold inconsistent beliefs, cognitive dissonance suggests that they almost always side with what is most comfortable instead of what is true in order to alleviate the arising tension.[22]

However, people can and do change their minds. There is no question the antidote to racism, sexism, anti-Semitism, and other hateful viewpoints is critical thinking. One approach is to "cognitively empower" people by encouraging them to think analytically and to consider available evidence more carefully.[23] Investments in young people's cultural awareness and media literacy and in countervailing messaging of tolerance and unity, which reassures victims and shuns perpetrators, will very likely take a bite out of hate-motivated attacks.

Social media companies could "de-platform" certain groups and individuals, thereby denying them access to a venue in which to espouse their hateful rhetoric in the first place. We saw this in January 2021, when President Donald Trump was de-platformed from Twitter and Facebook for inciting an insurrection with the intent to overthrow a fair and free election, and when Amazon's cloud computing service pulled support for the "free speech" social network Parler, an alternative to Twitter that was popular among Trump supporters and was implicated in the 2021 storming of the U.S. Capitol. De-platforming obviously works—it largely silenced a sitting U.S. president during his final weeks in office—but making editorial decisions does raise thorny moral and legal questions for tech companies, which until now have been treated as *platforms for*, not *publishers of*, third-party content, and have been loosely regulated to avoid not limiting debate.

Some people argue that de-platforming from mainstream sites will simply force people into darker and even less regulated sites, where the social media echo chamber is amplified. Research finds that "hate clusters" often regenerate and spread across platforms, even when they are banned.[24] However, Megan Squire, professor of computer science at Elon University and an expert in online extremism, argues that de-platforming seriously undermines hate because extremists need mainstream social media platforms to normalize their ideas and spread them to the largest audience.[25] They are helped in this when mainstream figures, even presidents, retweet extremists' words or refuse to denounce them.

When Twitter and Facebook let extremists' profiles remain active, the companies lend the credibility of their online communities to them. It is much harder for fringe groups and individuals to appear "normal," and for everyday people to be recruited into extremist groups, if those groups are buried in the depths of the internet. Mainstream platforms that combine both public and private means of communication, such as public posts, private groups, and direct messaging, also allow for a seamless pivot between front stage propaganda and backstage planning and organization. De-platforming thus disrupts both functions by deleting an extremist's Rolodex of fellow extremists.

Look at some of the most recent hate-motivated mass shootings, and you'll see that nearly every shooter posted some kind of indication of their hateful thinking on the internet in the days and weeks leading up to the event. Some shared complete "manifestos" online, stating their political or religious beliefs with undertones of malice and hatred. Others spelled out their violent intentions explicitly.

In the wake of the 2019 mass shooting in El Paso, which was preceded by the shooter posting a racist screed full of white supremacist talking points on 8chan, a hate-filled online message board, President Trump called on social media companies, who run massive platforms and can sift through the personal data of billions of people, to "detect mass shooters before they strike." The president wanted private enterprises to develop new algorithmic tools for surfacing "red flags" that could enable the government to act earlier to prevent mass casualties.

Determining whether threats of violence on social media are credible is time- and labor-intensive work. In most cases, law enforcement still relies on tips—someone saw the threat and contacted authorities about it. And while social media companies flag to law enforcement those items they suspect indicate a specific threat, there are no federal laws requiring them to alert authorities or to take any other action in response to threats of violence posted on their platforms. This leaves law enforcement either out of the loop entirely or forced to subpoena companies for more information as needed— a cumbersome process when time is of the essence.

We're at a critical juncture to change this. Technology companies such as Facebook (which also owns Instagram), Google (which owns YouTube), and Twitter are waking up to the reputational risks of being associated with hate speech and other harmful content and are increasingly devoting considerable resources to removing it. But as private companies, these platforms are beholden to their own internal hate speech and violence policies. The decision about whether to remove content or ban a user falls largely on hired content moderators, who manually review any flagged material using predefined guidelines.

Adjudicating among thousands of triggering and traumatizing posts that are in potential violation of company policy every day is difficult work,[26] made no easier by the fact there is little consensus on what actually constitutes hate speech and that any context or nuance can drastically alter the meaning of words posted online. The limits of free expression are difficult to craft into law, but if the government could do this, a significant advance will have been made.

If someone does post to social media immediately before they decide to unleash violence, it's often not something that would trip many company policies as they are currently written, because social media companies, champions of free speech, rarely punish what people say they might do, only what they've actually done. In August 2020, a militia page advocating for followers to bring guns to oppose a Black Lives Matter protest in Kenosha, Wisconsin, was flagged to Facebook at least 455 times after its creation, but it was cleared by no fewer than four moderators, all of whom deemed it "non-violating." The page and event were eventually removed from the platform . . . several hours after a seventeen-year-old allegedly shot and killed two protesters.[27]

With the benefit of hindsight, content moderators clearly got that one wrong. The question is: Can our hindsight become someone else's foresight? Banning accounts and/or flagging them to authorities *before* anyone makes a solid threat against a person or group moves us into *Minority Report* territory, where police apprehend criminals for crimes not yet committed based on precognition. Is America comfortable leaving it up to Silicon Valley to decide who is and is not the next mass shooter? After all, social media companies are precisely that: companies. They have a singular interest in creating shareholder value. Facebook, Twitter, and other social media platforms were created with the simple goal of connecting people online, but because more human attention and engagement mean more advertising dollars (their primary source of income in the absence of subscription and usage fees), they've done little to date to protect their users.[28]

Social media platforms are designed to profit from a form of confirmation bias, the natural human tendency to seek, "like," and share new information in accordance with preexisting beliefs. To keep us online, they rely on adaptive algorithms that assess our interests and flood us with content that is similar to what we liked before. This makes it difficult for extremists to kick old habits, like extremism. Even if someone wants to avoid hate online, personalized search results based on past click behavior and history instead create "filter bubbles" that make hate unavoidable.[29] The social media echo chamber provides reaffirmation for hate by silencing outside voices and contradicting any intervention's countervailing messaging. Algorithms promote content that sparks outrage and amplifies biases within the data that users feed them.

Algorithms are more a problem than a solution, it seems. There's an important difference between tipping authorities off when someone posts a concrete threat of violence and using "big data" to identify who could potentially be a shooter. This assumes the algorithms can even get it right. There is a tendency to think of machine learning as a cure-all to expedite decision-making and mitigate existing human fallibility in the process. The fact is, algorithmic tools are based on decisions and data, and that makes them no more objective than the humans who create them.[30]

An algorithm is only as good as its trainer, whose own preferences are baked into the codes they write, and deep learning is only as good as its data. Tech firms have a lot of data (probably too much), but that does not necessarily mean it is good data, fit for this purpose. We explicitly caution against using our data for predictive modeling—and we've curated the largest, most comprehensive database on mass shooters. The reason for this? Many of the factors correlated with mass shootings, from childhood trauma to gun ownership, are true for millions of people who never commit mass shootings. Mass shootings also are extreme and rare events. There are not enough outputs to balance all the inputs, which is precisely what predictive algorithms need to be able to predict.

In the end, the best defense against extremism is to be found within ourselves and in the cohesive and multicultural communities we create. Extremism is not something foreign to our society, but instead part of it. We don't have to hunt down hate to find it; we need only recognize that it is loosely directed even when it is tightly held. Perpetrators of mass shootings motivated by hate tend to have a loose affiliation and weak ideological belief system. Their true hatred is self-loathing, anger, frustration, and hopelessness. This opens the door to intervention because the people saying hateful and hurtful things, online and in person, are really just projecting an underlying unhappiness with themselves, not a strong conviction about others. To stop mass shootings motivated by hate, we must embrace the complex reality that online activity is rooted in real world experience. The online and offline lives of mass shooters are not mutually exclusive, but rather one and the same. For any intervention to be successful, it must reach people where they are at, both in digital space and in physical space. It must also reach them earlier, before lost souls ever go searching for hateful narratives to make sense of their lives, and before a mass shooting is ever on the horizon.

CHAPTER 8

OPPORTUNITY

In his book about the scourge of urban gun violence, *Bleeding Out*, Thomas Abt, a senior fellow at the Council on Criminal Justice, uses a powerful metaphor.[1] If a young man is rushed into an emergency room, dying from multiple gunshot wounds, the doctor doesn't start listing off all the social problems that got him there—a broken home, poverty in the neighborhood, a lack of education, employment, and training opportunities—even if, technically, they might be root causes. No, instead the doctor says, "We've got to stop the bleeding." Because that's the first step. You address the immediate emergency, and then you work outward from there.

Well, when it comes to mass shootings, in 2020 we stopped the bleeding. U.S. mass shootings hit a record high in 2018, with nine, including the Valentine's Day massacre at a high school in Parkland, Florida. The second-most shootings in a year prior to 2018 was seven in 2017, the year we started this research, which was also the deadliest year on record after the unprecedented shooting that took place in Las Vegas. There were also seven mass shootings in 2019, three with large death tolls in the month of August alone. And so the worst years on record for mass shootings were 2017, 2018, and 2019. (1999 also had seven shootings.)

The year 2020 started much like 2019 ended, with a mass shooting on February 26, when an employee at a brewery in Milwaukee killed five coworkers. Then, on March 15, a man killed four people at a gas station in Springfield, Missouri, before killing himself. America was at risk of bleeding out. But then, suddenly, unexpectedly, the United States fell into the grip of a global pandemic—and the shooting stopped.

The novel coronavirus created an interesting natural experiment. It did two things to mass shootings. One, it curtailed the opportunity for them. Criminologists once assumed that opportunity merely determined when and where a crime occurred. However, four decades of research show that opportunity actually causes crime.[2] With people's movements restricted;

with schools, businesses, bars and restaurants, places of worship, and other possible shooting sites all closed; and with the vast majority of Americans staying indoors, COVID-19 took the *masses* away from mass shootings.

The other thing the novel coronavirus did was stop the contagion. Prior to 2020, America's fear of and fascination with mass shootings was fueling other mass shootings in three ways. First, one mass shooting provided social proof for another mass shooting—and so the next mass shooting inevitably followed the last, whether in style or substance. Second, intense media coverage of mass shootings led to more people seeking to become copycat killers. And third, endless discussion and excessive worry over the risk of mass shootings fed daily mass shooting routines, such as active shooter drills, which, in turn, planted the seed that mass shootings were normal, a legitimate way of handling grievances if someone was angry and struggling. COVID-19 broke this cycle, not least because, in 2020, *everyone* was angry and struggling, keeping mass shooters out of the headlines and out of our heads.

We've seen this break in routine before. Northeastern University criminologist James Alan Fox recalls how the September 11, 2001, terrorist attacks deflected attention from an alarming sequence of school shootings in the late 1990s and early 2000s, including Columbine, and there wasn't another multiple-victim K–12 school shooting for four years.[3]

This time, unfortunately, the break didn't last. In March 2021, as the pandemic eased, just as businesses and workplaces began reopening and people started gathering in larger numbers, we had two mass shootings in a week—the first at three Atlanta-area spas that left eight people dead, then a shooting at a grocery store in Boulder, Colorado, that killed ten. The return to public life meant a return to the routine of mass shootings, in part because lawmakers did nothing in between to prevent them, but also because the pandemic exacerbated many risk factors for violence, such as social isolation and economic hardship.

But there is still an important lesson to be learned from mass shooting trends in 2020. We obviously cannot shut down public life and stay home permanently wrapped in personal protective equipment, trading one form of mass death for another. Because we've stopped the bleeding before, however, we can apply the same opportunity principle, grounded in the science of situational crime prevention, to help stop the bleeding again.

—

In the early twentieth century, the United Kingdom heated domestic ovens with coal gas, which contained lethal levels of carbon monoxide. By the late 1950s, more than half of all suicides there—about the same proportion as firearm suicides in the United States today—involved someone putting their head in an oven, to use the common expression of the day, because it offered a quick, painless, bloodless means of death.

Then, in the 1960s, the government began, incidentally, to replace manufactured gas with cleaner, natural gas from the North Sea, which was virtually free of carbon monoxide. By 1977, less than one half of 1 percent of suicides used domestic gas, and the overall national suicide rate fell by a third.[4]

Twenty years later, the United Kingdom also changed the packaging for a popular over-the-counter painkiller to require "blister packs" for packages of sixteen pills when they were sold in places like convenience stores, and for packages of thirty-two pills in pharmacies. Big bottles made it easy to pour out many loose pills at once and were implicated in hundreds of deliberate and accidental overdoses each year. Blister packs meant pills had to be popped out one by one, making it a long, slow process to pop out enough pills to die by suicide.[5] A study by Oxford University found that suicide deaths from paracetamol overdoses fell by 43 percent over the next decade.[6] A similar decline was found in accidental deaths from medication poisonings, and overdose-related liver transplants dropped by 61 percent.

In chapter 4, we wrote that someone in a suicidal crisis is like a balloon full to bursting—the goal is to let a little air out. Study after study finds that putting even the smallest obstacle between people and the means to kill themselves can do precisely that. The natural gas and the blister packs slowed things down. Firearms, however, the most common means of suicide in the United States and other countries where guns are prevalent, speed things up. They are fast and lethally efficient (resulting in death 85 percent of the time)[7] and leave little room for a change of heart or a lifesaving intervention.

Switzerland, like the United States, has a well-established gun culture. It boasts one of the highest rates of firearm ownership in the world—about one-third of all Swiss households owns a gun. That's because Switzerland has compulsory military service. The famous "Swiss Army" is a well-regulated militia with every able-bodied Swiss man between the ages of eighteen and forty-three expected to serve. Each conscript is issued a personal service rifle, which they keep at home. They have regular drills. And when soldiers complete their service, they have the option to purchase their military-issued rifle from the government at a discount. Many do so because Switzerland has a strong tradition of sport shooting and hunting.

Compared with other European nations, Switzerland also has a remarkably high number of firearm-enabled suicides, about 40 percent of which are committed with army weapons.[8] At least, until 2003. That was the year Switzerland introduced new reforms (titled "Army XXI") and civil service as an option for people who didn't want to serve in the armed forces. It was the closest thing to a national randomized controlled trial you could get. As a result of the reform, the number of troops was halved over the period of one year, from approximately four hundred thousand to two hundred thousand. That meant far fewer people with access to guns at home. It also meant far fewer suicides, specifically suicides by shooting.[9]

A 2010 study of the Israeli army found that requiring soldiers to leave their weapons on base over the weekend, as opposed to bringing them home, reduced the suicide rate among troops by almost 40 percent.[10] So, there was precedent for this, but in Switzerland, the change was so abrupt that Swiss psychiatrist Thomas Reisch and his colleagues couldn't believe what they were seeing. They ran the numbers and discovered that the drop in suicides was clustered among people between the ages of eighteen and forty-three—the same group that would have been serving in the military before the 2003 reforms.[11] And in a direct challenge to the talking point that if someone is intent on suicide but doesn't have a gun, they will find another way, Reisch found that 78 percent of the men who would have taken their lives with a gun did not substitute another method of suicide, such as poison or hanging. He observed comparable reductions in suicides after the installation of safety nets and access barriers that prevent people from jumping from bridges, similarly with little or no substitution effect or displacement to other bridges.[12]

From gas ovens to pill bottles to military arms to bridges, it turns out that reducing access to certain lethal means of suicide can have a dramatic effect on suicide rates. The implication is that if people can't get their hands on the easiest tools to harm themselves, there will be fewer deaths.

—

Simon Osamoh, a former police detective specializing in counterterrorism and security director at the Mall of America, in Minnesota, is a sought-after national trainer on church security. Like James, Osamoh is British, and the two of them first met not long after arriving in the United States, when a mutual friend clocked their accents and decided they could use their good old-fashioned humor to help each other survive the isolation of the harsh Minnesota winters. Osamoh is a huge believer in situational crime prevention, but he focuses more on its softer side. For example, reducing provocations. This is especially important in restaurants and bars and places of commerce and worship, where long lines or poor customer service could tip an already disgruntled visitor over the edge.

For years, Osamoh has trained ushers and greeters at churches—or anyone customer-facing, for that matter—in the subtle art of conversation. He explains his philosophy: "Walk into any Great Clips hair salon in America, and someone at the front desk will ask, 'What brings you here today?' The answer is obvious—a haircut. But the question gets people talking. It opens up a dialogue."

Dialogue is important, Osamoh argues, because it allows someone to begin to probe for verbal and nonverbal cues of harmful intent or actions incongruous with the space. He uses the 2015 Charleston church shooting as an example. "A white supremacist walks into a Bible study at a historically black church, carrying a bagful of guns and ammo, and not one person greeted him to ask what he was doing there." Osamoh is incredulous. "He sat in the parking lot and then in the building for nearly an hour. No one thought, *Wait a minute. He looks lost or out of place.*" Osamoh notes that when the FBI questioned the shooter, he said he was surprised by that and that "if someone had approached him that day, he might not have gone through with the crime. In fact, he'd been casing schools and shopping malls beforehand but had decided on the church because it was the softest target—there was no security."

Osamoh acknowledges that this can sound like victim blaming, especially when churches should be welcoming and nonjudgmental places, but he was referencing the fact that three months before the shooting, security officers at a shopping mall in Columbia, South Carolina, found the Charleston shooter asking employees at two stores unusual questions about staffing and operating hours. He was banned from the mall for a year. Security followed up by dropping off a flyer displaying the shooter's picture with each of the mall's tenants. Tenants were told to be on alert and to call security if they saw the young man in the mall again. When he was spotted at the facility a month later, he was charged with trespassing and placed on a new, three-year ban.

Osamoh explains that situational crime prevention is about being proactive and prepared for the worst. "You don't leave your car unlocked with the engine running, so why would you leave the church door wide-open with no one watching the entrance?" He explains that the methodology is not about profiling people or creating a hostile space—in fact, it's quite the opposite. It's about making sure everyone feels seen, which reduces anonymity, a risk factor for violence. It's also about making sure people feel heard, which de-escalates tensions.

It takes courage to confront a stranger proactively and ask them how they're doing, Osamoh says, which is why this sort of behavior-detection approach is more commonly deployed by trained professionals at airports and concert venues, locations where security screening is expected. Osamoh wants to change that. He believes that, with good training, anyone could be more situationally aware. He quotes the famous "Moscow Rules" for CIA operatives: "Never go against your gut; it is your operational antenna. If it feels wrong, it *is* wrong."

—

Situational crime prevention helps us understand why mass shooters target one space over another.[13] Our data show that shooters target certain sites if they are identified with or representative of a specific grievance—the school or workplace, for example. Shooters target iconic or symbolic sites like churches and military bases for similar reasons but also to send a wider message to society. They also target sites they know certain people frequent. The routine of religious adherence means that an estranged husband knows where his wife and children will be on a Sunday morning, and a disgruntled worker knows when he can confront his boss outside office hours. The 2019 El Paso shooter even drove eleven hours to a border community from his hometown near Dallas, Texas, to fire at shoppers inside a Walmart. Most of the twenty-three people killed that day were Latinx. The shooter confessed to police that he was targeting Mexicans, and in a statement he had posted to the online message board 8chan, he called the Walmart attack "a response to the Hispanic invasion of Texas."

The site of Perpetrator A's shooting, an Italian restaurant, "wasn't his first choice," explained Marco, the business manager of a site where, nearly thirty years ago, four people were killed and six others were injured. His "first choice" was the steak house down the road, but it was so busy that night that Perpetrator A couldn't find a parking spot. So, instead, he visited the nearby Italian eatery, Mario's. Perpetrator A targeted Mario's in part because it was familiar—it was well-known and only a mile from home. It was also easier—more accessible and less protected than other sites, like the grocery store across the street with an off-duty cop working security. Mario's was also busy that warm summer evening, and occupied sites have more potential victims in them than other targets.

We were lucky to meet Marco. For obvious reasons, we tended to book our interviews weeks, sometimes months in advance. We also tended to schedule them with plenty of breathing room afterward, because the interviews often got heavy, and we needed the time and space to process and decompress. As working parents, however, whenever we travel, we also tend to over-schedule ourselves in an effort to get done in three days what should really take four, so we can get back home to our kids. And so it was, one summer, when we were traveling in the South and an interview we had scheduled about a different mass shooting, at a college, got canceled. We looked at the time and made a quick decision to drive an hour south to eat lunch at Mario's, on the off chance that someone there might remember the tragedy that took place nearly thirty years before.

Pushed for time between interviewees, we arrived at the restaurant rather frazzled because Jill was pulled over for speeding en route—our upgraded sporty rental car drove faster than she was accustomed to. We were also second-guessing our choice the entire journey down, fearing that we'd come off as morbid mass shooting tourists from Minnesota or would retraumatize someone by showing up out of the blue.

We were seated in a corner booth, and as we ordered our lunch, we told the young waitress about our research. (Looking back now, we see it was not our finest elevator pitch.) But she took pity on us. "I bet I could get Marco," she replied. Marco shows up around the same time as our Caesar salads. He sits down and pours himself a sparkling water into a wineglass and garnishes it with a lemon slice. He's Greek, with olive skin, distinguished but casually dressed in a loose-fitting T-shirt and shorts. "Pardon my appearance; I'm just here for lunch," he says. Within minutes we can see that Marco is a pillar of the community. He knows everybody's name, and they all know his. Patrons stop by to shake hands, and he talks to each and every one of them in a way that makes them feel like they're the only person in the room. He talks to us that way, too, for nearly two hours.

Marco remembers the night of the shooting as if it were yesterday. He has the date committed to memory. There were about thirty people in the restaurant that night, he says. He had just finished his shift and was sitting at a booth, eating dinner with his wife and her parents, the restaurant's beloved owners, who had lived in the community for fifty-four years and had introduced pizza to the town. At approximately 10:15 P.M., he says, he heard gunshots outside. (He knew they were gunshots and not firecrackers because he had served in the Greek military before moving to the United

States for graduate school.) He peered out a side window to see Perpetrator A outside armed with two shotguns, a rifle, and a bag of ammunition. Marco rushed to the kitchen to lock the back door, but before he could reach it, Perpetrator A had pushed it open from the outside. Marco retreated into the restaurant and told everyone to get out. It was then that Perpetrator A shot and killed the cook.

Marco's wife and in-laws dived under their table. Marco remembers seeing his wife cling to the table leg for dear life. Perpetrator A kicked open the saloon-style doors that separated the kitchen from the main dining room "like something out of an old Western," and Marco escaped out the front door. A few hours before the shooting, Perpetrator A had watched a revisionist Western film. He told us via letter:

> *I was drinking along with Clint Eastwood in "Unforgiven." I had peeled the label from my bottle and knocked the plastic from the cork so that my bottle looked just like the whiskey bottle that Clint was drinking from.*

Marco fled right into the arms of an off-duty police officer who had heard the shots and had run across the street from the grocery store where he was moonlighting. They heard more shots, nineteen in total. Marco wanted to go back in, but the cop held him back. "I've called for backup," he said. "More of us are on the way." He then shot Perpetrator A through the window from outside, hitting him in the leg. Perpetrator A went down, but he got back up and continued firing. He shot Marco's father-in-law in the face and his mother-in-law point-blank in the head. Marco's wife watched both her parents die before she, too, was shot in the thigh. Then the shooting stopped. Perpetrator A's rifle had jammed. This afforded one of the first responders on the scene time to crawl through a rear door of the restaurant and shoot Perpetrator A again, disabling him.

Marco is comfortable with long moments of silence. It's the what-ifs that occupy his thoughts. What if the steak house parking lot hadn't been full that evening? What if he'd gotten to the back door sooner? What if his family had run out with him, instead of hiding? What if his children had been there that night, as they were most nights, instead of safe at home with a babysitter? What if he had had a gun?

Marco now carries a gun at all times. His whole family does—everyone except his wife. She survived the shooting but "walks with a limp." She hates guns. She "recovered physically, but not psychologically," Marco says, his watery eyes spilling over. "You never really recover." He recalls a family vacation to Greece where the sound of a local farmer using a pneumatic captive bolt pistol to stun goats prior to slaughter triggered his wife's PTSD. Even for Marco, "whenever a car backfires, it takes me back."

But Marco is comfortable around guns, and confident. He's a hunter, military trained, the quintessential "good guy with a gun." Such a good guy that he even picked up the tab for lunch before taking us on a tour of his restaurant, which had rebounded stronger than ever after the shooting.

"The media and the community really rallied around us," Marco explains. The restaurant is now double its original size, more upscale, with dark woods, wine racks, and pictures on the walls. Amid the framed Mediterranean vistas are newspaper clippings from that fateful night and photographs of family and friends lost. So much beauty in the pain of tragedy.

—

Situational crime prevention works, but no one wants to live in a police state, under a perpetual COVID-like lockdown to stop mass shootings. The question is: How much liberty are we willing to sacrifice for our security? In the United States, firearms are perhaps the ultimate expression of liberty and, in the minds of many, the greatest tool for security. That includes security from mass shootings.

In recent years, several state legislatures have written or revised firearm laws to make it easier for people to carry guns in schools or houses of worship, especially people with a background in the military or law enforcement. Arming teachers is perhaps the most controversial prospect, but there are already a surprising number of armed personnel in America's schools.

Millions of dollars have gone into federal Community Oriented Policing Services (COPS) grants to fund additional school police over the past twenty years, and within six months of the 2018 Parkland school shooting, more than $1 billion was added to school security budgets by state legislatures, with funding for school resource officers (SROs) being one of the largest items. The American Civil Liberties Union (ACLU) now estimates that 1.7 million students are in schools with police but no counselors, 6 million students are in schools with police but no school psychologists, and 10 million students are in schools with police but no social workers.[14]

Measuring the impact of SROs on mass shootings is tricky. We examined every recorded incident in which more than one person was intentionally shot in a school building during the school day, or in which a perpetrator came to school heavily armed with the intent of firing indiscriminately, as reported by the public K–12 School Shooting Database since 1980. Out of 133 cases, 29 (24 percent) had an armed officer on scene when the shooting began. These tended to be larger high schools. We found that armed security yielded no significant reduction in rates of injuries, and, in fact, after controlling for other factors like the school size, the number of shooters, and the number and type of firearms, the rate of deaths was nearly *three times higher* in schools with an armed police officer or a security guard present.[15] Looking at mass shootings in any location, we similarly found that more people were injured when there was an armed person on scene than when there wasn't (an average of ten people injured versus seven, if you exclude Las Vegas, whose victim count was so high it skews the data).

SROs can respond to mass shootings in unpredictable ways. The armed officer at Parkland, for example, did not enter the school, staying outside for forty-five minutes both during and after the shooting despite seventeen people having been murdered. There are also concerns about the visible presence of police officers in schools negatively affecting the entire school climate and impeding educational progress. Sociologist Aaron Kupchik, author of the 2010 book *Homeroom Security*, finds that "the presence of police in schools is unlikely to prevent another school shooting and the potential for oppression of students—especially poor and racial/ethnic minority youth—is a more realistic and common threat than Columbine."[16] That's because, when in schools, police officers do what they are trained to do, which is to detain, handcuff, and arrest. This contributes to a larger social problem known as the "school-to-prison pipeline," in which even minor infractions at school are adjudicated by the criminal justice system.[17]

There are examples of SROs on campus reducing the severity of school shootings. One example is the officer at the Santa Fe High School shooting in Texas in 2018, in which ten students were killed: That school resource officer drew attention away from the perpetrator while students and teachers escaped. Another example comes from one of our key case studies. When Perpetrator B arrived at the site of his crime, his former high school, and opened fire, his 9mm carbine jammed. He was apprehended by a deputy sheriff assigned to the school and a retired highway patrol officer who taught driver's education. Lacy, the object of Perpetrator B's affections, whom we met in chapter 5, tells us this intervention took everyone at the school by surprise, because students would make fun of the SRO for being so "dopey." High school students can be cruel, but, she says, "Seriously, we never thought he could even run," let alone tackle an active shooter.

By definition, however, armed security was no deterrent to violence in cases in which a shooting still happened. We think this has something to do with the fact that so many mass shooters are actively suicidal and intend to die in the act. A shooter may actually be drawn to a location like a school precisely *because* there is an armed officer on scene, given that they wish to be killed. In December 2019, a gunman killed two people at a church in White Settlement, Texas, before an armed volunteer, a firearms instructor, shot and killed him six seconds later. It was the perfect test case for the "good guy with a gun," but what was lost on the gun rights advocates who celebrated this act of heroism was that having a concealed handgun failed to deter the crime in the first place and was no advantage to the first guard who engaged the gunman; he was killed. Most people in life-or-death situations freeze or shut down entirely, even the good guys. (Case in point: Parkland.) The chances that a regular armed civilian will shoot an innocent person by accident are high; so, too, are the chances of arriving officers' mistakenly shooting the good guys because they are seen with a weapon in the aftermath of a shooting incident.

—

Gun safety advocates balk at the idea that the solution to guns is more guns. They argue that, in much the same way the coronavirus pandemic proved that there can be no mass shooting without masses, there can be no shooting at all without guns. And study after study finds that ready access to lethal weapons in the United States creates *opportunity* for lethal violence to occur,[18] including mass shootings with excessive casualties. In one of his letters, Perpetrator A told us that his weapon of choice was simply convenient:

> *The shotgun I used was one that I was given on my 15th birthday and used it to hunt deer and various small game animals. I had it and the ammo there at my fiancée's house.*

Fifteen-year-old Gracie Anne Muehlberger and fourteen-year-old Dominic Blackwell were killed in November 2019 at Saugus High School in Santa Clarita, California. A fellow student with a pistol opened fire in the outside courtyard, or quad, shooting five students in total, two fatally, before turning the gun on himself. Gracie's father, Bryan, walked us through the heart-wrenching story of that day, including how he was forced to use his Find My iPhone app to cut through the chaos of the scene to locate his daughter's body in the hospital. Bryan, a technologist, is a big proponent of "root cause analysis," a method of problem-solving used for identifying the source of faults. He was still trying to comprehend how the shooter, who was too young to pass a background check or purchase a gun legally in California, was able to source off the internet a do-it-yourself kit of interchangeable parts and build the .45-caliber "ghost gun" that killed his little girl.

A ghost gun is any sort of firearm built at home without a manufacturer's serial number, which makes it practically impossible to trace. The U.S. Bureau of Alcohol, Tobacco, Firearms and Explosives doesn't consider the do-it-yourself kits to be firearms, so buyers don't have to undergo the usual background checks, although President Joe Biden has proposed new restrictions on ghost guns, and California attorney general Xavier Becerra, backed by Bryan Muehlberger, is suing the ATF to change its policy.[19] In the Santa Clarita shooting, it is unclear whether the gun was assembled by the shooter or his father, an avid hunter who died in 2017 and left guns in his wake. What is clear is that whoever assembled the weapon bypassed both many existing regulations regarding the definition and registration of firearms and the associated background checks for possession and transfer.

Bryan himself proved this fact by buying his own ghost gun online—in his deceased daughter's name, he told us. And assembly isn't difficult: An unfinished firearm receiver comes about 80 percent complete, and there are instructional videos online that walk you through the finishing process. The parts and playbook, both found online, created the opportunity for violence to occur. Without them, Bryan's daughter might still be alive.

Firearms used in mass shootings

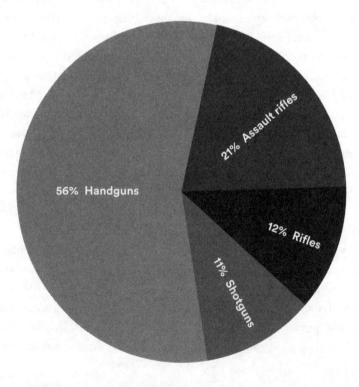

How mass shooters got their guns

63% Legal purchase

9% Stolen from family/friend

28% Illegal purchase

If the prevalent weapon in a community is a knife, then stabbings are higher. If it is a gun, then more people are shot. In our database, 172 mass shooters used a total of 377 firearms to commit 169 mass shootings. Is this just the price America has to pay for protecting everyone's Second Amendment right to bear arms? We don't think so. There is nothing in the Second Amendment prohibiting sensible firearm regulations that curb opportunities for shootings to arise. As Justice Antonin Scalia, champion of constitutional originalism, wrote in his 2008 opinion for *District of Columbia v. Heller*, the landmark Supreme Court decision that expanded the scope of the Second Amendment to the possession of firearms for the purpose of personal self-defense, not simply the common defense. "Nothing in our opinion should be taken to cast doubt on longstanding prohibitions on the possession of firearms by felons and the mentally ill, or laws forbidding the carrying of firearms in sensitive places such as schools and government buildings, or laws imposing conditions and qualifications on the commercial sale of arms."

The United States has regulated firearms for years, albeit loosely. The 1934 National Firearms Act, the first major federal gun law, and the 1938 Federal Firearms Act together created a licensing system for dealers and imposed tax and registration requirements on the "gangster guns" favored by Prohibition-era organized crime and on display during the 1929 Saint Valentine's Day Massacre. The 1968 Gun Control Act, passed after the assassinations of Robert F. Kennedy and Martin Luther King Jr., restricted the importation of military-surplus firearms, banned mail-order gun sales—President John F. Kennedy was killed with a mail-order gun—and prohibited gun dealers from selling to "dangerous" categories of persons, such as people with felony convictions or those with prior psychiatric hospitalization.

Efforts at the federal level to regulate firearms have gone nowhere in recent years, however, owing in large part to the power of the National Rifle Association. There was a time when the NRA, founded in 1871, focused principally on hunting, marksmanship, and conservation, and was willing to compromise on gun legislation. The NRA in fact endorsed the laws of the 1930s and 1960s. But in the late 1970s, its moderate leadership fell to a cadre of absolutists opposed to any hint of regulation.[20] In the 1980s, the attempt to assassinate President Ronald Reagan and the shooting of his press secretary, James Brady, led to a call for gun control. The NRA was vehemently opposed, and gun laws largely got weaker, not stronger, in the years since.

In 1986, for example, the Firearms Owners Protection Act repealed parts of the 1968 Gun Control Act by invoking "the rights of citizens . . . to keep and bear arms under the Second Amendment." Individual states responded by widely adopting "concealed carry" and "stand your ground" laws, the latter of which exonerated from prosecution citizens who used deadly force when confronted by an assailant, even if they could have retreated safely. In 2005, President George W. Bush signed a law protecting firearms manufacturers, importers, and dealers from lawsuits by victims of crimes involving guns. Three years later, in *District of Columbia v. Heller*, the U.S. Supreme Court ruled unconstitutional a Washington, DC, ban on handguns in the home for self-defense. States have the right to pass their own gun control measures; they just can't deny firearms outright, the Court said.

Federal law is the floor, not the ceiling, on gun control, which is why America is a "confusing patchwork" of gun legislation.[21] It's why a teenager who can't buy a gun in California can go buy one in neighboring Nevada, drive back to California, visit a popular garlic festival, kill three people, wound seventeen others, and then take his own life. It's why most of the guns used to perpetrate the worst mass shooting in Canadian history, the 2020 Nova Scotia attacks that killed 22 people, came from the United States. Still, according to the federal government and the Brady Handgun Violence Prevention Act of 1994, named for the staffer disabled in the Reagan assassination attempt, it is illegal to sell guns to juveniles, convicted felons, fugitives, undocumented Americans, drug users, former mental patients, and dishonorably discharged veterans. People convicted of domestic violence or living under a particular type of restraining order also are prohibited. Under the common-law concept of "negligent entrustment," a gun also cannot be sold to a person if the seller knows, or reasonably should know, that the buyer poses an unusually high risk of misusing it.

NRA enthusiasts argue that we don't need new gun laws; we just need to enforce the existing ones. It is illegal for a gun retailer to sell a firearm to anyone we've just listed. These dealers need a federal license and must run background checks to see if the buyer meets any of the criteria just given. However, a privately owned gun can be transferred legally in ways that bypass gun dealers, and our data show that a combination of strange state-versus-federal loopholes and poor enforcement of existing gun laws keep contributing to mass shootings.

For example, the 1990 General Motors Acceptance Corporation office shooter, who killed eleven people over a twenty-four-hour shooting spree, had killed someone years before, but because the judge withheld a guilty verdict on the condition that the shooter complete probation, the shooter was not considered a convicted felon under state law and was free to purchase guns.

The 2007 Trolley Square shooter, who killed five and wounded four in Salt Lake City, purchased a shotgun with a pistol grip from a pawnshop. You have to be eighteen to purchase a rifle or shotgun in Utah, but twenty-one to purchase a handgun. The question is: Is a shotgun with a pistol grip a shotgun or a pistol? Some argue that it's a handgun because the existence of the pistol grip means it no longer qualifies as a weapon to be fired from the shoulder. Others say it's a shotgun because the pistol grip is removable. In the end, the clerk who sold the gun was charged with unlawful transfer of a firearm to someone under twenty-one, but the charges were dropped when he pled guilty to a misdemeanor paperwork violation (he forgot to check a box on the form to confirm that he had seen two forms of ID), meaning the shotgun/pistol debate was never adjudicated.

See how easy it is? The Virginia Tech shooter had been court-ordered to receive mental health treatment, thus shouldn't have been eligible to buy a gun under federal law. In fact, of the thirty-four perpetrators in our database who had been hospitalized for psychiatric reasons, 88 percent were hospitalized involuntarily, which should have prohibited them from possessing firearms. However, Virginia commonwealth statute was worded in such a way that it did not apply to the shooter's situation, and in this and other cases he was still able to pass a background check.

The 2015 Charleston church shooter had a prior arrest during which he confessed to using drugs. When he tried to buy a gun, the dealer asked the FBI for approval, but the FBI declined because they wanted to investigate further. By law, the FBI has three business days to allow or deny a gun purchase, after which the gun dealer is free to sell the gun whether they have heard back from the FBI or not. Three days passed, and even though the FBI had not yet completed their investigation, the dealer sold the young man the gun. A few months before the shooting, the Charleston shooter was also caught by police in possession of a forearm grip for an AR-15, but he was not charged because the tool is lawful in South Carolina.

The 2017 Sutherland Springs church shooter was court-martialed by the air force for beating his wife and fracturing his toddler stepson's skull. The shooter was given a "bad conduct" discharge, and the air force was supposed to report his domestic violence conviction, which, on six separate occasions, would have disqualified him from purchasing a gun, but never did. The shooter lied on his background checks and said he had never been convicted of a felony, though he functionally had, because the military does not classify crimes committed by service members as "felonies" or "misdemeanors."

The shooter who killed five and injured seven at Henry Pratt Company in Aurora, Illinois, in 2019 had a prior conviction for aggravated assault for beating his girlfriend with a baseball bat. Despite this, he was able to obtain an Illinois Firearm Owner's Identification Card (FOID), which is a prerequisite for buying a gun in the state, presumably because his felony record was not properly submitted to the federal database. With FOID in hand, the shooter bought a gun and applied for a concealed-carry permit. That was when the state discovered the felony record. It revoked the shooter's FOID but never confiscated the gun he had bought with it. Why not? Illinois law states that when someone's FOID is revoked, they are asked to confirm that they no longer possess guns. The problem is no one checks that information.

Finally, the 2017 Rancho Tehama Reserve shooter, who killed five and injured twelve, was previously arrested for stabbing his neighbor. He was subject to a civil harassment restraining order as well as a criminal protective order and was asked to turn over all his firearms. He turned in a pistol and said he owned no other guns, exploiting the infamous "honor system," given that officials had no way of knowing how many guns he owned and no responsibility to check because he was not a felon. Little did they know, the shooter had two AR-15s he had built from parts, a handgun, and his wife's handgun at home. Neighbors even told police that the man had guns at home—they could hear him doing target practice—but because no one ever caught him red-handed, there was nothing law enforcement could do.

By our calculation, background checks on all gun sales or transfers may have prevented at least sixteen mass shootings (about 9 percent of the total), saving more than one hundred lives,[22] while ending the "default proceed" option on federal checks that take longer than three days may have averted the 2015 Charleston church shooting. Leading experts in criminology, public health, and law consider background checks performed by a licensed firearms dealer, law enforcement agency, or other neutral third-party arbiter to be the most effective way to reduce all gun deaths.[23] About 80 percent of all Americans support background checks for private sales and at gun shows.[24] However, a 2017 survey found that 22 percent of current U.S. gun owners who acquired a firearm within the past two years had done so without one and that the rate was 57 percent for people living in the thirty-one U.S. states without regulations on private firearm sales.[25]

More comprehensive than universal background checks, the most effective mass shooting prevention measure would be permit-to-purchase laws,[26] which exist in some form in thirteen states and require prospective gun purchasers to apply for a permit in person at a law enforcement office. Anyone granted a permit can then purchase guns for a set period of time without undergoing repeated background checks, as they would have to otherwise. One 2015 study found that Connecticut's permit-to-purchase law, introduced in 1995, was associated with a 40 percent reduction in the state's firearm-related homicide rate, while Missouri's removal of its permit-to-purchase law in 2007 was associated with a 25 percent *increase* in its firearm homicide rates over the next five years.[27]

For those buying a gun impulsively, permit-to-purchase laws create a temporary barrier, a bit like mandatory waiting periods. Mandatory waiting periods of three to ten days are the functional equivalent of counting to ten before doing something impulsive that could ruin your life and career, such as sending an angry email to your boss—only, in this case, it can stop you from shooting someone. Critics argue that waiting for a gun is inconvenient, especially in an era of online shopping and instant gratification, but you have to ask: Who needs a gun immediately unless they intend to use it right away? Nearly a third of mass shooters purchased a gun within a month of their crimes. The 2021 Atlanta spa shooter bought his gun just hours before the attack—no waiting required. That same day, over a thousand miles away, a twenty-one year old man bought a Ruger AR-556 pistol, a semi-automatic weapon with a capacity of thirty rounds, and six days later he used it to kill ten people in a Boulder supermarket. One Harvard study found that waiting period laws that delay the purchase of firearms by a few days reduced gun homicides by roughly 17 percent.[28] That seems worth the wait.

30%

of firearms used in mass shootings were purchased within a month of the shooting

Of course, it's not just procedures and policies that fail to stop mass shootings. People do, too. The 2018 Nashville Waffle House shooter had legally bought his guns. They were then taken away by police after the Secret Service arrested him while trying to break into the White House. The guns were given to the shooter's father for safekeeping, but he just gave them right back to his son.

Our data show that 80 percent of school shooters get their weapons from family members. There are many examples: A teen in Marysville, Washington, used one of his father's handguns to kill four classmates and himself in 2014. The shooter at Sandy Hook Elementary School in Newtown, Connecticut, in 2012 used firearms that belonged to his mother to kill twenty-seven people, mostly small children, but also his mother, before killing himself. The gunman who killed ten people in a Santa Fe, Texas, high school in 2018 had taken a shotgun and a pistol that belonged to his father.

There are no federal laws and few state laws requiring safe storage of guns, and no federal standards for firearm locks, which are distributed by law with every sale with no mandate to use them. Only six states (California, Massachusetts, Minnesota, Nevada, New York, and Virginia) and the District of Columbia have laws requiring the safe storage of guns in the home. Under California law, for example, parents can be criminally charged if they keep an unlocked firearm on their property where kids can get ahold of it. However, the laws are nearly impossible to enforce without going from door-to-door with a warrant.

So-called smart guns, which use biometrics and technology (e.g., radio frequency identification, or RFID, chips; fingerprint recognition; magnetic rings) to personalize a firearm the way one would a smartphone, thereby preventing unauthorized use, are one solution to this problem, but legal and logistical issues are still being ironed out.[29] In the meantime, research shows that secure storage policies can help prevent gun thefts, suicides, accidental shootings, and, by extension, mass shootings. One study found that keeping firearms locked up can reduce shootings in the home by 75 percent.[30] Proposals requiring secure storage at home are also generally popular. A 2019 survey by the Johns Hopkins Center for Gun Policy and Research found that most gun owners agree that people who buy a firearm for the first time should have to take a course on the safe handling and storage of the weapon.[31]

When asked, a majority of gun owners confess that they do not safely store all their firearms.[32] According to a 2015 national study, about one in five gun-owning households with children under age eighteen stores at least one weapon in the least safe manner: loaded and unlocked.[33] A 2018 survey of U.S. veterans put that number at one in three.[34] That means that up to 10 percent of U.S. children, roughly five million, live within reach of a loaded gun.

There isn't much research available on the effectiveness of safe storage awareness campaigns.[35] The Brady campaign's public health effort to "end family fire" has found that parents are much more likely to ask other parents whether they have guns in the house after receiving information about securing firearms. This is something we all can do. Every parent can make sure any gun they have in their own home is secured, and when their children visit a friend's house to play, parents can ask other parents if they have guns, and if so, if they are stored safely. And relatedly, just as we now accept that friends don't let friends drive drunk, a national public health campaign could instill the message that friends don't let friends borrow their guns.

—

Just days after a terror attack on two mosques in Christchurch, New Zealand, in 2019 that left fifty-one people dead and was streamed live on Facebook, Prime Minister Jacinda Ardern announced a temporary ban on military-style semiautomatic weapons and assault rifles. Weeks later, all but one of Parliament's 120 lawmakers voted to make the ban permanent.

This is the sort of swift, decisive action on guns that, for years, a majority of Americans have been calling for. In fact, a 2018 survey found that a clear majority of Americans favor regulating the lethality of firearms available to the public. Six in ten people supported banning AR-15s. Similar views were expressed regarding banning the sale of other assault weapons, high-capacity magazines, and lethal firearm attachments.[36] However, support among Republicans, conservatives, and NRA members was far lower.

America has become so fractured along political and ideological lines that the prospect of bipartisan legislation on firearms seems slim—but it has been done. Nine months after a well-armed man shot and killed six passengers and wounded nineteen others aboard a Long Island Rail Road train, then President Bill Clinton signed the Public Safety and Recreational Firearms Use Protection Act, better known as the federal assault weapons ban, which was a part of the bipartisan Violent Crime Control and Law Enforcement Act of 1994.

The act changed the federal criminal code "to prohibit the manufacture, transfer, or possession of a semiautomatic assault weapon"—that is, any gun that can accept a detachable ammunition magazine and that has one or more additional features considered useful in military and criminal applications but unnecessary for sports or self-defense, such as a folding rifle stock.[37] It was law for a decade before expiring in 2004. It banned more than a dozen specific firearms and certain features on guns, but because there are so many modifications that can be made on weapons and because the law did not ban all semiautomatic weapons outright, many such guns continued to be used legally. The law also contained various loopholes, and it applied only to types of weapons and large-capacity magazines that were created *after* the bill became law, meaning that there was nothing illegal about owning or selling items created *before* the law was signed.

The assault weapons ban was clearly imperfect, but a recent study using our data estimated that after controlling for population growth and homicides in general, the law prevented eleven mass shootings in ten years, and a continuation of the ban would have prevented thirty more mass shootings that killed over three hundred people.[38] Between 1966 and September 1994 (twenty-eight years), before the assault weapons ban, assault weapons were used in fourteen of fifty-five shootings (25 percent), with the first case in 1977. Between October 1994 and September 2004 (ten years), when the assault weapons ban was active, assault weapons were used in seven of thirty-three shootings (21 percent). And between October 2004 and July 2020 (sixteen years), when the prohibition expired, assault weapons were used in twenty-three of eighty-one shootings (28 percent). However, there was a statistically significant increase in assault weapons used in mass shootings between 2014 and 2019, which also coincided with shootings becoming deadlier.

There is a certain mythology surrounding assault weapons in mass shootings, especially the AR-15. AR stands for "ArmaLite rifle" (not "assault rifle," a common misconception), referring to the gun's original manufacturer, which sold the rights to Colt in the 1950s. Colt suspended production of the original AR-15 for the civilian market in 2019, but its patents expired decades ago, and other manufacturers, like Ruger, Smith & Wesson, Bushmaster, and Sig Sauer, make imitation "AR-15-style" weapons.

Gun purists hate when an AR-15–style weapon gets called an "assault rifle" because the term technically is reserved for fully automatic weapons, which have been illegal to own in the United States without a federal permit since 1934. (An AR-15 is the civilian version of the military's fully automated M16.) For firearm enthusiasts, the AR-15 also is the pinnacle of design and engineering. As with any semiautomatic firearm, when you pull the trigger, it fires; if you depress the trigger, it automatically reloads; and if you pull the trigger again, it shoots again. But the weapon is lightweight, ergonomic, and easily modified. It's also highly accurate and reliable. And deadly.

Assault rifles are rarely used in the commission of crimes—only about 1 percent of all firearm homicides are perpetrated with one.[39] But when it comes to mass shootings, assault rifles are massively overrepresented; that number is 26 percent. The 2017 Las Vegas shooter brought twenty-two of them to the scene of his crime. Mass shooters who use assault rifles follow in the footsteps of other mass shooters who have used them to achieve high body counts. The weapon evokes the military, looks scary, and is implicitly associated with mass destruction. It communicates fear and intimidation of others, which is precisely the goal of mass shootings.

High-capacity magazines, most commonly defined as any ammunition-feeding device holding more than ten rounds of ammunition, also feature in a number of mass shootings, including all eight mass shootings with twenty or more fatalities. A ban on high-capacity magazines would affect the number of bullets loaded into any semiautomatic weapon and, it seems, reduce the number of fatalities in mass shooting incidents.[40] Some of the high-capacity magazines used in mass shootings are already legally suspect. The 2017 Sutherland Springs church shooter bought an AR-15 in Texas with a "standard" thirty-round magazine, but he lived in Colorado at the time, which has a fifteen-round limit. Federal prosecutors decided the sale was illegal and should have stayed with Colorado's fifteen-round limit.

The 2016 Cascade Mall shooter had a twenty-five-round magazine in a .22 Ruger, which normally comes with a ten-round magazine. The 1998 Thurston High School shooter used a .22 Ruger with a fifty-round magazine. The 2011 Tucson shooter, who shot U.S. representative Gabby Giffords, used a Glock 19 with a thirty-three-round clip, over double the standard fifteen-round capacity.

The 2012 Aurora movie theater shooter had a one-hundred-round drum magazine for his AR-15, something that Colorado Republican senator Bernie Herpin said was a "good thing" because it jammed after *only* seventy-six bullets were fired.[41] The 2019 Dayton shooter also used an AR-15 with a one-hundred-round drum. He was fatally shot by responding police officers just thirty-two seconds after first pulling the trigger, but still managed to shoot twenty-six people, nine fatally.

A recent study estimated that restrictions on large-capacity magazines could potentially reduce mass shooting deaths by up to 15 percent, and total victims shot in these incidents by one quarter[42]—our data suggest that this might be an underestimate. Mass shootings committed with large-caliber firearms (43 percent), such as .40s, .44s, .45s, and 10mm and 7.62 x 39mm weapons (an AK-47 round), also result in far greater fatalities and injuries than those with smaller-caliber guns like .22-, .25-, or .32-caliber, or medium-caliber guns, like .38s and 9mms. Caliber is a measure of the diameter of the bullets fired by a particular gun. It's clear that if large-caliber guns had been replaced with smaller-caliber, less deadly weapons, the result would have been a reduction in homicides, assuming everything else was unchanged.

Still, an assault weapon ban or high-capacity magazine ban is just one way to curb mass shootings. In the wake of two mass shootings in Texas and Ohio in August 2019, which killed twenty-nine people in twenty-four hours and briefly shook the nation from its usual "thoughts and prayers" approach to gun violence, "red flag" laws emerged as a rare point of agreement across the political aisle.

Red flag laws—properly known as "extreme risk protection orders," or ERPOs—allow family members to petition a court to remove a person's access to firearms temporarily if they are thought to pose a threat to themselves or others. It is telling that it took two mass shootings, and not decades of rising firearm suicide rates, to bring ERPOs into the public consciousness, but the evidence suggests that they are as effective a suicide prevention tool as the United States can realistically hope for. In Connecticut, ERPOs were associated with a 13 percent reduction in firearm suicides between 2007 and 2015, and the proportion of gun-removal subjects receiving outpatient mental health treatment doubled within a year of the law's being introduced.[43]

Perpetrator B was discharged from military basic training owing to depression and suicidal ideation, yet he was able to buy a gun at Walmart. He was later arrested by police and hospitalized, and his social worker was sounding the alarm about his Columbine obsession, but Perpetrator B still maintained access to his firearm. A well-enforced ERPO could have averted the shooting he perpetrated with it just a few weeks later.

A small wave of states adopted red flag laws in the wake of the school shooting in Parkland, Florida, in 2018, but there are still only seventeen states with some form of the regulation on the books. And only two states, Maryland and Hawaii, plus the District of Columbia, allow doctors, often the first to spot signs of mental health in children and adolescents, to petition for one.

It's clear that many laws and protections would help reduce mass shootings without significantly infringing upon the rights of gun owners. Some of these laws don't need NRA approval and might even appeal to gun owners' sense of personal responsibility. And for guidance on how to get it done, we can look again to that other nation of gun lovers, Switzerland.

In 2001, a gunman walked into the parliament building in the Swiss city of Zug and opened fire. There were about ninety people in the room at the time, and he killed fourteen of them and injured eighteen more before turning the gun on himself. It remains the deadliest attack of its kind in Switzerland.[44]

The shooter had a history of threatening behavior, yet he was able to buy several guns in several different jurisdictions, called cantons, just days before the massacre because he had a permit and no criminal record. Because he bought them in several different locations, no one was wise to the fact that he was amassing an arsenal.

After the attack, the Swiss changed their laws. Military weapons could stay in the home, but not their ammo. The government also created a national gun database and required people to register their weapons whenever they bought them at a gun store. The creation of such a registry is anathema to many Americans, but the Swiss did it. And they still have their guns. They also have gun training and background checks. Today, Swiss police know when someone is buying weapons in quick succession, and they have a duty to intervene if they feel something strange is going on.

As we've shown throughout this book, firearms are not the only factor in mass shootings; far from it: Mass shootings have complex roots. But guns are a factor that is easily malleable. Like coal gas and over-the-counter medication, they can be removed from the equation, and thus the opportunity for a mass shooting can be greatly diminished. It won't be easy, but support for stricter gun laws is higher today than it has been in nearly thirty years.[45]

CHAPTER 9
HOPE

We drive miles down dirt roads to reach Caitlin's farm, located on the outskirts of a small town in the Midwest. We sit on her back porch, surrounded by wandering dogs and chickens. A tornado has recently ripped through her lot, and Caitlin has spent the morning clearing debris and rebuilding chicken fences; her hands are caked in dirt. But she's upbeat because her new flytraps have just arrived, which she's been waiting for, because the old ones stink. Caitlin is funny, friendly, and straightforward. "I just tell it like I see it," she says.

Several years prior to our meeting, she lived in an apartment building in town and was attending the local community college to become a police officer. She was washing dishes one wet afternoon when she saw a teenage boy, casually dressed, carrying a backpack and takeout from Taco Bell, cutting across her back lawn. He was headed to the storage units behind her building.

"There was just something about him that didn't feel right. I don't know, a gut feeling, I guess," she says. "He was wearing tennis shoes even though it was sleeting, and he stepped in this huge puddle—the water was really deep—but he didn't even slow down to check his shoes. He was just beelining for this storage unit. Something was off about it."

Caitlin called up her cousin, who lived in the same building, one floor below. They sat at her tiny kitchen window watching the boy trudge through calf-deep puddles of mud to the storage unit and struggle with the lock for nearly ten minutes. "I thought he was breaking in." When he eventually got it open, Caitlin could see lanterns and garbage bags inside. "Then I thought he was either living in that unit or cooking meth, because that's what people do in small towns."

They also shoot, she tells us. Guns are a way of life out here. Caitlin grew up around them, and her husband is an avid hunter. On our drive in, we passed a large sign for a gun shop with more than five thousand guns for sale. A common pastime for high-schoolers here is shooting Tannerite explosive targets and "blowing shit up," Caitlin jokes.

Still, Caitlin wanted to call the police. Her cousin thought she was overreacting, but eventually, still convinced that something wasn't right, she dialed the nonemergency number and reported what she was seeing: "There's a young man in a storage unit behind my building. He might be living in it. You might want to check it out."

Minutes later, two squad cars arrived on the scene and confronted the boy. Caitlin watched as he was arrested and driven away. It was a week later when a police sergeant finally called her to explain what had happened: She had foiled a mass shooting. The storage shed was stock-piled with guns and bomb-making supplies, and at the boy's home the police had found hundreds of rounds of ammunition and a notebook with detailed plans to kill his high school classmates, his parents, and then himself.

"You did a really good thing," the sergeant told her.

Media requests and an outpouring of flowers, gifts, and emails from across the country followed. Family members whom Caitlin "hadn't spoken to in years" called to thank her. She is still hailed as a hero in her small town, and one guy still buys her a drink whenever she visits the local tavern. But she doesn't think that what she did was that remarkable, deserving of the "hero" tag.

"I was just being a cautious person, doing what I felt was right," she says. "Something didn't seem right, so I reported it." Caitlin saw something and said something; it was that simple. "Thank God he walked through my yard that day."

The experience changed Caitlin, who's now a mom to two young boys. She switched her major from law enforcement to social work because she wants to help people like the boy whose odd behavior she reported, beyond just putting them in jail. "He needed some real help," she reflects. "Some type of long-term intervention."

—

We started this book by announcing that mass shootings are not an inevitable fact of American life but, rather, are preventable. Throughout this book, we've identified numerous off-ramps along the road to mass violence that can help people exit. Now the work begins. We must build these off-ramps on the road ahead at the individual level, the institutional level, and the societal level.

One obvious place to start is opportunity. Like Caitlin, we can all be willing as individuals to step in when we sense that something is not right. As individuals, we can recognize that it's better to overreact than underreact when we have a gut feeling, and to identify a trusted resource we can report to. But the operative word here is *trusted*. No one will speak out if they fear an under- or overreaction from people in power. We must have full faith in our institutions to do the right thing, and that takes leadership, transparency, and accountability.

At the institutional level, we can curb opportunity through situational crime prevention, by establishing systems for checking in on the people entering our schools, workplaces, and churches, such as employing trained greeters to welcome people as they walk through the door.

At the societal level, we can elect policy makers who acknowledge the American roots of mass shootings, who condemn the violence in no uncertain terms, and who will pass the commonsense gun laws that the majority of Americans agrees will make it easier to keep guns away from people who shouldn't have them—like the fifteen-year-old high school student in Caitlin's small town. We can push for policies such as red flag laws; close legal loopholes through universal background checks or permit-to-purchase laws and mandatory waiting periods; recognize the risks posed by ghost guns; and enforce safe storage.

This same tiered approach applies to stopping the social contagion and hateful rhetoric that embolden angry, rejected young men and encourage violent retribution. As individuals, we can avoid clicking on, "liking," or sharing news stories that show the perpetrators' faces, provide details about their crimes, or include personal writing or videos that the perpetrators were hoping would be widely distributed. Our institutions can teach media literacy to young people, starting in elementary school, so students know how to stay away from hateful rhetoric online and identify false claims. Mainstream media can follow the No Notoriety protocol and avoid turning mass shooters into celebrities, and advertisers can divest from the networks and newspapers that do. Government can hold social media companies responsible for acts of mass violence that are organized and disseminated on their platforms, and we can lobby those companies to de-platform and disrupt online hate groups.

—

We fly out to meet with Ann and Valerie, the mother and sister of a perpetrator of a recent mass shooting. Ann sent us an email after reading about our work, wanting to get involved. We sit in the conference room of an upscale downtown apartment building. In the common room next door is the Friday night reception for residents of the building: wine and cheese plates. Laughter and conversation are muffled through the wall of windows separating the two spaces. Our room is quiet. Ann and Valerie are both nervous, guarded, and scared. Their pain, guilt, and shame are palpable. They speak slowly and quietly.

"I just drove down the highway the other day, driving past the last place that I saw [my brother]," Valerie, the sister of the perpetrator, tells us. "I get overwhelmed and emotional every time. Even years later. We had dinner there days before it happened. I've gone over that dinner so many times: Was there a sign? Was there something I could have said? A question I should have asked? Should I have known somehow? I feel like he was settled at that point. His plans were impenetrable. Everything seemed so normal."

"It was all so rushed. We were all so busy," Ann adds, trying to comfort her daughter, to ease her guilt. "I was so focused on work. I should have paid more attention then. I should have spent more time. He wanted love. He wanted kindness. He wanted compassion."

Ann's voice is pained, her eyes brimming with tears, "In elementary school, they said he needed help. But financially we couldn't afford it. I didn't know that if we got him evaluated, he could get resources for free.

We didn't know about any of it. We need good mental health care in this country. It has to be accessible. We need to help mothers and fathers know where to go when they are worried about their child."

"Did you have any sense that something was wrong in the weeks before it happened?" Jill asks.

Ann nods and takes a deep breath: "Before the shooting I was worried about him. I called the mental health crisis line to go check on him, but they sent the police. The police didn't ask him anything. They basically knocked on the door, he said he was fine, and [they] asked me, 'Why did you call us?'"

Valerie cuts in, her voice more frustrated: "What if a social worker had responded? Would it have gone differently? Would they have discovered something was terribly wrong?"

—

Mike shared similar sentiments when he spoke with us at Jill's office. He had also seen news coverage about our work and had reached out wanting to know if he could help.

Mike is visibly emotional when he arrives to tell us about his son, Bobby. He hesitates at the door, too nervous even to sit down, and leaves to get a drink of water before coming back in. He is carrying a piece of paper and visibly shaking.

He explains to us that Bobby grew up in a chaotic household. His mother, Mike's wife at the time, was violent and unpredictable, suffering from undiagnosed serious mental illness. (Mike now believes it was schizophrenia.) Bobby's maternal uncle went to prison for murder after stabbing a man forty times and rolling him up in a carpet. When Bobby was eight, his uncle was released from prison and moved in with his sister, Bobby's aunt, down the street from them. Bobby would spend a lot of time at their house, which Mike describes as a "crack den, where everyone was always high and drunk." Mike thinks Bobby might have been sexually molested in that house, but he's never been sure.

Bobby was bullied throughout school. He was always fascinated by weapons and carried a screwdriver with him to school every day to "feel safe." In eighth grade, he posted a threat of school violence on his Facebook page that a teacher saw. The police showed up at their house, arrested Bobby, cuffing him and putting him in the back of a squad car. The cops eventually decided not to charge him, and he was transferred to a local hospital for inpatient treatment. At that point, Mike found out that his son had been hearing voices, and Bobby was placed on suicide watch. After a week in the hospital, he was diagnosed with "major depression with psychotic episodes" and then released.

Soon after that incident, Mike divorced Bobby's mom. He was proactive about keeping Bobby in regular therapy. They did weekly father-and-son therapy sessions with a psychologist, and Bobby had a separate therapist individually; he also took medication. When Mike remarried, to a woman who had her own son about Bobby's age, Bobby decided to move up north to the rural area where his mother lived.

"The problem was that there was no access to mental health care up north; the nearest therapist was a one-hour drive away," Mike recalls. "I would drive up Wednesday to drive him one hour to a therapy appointment and then drive home on Thursday. The doctors up north wouldn't prescribe medication for his hearing voices, and he never told his new therapist about them. And the school up there was ill-equipped—no mental health resources at all."

Bobby eventually got kicked out of school for "writing things that scared people." He moved to the next state over and quit mental health treatment altogether. He bought a "cache of weapons—pistol, shotgun, Mace, brass knuckles" and told Mike to "stop digging around in my business." Mike says he was walking on eggshells, but at this point Bobby was an adult.

"I was terrified he was going to kill himself," Mike says. "I couldn't take the risk of hurting him or pushing him over the edge."

At the age of twenty, Bobby took his own life by shooting himself. He left his dad a long note. It's the piece of paper Mike has carried with him into our meeting. He's never shown it to anyone before:

Dear Dad,

I'm gone. Some may say too soon, but I feel like it was past overdue.

We have very few things in common. We both have our own set of morals, principles we live by, but we're coming from such different schools of thought, I've felt like every day that I've learned a new lesson, we've drifted more apart. But that may be the case with everyone in this life. With every day, each passing hour, I've drifted further and deeper into this void, one too dark for this world. That's why I need to go. Why I am gone now. My ideas are too archaic. A disgusting barbarian has lived inside my head and taken over. He's ruled my mind like occupied territory since I was age 6 or age 7. This is me winning the war. I'm not letting him win.

If I had it my way, I would have the heads of my enemies cut off by swords and anyone who's done anything to hurt or embarrass me would be on that list. We spoke of monsters recently. I want to protect others but I feel dangerous. Like I'm on the verge of becoming a monster. Something inhuman. I'm ending my life so I can ensure no one gets hurt. Both of my families will be saddened by my passing, but there will be an unknown number of families spared the pain of losing loved ones to a bogeyman.

Mike's eyes fill with tears as we read it. Like Ann and Valerie, Mike lives with a lot of what-ifs: What if Bobby hadn't moved up north and, instead, had continued his treatment twice a week in the city? What if he had been able to access high-quality treatment up in that rural area or if there had been mental health treatment available at his school? What if Mike had gotten him hospitalized when he was so worried about him and he had been unable to purchase guns?

—

Addressing trauma and crisis feels daunting, but there are things that each of us can do. As individuals, we can prioritize developing healthy, honest, long-term relationships with young people—our children, relatives, neighbors, and members of our community. We can volunteer as mentors and be willing to walk with children through their hardest moments, listen deeply and authentically, and connect them to resources when needed. We can all be trained in the skills of crisis intervention and suicide prevention. We can know how to recognize the signs of a crisis and intervene with verbal and nonverbal skills to "let air out of the balloon" and help someone in crisis get through the moment. We can become comfortable asking people if they are suicidal; we can learn to listen and validate feelings and know what resources are available in our communities and how to facilitate connections to them.

At the institutional level, we can create warm and welcoming environments where young people feel seen and supported. We can also start screening for trauma in doctor's offices and schools so that young at-risk people can be identified early on and connected with free, accessible resources. We can establish crisis response teams in schools, universities, workplaces, and places of worship so that the community can report people they are concerned about without the threat of arrest or punishment. We can establish anonymous reporting systems to gather information and referral mechanisms to connect people in crisis to needed resources.

We should offer this care and support to anyone who is struggling, not just because it might avert a shooting tragedy. We need to increase knowledge and awareness of these resources and remove the stigma associated with receiving help. Our schools need funding to provide students with adequate on-site services such as counselors and social workers, and to train teachers to respond to trauma and crisis when they see them in their classrooms. Teachers also need an evidence-based national curriculum focused on social-emotional learning, specifically teaching young boys coping skills, communication, health relationships, and empathy.

Big picture: We need serious investment in the social determinants of health and well-being—the social and economic conditions in housing, employment, food security, and education that have a major influence on individual and community health. We need a stronger social safety net in the United States, so that the loss of a job doesn't mean the loss of one's home, identity, or health insurance. Universal health care, paid maternity leave, and access to affordable child care are examples of policies common in other wealthy democracies that reduce the stress and financial strain on new mothers.

At the society level, well-resourced social service providers are needed. As Ann noted in her interview, this includes affordable, accessible, high-quality mental health treatment in schools and in the community. For most of American history, people with serious and persistent mental illness were locked away in hospital-like institutions.[1] Starting in the 1950s, most of these facilities were shut down due to inhumane treatment and rampant physical and sexual abuse. But only half of the community-based mental health treatment and assistance services touted to replace the old state-run mental health institutions were built, and none of them was fully funded.[2] Current options either are difficult to access because we have such a shortage of qualified health care providers in this country, or are prohibitively expensive because they are not always covered by private insurance. For people experiencing psychosis for the first time, one of the biggest barriers to getting treatment is not knowing where to seek help.[3]

Law enforcement has become the de facto first responder to many mental health crises. But the police really only have two options at their disposal: arrest (though the problems at hand do not call for legal intervention, so that just criminalizes mental illness) or hospitalize. Police officers have the authority to take a person into custody for medical treatment if they are in need of a mental health evaluation and are in danger of harming themselves or others if not immediately detained. However, even this is a temporary fix, because the goal of psychiatric hospitalization is really only stabilization.

There is some misperception among the general population that an involuntary psychiatric hold can cure mental illness. The reality is that hospitals are very limited in what they can impose on people. They can't force treatment and they can't coerce patients into attending follow-up appointments. They also can't medicate someone against their will without safety concerns. Even if an antipsychotic medication is prescribed, it takes seven to ten days before any real effects are felt—long after discharge from the hospital in most cases. The average length of stay in a psychiatric hospital is two to three days in some places and five to seven in others. But admittance is the exception, not the rule. We witnessed this firsthand when we partnered with a suburban police department in Minnesota and spent several days and nights doing ride-alongs with police responding to crisis calls.[4] Police would send people experiencing a mental health crisis to the hospital in an ambulance, but within hours that person would be home again, redialing 911. We interviewed the doctors and nurses at the largest psychiatric emergency department in town, and they told us they turned away over 80 percent of people who were sent to them, either because the patients were not in acute danger of hurting themselves and others or because the hospital didn't have the bed space.

Within our current system, people are cycling in and out of hospitals, with only a large ambulance bill to show for their trouble. The hospitals are frustrated, the police are frustrated, the people in crisis and their families are frustrated. This is a systemic problem that needs systemic solutions. We need to actually deliver on the promise of the Community Mental Health Act and the enduring vision of President John F. Kennedy, who signed it one month before he was assassinated in 1963: to build and fund affordable, community-based mental health treatment and assistance services that can be easily and readily accessed by the people who need them.

—

Missy, the former math teacher and survivor of the 2005 Red Lake school shooting, has vivid, terrible memories of that day. The perpetrator was suspended at the time of the shooting, on homebound services, and not allowed in the school. His grandfather was a cop, and the perpetrator used his grandfather's guns, bulletproof vest, and squad car the day of the shooting. He entered the school at 2:50, during seventh period. First, he killed the unarmed security guard at the front door. He came to Missy's room then. Missy was having trouble with students walking into her classroom who weren't supposed to be there, she recalls, so she had locked the door earlier in the day. A student ran up to her locked door, screaming that there was a shooting taking place at the school. Missy assumed it was gang related, because some of her students had gotten mixed up in that violent way of life. So she turned off the lights and lined her students up against one wall.

She had a window next to her locked door with her name on it. When she saw the familiar face of the perpetrator standing on the other side of the glass, the student who three years before had told her he liked Hitler and who had been cutting himself, "I knew we were in trouble," she says. He was wearing a blue bandana, a bulletproof vest, and combat boots. Missy saw his eyes reveal a sudden flash of insight: that he could shoot out the glass. Three shots, and the glass was out. To this day, the sound of glass crunching underfoot still triggers Missy's PTSD.

The perpetrator entered her classroom and asked a few people, "Do you believe in God?" There were fifteen students and three adults in the room, all lined up against the wall, praying for salvation. He just started shooting down the line. Guttural screams filled the room.

"I heard *pop, pop, pop, pop, pop,*" Missy describes, the pain palpable in her voice.

Then the shooter pointed the gun at Missy and fired, but there were no bullets left.

"He looked possessed during the shooting," Missy tells us. "There was a dead look in his eyes. I saw evil that day."

During the break in gunfire, a sophomore named Jeff May, one of Missy's favorite students and her "hero," lunged at the perpetrator with a No. 2 pencil, then tried to wrestle him to the ground. The perpetrator shot Jeff in the face point-blank, but Jeff's selfless actions shook the perpetrator and seemed to "wake him up for a bit." He fled Missy's classroom.

When he left, it was "total chaos," Missy says. The lights were off, and the smoke alarm was blaring. "I froze." The perpetrator had left one rifle in her classroom, and he came back in minutes later to get it. He pointed the rifle at his head and shot himself.

After the shooting, students and faculty converged on Missy's house as a gathering point. Without having to ask, everyone knew who the shooter was. "Everyone knew it had to be him. You know the kids. We knew," Missy reflects. She went back to her classroom later that day, to help the FBI identify the bodies lying on the floor. "My babies," as she calls them.

Missy never returned to teaching. She's been in therapy for the past fifteen years, "about a thousand hours," she says.

—

After our first interview, Missy felt inspired to do more. She attended parent training on threat assessment and emergency planning with Safe and Sound Schools, a nonprofit founded by parents who lost children at Sandy Hook. She then drove to North Dakota to attend training by the Readiness and Emergency Management for Schools Technical Assistance Center. During the lunch break, she approached the trainers and told them who she was. They were shocked and apologized that some of their slides included information about her school's shooter and photos from the shooting. A few months later, they invited Missy to be the keynote speaker at a national training event.

Missy has also worked with the "I Love U Guys" Foundation, founded in 2006 by John-Michael and Ellen Keyes following a school shooting that took the life of their daughter, Emily. Emily texted "I Love U Guys" during the ordeal, which became a rallying cry for the organization: to promote school safety and preparedness through the lens of kindness, community, and responsibility. The organization's measured "standard response protocol" for all threats to student safety, including weather emergencies, is the antidote to the traumatic ALICE protocol discussed earlier in the book. Missy has spoken at "I Love U Guys" events nationally. During the pandemic, as all her speaking engagements were canceled, she wrote her own children's school's emergency operation plans and started to get involved in statewide policy.

Missy has told her story to rapt audiences at several of the Violence Project's trainings, and each time she tells it, her voice gets stronger. She describes our research as "her missing piece." She explains: "We had security. I think we had a good culture and school climate. We had community liaisons. But we didn't have mental health. And we didn't have formal systems where the teachers and administration were talking to each other about students they were concerned about."

After one presentation, at which a parent who lost her son at Sandy Hook was in the audience, Missy approached Jill in the hallway, her voice a whisper and shaking with emotion: "When I meet parents from the Sandy Hook shooting, I always feel the need to apologize. Why didn't we stop it? I'm so sorry we didn't stop it. Y'all came after us. Why didn't we stop it?"

During the course of this research, we became aware of "survivor networks" like this: informal and formal groups of "similar others" who have experienced the tragedy and trauma of a mass shooting and who provide for one another a range of social and emotional supports to assist in healing and recovery.[5] It was a humbling experience to sit with survivors and victims united in grief but also in purpose: to help each other through the day and ensure that what happened to them never happens again. It's a club to which no one wants to be a member and that no one can ever leave. Survivors and victims share an unspeakable bond. "This is sadness that sinks into your bones and never goes away," Tom Teves from No Notoriety told us when we asked about his contact with other victims' families. Every anniversary of the shooting, every missed birthday or milestone, every back-to-school day and graduation, the grief comes back in waves. "We're never untraumatized. Which means we can't be retraumatized. It's not like I broke my arm but now it's healed. You just cope," Tom says.

—

Over a year later, Missy and Jill meet in Jill's university office. Missy is in town to visit family. "What's next for you?" Jill asks.

Missy laughs. "I'm not sure what's coming next for me. I can never go back to the classroom; that's not in the books for me. I don't know exactly why—guilt, I guess. And fear."

Jill presses her: "What do you think we need to be working on in terms of prevention in schools? What needs to happen to stop this from happening again?"

Missy pauses. "I'm a math teacher with a math brain. I think of things as black-and-white, something to be solved. I've been trying to solve this. But this is fuzzy. It's complex. I've had to learn to accept that."

—

It *is* complex. There are no quick fixes to systemic social problems. For too long, America has either viewed possible solutions in isolation or created false dichotomies that are pitted against each other, from gun safety measures to mental health treatment. Even when solutions have merit, they are then wrongly dismissed for being imperfect. The reality is that imperfections do not render solutions completely useless. There is no one solution to rule them all. As with Swiss cheese, there are holes—but if you layer the slices, one on top of the other, the holes start to get covered up. And layering imperfect solutions, holistically, is the only way to prevent mass violence.

After every mass shooting, the media like to fixate on "motive," but in reality, the pathway to mass violence is long and winding. At the moment of their crimes, mass shooters usually have suffered trauma. They've experienced an existential and often suicidal crisis in the days and weeks leading up to the shootings. They've searched for validation for their feelings and have found it in America's cultural script for mass violence: its long history of firearm-enabled violence, its values of rugged individualism and success at any cost, and the words and deeds of mass shooters past and present. And they've had the opportunity to shoot, often because of lax gun laws.

This complexity doesn't mean we give up. The voices of the victims, survivors, families, and perpetrators themselves have shown us the many possible off-ramps that could be taken along the way.

To recap, here's what we all can do to stop the mass shooting epidemic:

As Individuals	
Trauma	Build relationships and mentor young people
Crisis	Develop strong skills in crisis intervention and suicide prevention
Social Proof	Monitor our own media consumption
Opportunity	Safe storage of firearms; if you see or hear something, say something

As Institutions	
Trauma	Create warm environments; trauma-informed practices; universal trauma screening
Crisis	Build care teams and referral processes; train staff
Social Proof	Teach media literacy; limit active shooter drills for children
Opportunity	Situational crime prevention; anonymous reporting systems

As a Society	
Trauma	Teach social emotional learning in schools. Build a stronger social safety net with adequate jobs, childcare, maternity leave, health insurance, and access to higher education
Crisis	Reduce stigma and increase knowledge of mental health; open access to high quality mental health treatment; fund counselors in schools
Social Proof	No Notoriety protocol; hold media and social media companies accountable for their content
Opportunity	Universal background checks, red flag laws, permit-to-purchase, magazine limits, wait periods, assault rifle ban

These off-ramps have a broad diffusion of benefits. Not only will they likely impact mass shootings, but they will also reduce other forms of deaths of despair like suicide, reduce other forms of violence, increase reporting of concerns, curb the spread of hateful rhetoric, reduce the impact of trauma, and improve our mental well-being.

—

In one of Perpetrator A's last letters, he reflected on the difficult time he had answering all of our questions:

"This has turned out to be much more difficult than I expected. Some of the memories I'm forcing myself to recall are not easy to deal with."

In prison, he sees a psychologist and takes antidepressants. He concludes,

"I pray these responses help in some way further your study. Thank you very much for allowing me to contribute!"

In his final letter, Perpetrator B, the school shooter, signed off:

THANK YOU FOR WRITING TO ME AND FOR SEEKING MY ASSISTANCE. THANK YOU FOR DOING THIS RESEARCH AND THE TIME YOU AND YOUR HELPERS HAVE PUT INTO THIS. TAKE CARE NOW AND MAY GOD BLESS YOU! I WILL ALWAYS PRAY FOR YOU.

Exorcising the mass shooting monster will take all of us, working individually and collectively, to create the safe and connected world we want to live in.

ACKNOWLEDGMENTS

This book is full of personal stories. Many were hard to tell. We are forever indebted to the people who shared them with us and will never forget how they sacrificed a little bit of themselves in an effort to make the world a better place. For your honesty, hospitality, and humility, we thank you. The time we spent together has changed us for the better.

Research reported in this book was generously supported by the National Institute of Justice, the research arm of the U.S. Department of Justice, under award number 2018–75-CX-0023. Please note, the opinions, findings, conclusions, and recommendations expressed in this book are ours and not those of the Department of Justice. Thanks especially to Basia Lopez and all the participants at NIJ's 2019 Topical Meeting to Advance Research on Mass Violence, for vital input on the early stages of this project.

NIJ provided the financial capital, but a team of incredibly smart and skilled undergraduate students at Hamline University was the human capital behind this project. To Amanda Jensen, Kyle Knapp, Stasia Higgins, and Elliot Fay: Thank you for your steadfast commitment to the facts, careful attention to the details, and perfect combination of flexibility and tenacity in your pursuit of all leads. For the late nights, early mornings, and vibrant exchange of ideas: Thank you. Thanks also to Jessica Lindgren, Hannah Klumb, Hannah Peterson, and Grace McMahon.

Thank you to Hamline University for providing everything we needed for a project like this to thrive. Thank you also to the late David Steele, for convincing us to apply for the grant that changed our lives. To Marcela Kostihova, Shelly Schaefer, Gina Erickson, Sarah Greenman, and other Hamline colleagues: Thank you for supporting us from the beginning. Likewise, a shout-out to Metropolitan State University and the team at the School of Law Enforcement and Criminal Justice for your equally enthusiastic support. Thanks especially to Andrew Johnson for reviewing an early draft of the book and helping us see the forest for the trees.

To our partners in crime at the Violence Project Research Center, Missy Dodds, Jeremy Kalin, and Katie Pekel: Thank you for your friendship and for living the mission of this project. We hope we make you proud. Thanks also to Mary Dillon for all the small things that make a big difference.

Special thanks to the team at Abrams Press for helping bring this book to market, especially our editor, Garrett McGrath, for seeing something in this project and pushing us to fulfill its potential with insightful comments and good humor.

A huge thank-you goes to our agent and biggest champion, Veronica Goldstein, and the team at Fletcher and Company for taking a chance on us, always believing in us, and making our first foray into trade publishing a truly magical experience.

To our friends and mentors, especially Analisa Calderon: Thank you. To anyone who ever attended one of our trainings and asked us a critical question, or one of our classes and asked us for clarification; to anyone who challenged our work in the ivory tower and the public square: Thank you. You all helped us fine-tune the ideas in this book and make the final product that much better.

Writing a book is a labor of love and would not be possible without the patience and understanding of our families. James's father died suddenly, unexpectedly, the summer we wrote this book, and so the meaning of family took on renewed importance for us. To our parents and siblings: Thank you for building the foundation for everything that came next. Kevin and Emily: Thank you for believing in us and in this project, for your constant support, and for holding down the fort while we were interviewing and writing. And to our incredible children: We do this work for you, to help build the safe and compassionate world we want you to live in. May you always ask the hard questions and see the humanity in others.

AFTERWORD

Individuals who commit, or intend to commit, mass shootings have among the highest public profiles of all violent offenders. The Violence Project began as a code name for our research into their lives, to protect the identities of our research subjects. It has since grown into its own nonpartisan, nonprofit research center. At the Violence Project, we are dedicated to advancing data-driven solutions to vexing social problems and ending the scourge of violence in our communities. To learn more about our work or get involved, follow us on Twitter and Instagram at @theviolencepro, or visit us at www.theviolenceproject.org.

Our interviews with incarcerated mass shooters began in 2018 after we received funding from the National Institute of Justice and approval from Hamline University's Institutional Review Board. We wrote to 31 mass shooters living in prisons (as opposed to psychiatric hospitals, where consenting to research is difficult), the entire sample universe we were aware of at the time, plus a handful of homicide offenders who attempted mass shootings but fell below the threshold of four killed. Initially, nine perpetrators responded to our recruitment letter, which described the project and asked each potential participant if they were interested in being interviewed anonymously for a research study about their life histories, without any pay or compensation. Three letters were returned to us because the recipients were not allowed to read mail. Two of the nine responding perpetrators declined to participate, and others had their attorneys contact us to decline due to pending litigation. Seven agreed to be interviewed. A written consent form was then mailed to each participant detailing the benefits and risks of the study. Brief phone calls were subsequently held to answer any questions about the consent form or the research project.

Research in prisons is inherently challenging, especially when some of their most notorious and dangerous inmates are the subject of your research. Owing to constraints imposed by state and federal corrections departments, we were denied access to two of the participants, and face-to-face interviews were not permitted. Five of the perpetrators were able to sign the consent form and send it back to us. We conducted interviews via telephone and/ or written correspondence. In most cases, we exchanged one or two phone calls and, in some cases, up to twenty letters examining the lives and crimes of our interviewees. Interview questions asked about their childhoods and adolescence, their families, their education and work histories, their health and mental health histories, their access to firearms, and other factors of interest. In two cases, interviewees voluntarily signed a release form to allow us to gather records from hospitals, schools, and social services that corroborated their firsthand accounts.

While five mass shooters are hardly representative of all mass shooters, they amount to about a sixth of all mass shooters currently alive and incarcerated; thus the important insights provided do have significance.

For our community interviews, participants were recruited via a mix of what researchers call "purposive" and "snowball" sampling techniques. In total, we interviewed forty-four people: Sixteen were personally connected to mass shooters as family, friends, romantic partners, work colleagues, or survivors of their shootings; six were grieving family members who offered victims' perspectives; five provided personal insights into averted mass shootings; the rest were either first responders or community stakeholders in shooting tragedies or provided some other professional insight or expertise pertinent to our investigation. The interviews were semi-structured and lasted ninety minutes on average, although some people we interviewed multiple times, and some interviews lasted as long as eight hours. Owing to approved ethical protocols, no interviews were recorded, so quotations captured by hand and used in this book are not strictly verbatim but rather are faithfully reconstructed from shorthand notes. In no way do they distort the language or intentions of our interviewees. Two people were present at each interview, one to ask questions and the other to take notes.

All statistical data on mass shooters and mass shootings reported on in this book are derived from the Violence Project's database of mass shooters in the United States, which is publicly available, for free, on our website. There you will also find a detailed methodology and codebook for the more than 150 variables in the database, plus separate tabs on the more than 370 firearms used in mass shootings and the 1,200 victims who lost their lives to them. Each variable is hyperlinked to online sources, meaning you can trace the origins of our interpretations and fact-check them. Like thousands of other researchers, graduate students, and journalists, you can download the database as a spreadsheet and run your own analyses.

Also on our website is a link to our "Off-Ramp Project," a hub for violence prevention education and training (www.off-ramp.org). There you will find a series of online training modules for educators at K–12 schools, colleges, and universities; for workplace employees and supervisors; and for law enforcement and private security professionals, to become certified in crisis intervention and de-escalation, suicide prevention, and some of the other practical skills discussed in this book. The website also includes downloadable and customizable protocols for building a working crisis team in your organization and a list of resources to help divert people away from the pathway to violence.

American Psychological Association (https://www.apa.org/helpcenter
/crisis)
Click on your state in the APA's "Crisis Hotline and Resources" to find a
mental health professional in your area.

Boys & Girls Club of America (https://www.bgca.org/)
A national organization of local chapters that provide voluntary after-school
programs and mentoring for young people.

Brady Center to Prevent Gun Violence (https://www.bradyunited.org)
A nonprofit organization, the Brady Center to Prevent Gun Violence advocates for gun control and against gun violence.

Childhelp National Child Abuse Hotline (https://www.childhelp.org
/hotline/)
(800) 422–4453 / Available: 24/7
The hotline offers crisis intervention, information, and referrals.

Choose Love Movement (https://chooselovemovement.org/)
Choose Love is a community-led movement offering free "social and emotional learning" (SEL) to help people thoughtfully respond to any situation
or circumstance.

Cognitive Behavioral Therapist (http://nacbt.org/find-a-therapist/)
(800) 253–0167 / Available: 24/7
Call to be referred to a licensed cognitive behavioral therapist in
your area.

Crisis Text Line (https://www.crisistextline.org)
Text HELLO to 741741 / Available: 24/7
A live, trained crisis counselor receives the text and responds from our
secure online platform. The volunteer crisis counselor will help you move
from a hot moment to a cool moment.

Everytown for Gun Safety (https://everytown.org)
The parent organization of Moms Demand Action, Everytown advocates for gun control and against gun violence.

Giffords (https://giffords.org)
An American advocacy and research organization focused on promoting gun control, Giffords is named for mass shooting survivor Gabby Giffords, a former Democratic member of the U.S. House of Representatives.

The "I Love U Guys" Foundation (https://iloveuguys.org)
A foundation focused on school safety, known for its widely adopted "standard response protocol."

Inclusive Therapists (https://www.inclusivetherapists.com)
Their mission is to expand all mental health services to LGBTQ+ people and Black people, indigenous people, and people of color, connecting them to a culturally responsive licensed therapist.

March for Our Lives (https://marchforourlives.com)
A movement dedicated to student-led activism around ending gun violence.

MENTOR National (https://www.mentoring.org/)
Helps aspiring mentors connect with people who want a mentor and tailors its mentoring to an individual's needs and decisions.

Moms Demand Action (https://momsdemandaction.org)
A grassroots movement fighting for public safety measures to protect people from gun violence.

National Alliance on Mental Illness (NAMI) HelpLine (https://www.nami.org/help)
(800) 950-NAMI / Available: Monday to Friday, 10 A.M. to 6 P.M. Eastern Time

The NAMI HelpLine is a free, public nationwide peer-support service providing information, resource referrals, and support for people living with a mental health condition, their family members and caregivers, and mental health providers.

National Domestic Violence Hotline (https://www.thehotline.org/)
(800) 799–7233 / Available: 24/7
Our highly trained advocates are available around the clock to talk confidentially with anyone experiencing domestic violence who is seeking resources or information or is questioning unhealthy aspects of a relationship.

The National Grad Crisis Line (https://gradresources.org/crisis)
(877) 472–3457 / Available: 24/7
The National Grad Crisis Line helps graduate students reach free, confidential telephone counseling, crisis intervention, suicide prevention, and information and referral services provided by specially trained responders.

National Suicide Prevention Lifeline (https://suicidepreventionlifeline.org/)
(800) 273–8255 / Available: 24/7
The Lifeline provides free, confidential support for people in distress, prevention and crisis resources for you or your loved ones, and best practices for professionals.

No Notoriety (https://nonotoriety.com)
Promoting a "No Notoriety" protocol, this organization calls for responsible media coverage of acts of mass violence as a deterrent to future such acts.

Psychology Today (https://www.psychologytoday.com/us/therapists)
Check out their "Find a Therapist," a national, searchable database of mental health professionals across the United States.

The Rebels Project (https://www.therebelsproject.org)
Formed by a group of Columbine survivors in the wake of the Aurora theater shooting in 2012, this "survivor network" seeks to embrace, support, and connect survivors of mass shootings.

Safe Schools for Alex (https://safeschoolsforalex.org)
A nonprofit focused on best practices in school safety, named for Alex Schachter, one of the victims of the 2018 Parkland massacre.

Sandy Hook Promise (https://www.sandyhookpromise.org/)
Protecting America's children from gun violence in honor of the precious lives lost at Sandy Hook Elementary School on December 14, 2012, Sandy Hook Promise empowers youth to "know the signs" and "say something" and runs an anonymous reporting system.

Stop It Now! (https://www.stopitnow.org/ohc-content/crisis-hotlines)
This site provides resources for anyone in crisis or their loved ones.

Substance Abuse and Mental Health Services Administration (https://findtreatment.samhsa.gov/locator)
A behavioral health treatment services locator. A national, searchable map to find substance use care, mental health care, or a mental health hospital in your area.

The Trevor Project (https://www.thetrevorproject.org)
(866) 488–7386 / Available: 24/7
The leading national organization for the LGBTQ+ community, the Trevor Project provides crisis and suicide intervention.

Veterans Crisis Line (https://www.veteranscrisisline.net/)
(800) 273–8255 / Available: 24/7
Connect with the Veterans Crisis Line to reach caring, qualified responders with the Department of Veterans Affairs. Many of them are veterans themselves.

NOTES

CHAPTER 1

1. Jerome P. Bjelopera et al., eds., "Public Mass Shootings in the United States: Selected Implications for Federal Public Health and Safety Policy," https://fas.org/sgp/crs/misc/R43004.pdf.

2. J. Murray, "Mass Media Reporting and Enabling of Mass Shootings," *Cultural Studies—Critical Methodologies* 17 (2017): 114–24.

3. B. Obama, "Statement by the President on the Shootings at Umpqua Community College, Roseburg, Oregon," *The White House of President Barak Obama*, October 1, 2015, https://obamawhitehouse.archives.gov /the-press-office/2015/10/01/statement-president-shootings-umpqua -community-college-roseburg-oregon.

4. "One-third of US Adults Say Fear of Mass Shootings Prevents Them from Going to Certain Places or Events," *American Psychological Association*, August 15, 2019, https://www.apa.org/news/press/releases/2019/08 /fear-mass-shooting.

5. N. W. Aronowitz, "Fake Blood and Blanks: Schools Stage Active Shooter Drills," *NBC News*, February 14, 2014, https://www.nbcnews.com /news/us-news/fake-blood-blanks-schools-stage-active-shooter-drills -n28481.

6. S. Annear, "'Absurdity and Horror': School Uses Nursery Rhyme to Teach Kindergarten About Lockdowns," *Boston Globe*, June 7, 2018, https://www3.bostonglobe.com/metro/2018/06/07/jarring-nursery

-rhyme-somerville-school-teaches-kindergartners-about-lockdowns/tVSkONmr4QeQfZU5HgBbnI/story.html?arc404 rue.

7.   A. Herron, "It Hurt So Bad: Indiana Teachers Shot with Plastic Pellets During Active Shooter Training," *Indy Star*, March 21, 2019, https://www.indystar.com/story/news/politics/2019/03/21/active-shooter-training-for-schools-teachers-shot-with-plastic-pellets/3231103002/.

8.   F. Ritchin, "Columbine Students Are Asking: Will Sharing Photos of the Dead Change Our History of Violence?," *Time*, April 18, 2019, https://time.com/longform/columbine-gun-violence-campaign/.

9.   J. Densley, *How Gangs Work: An Ethnography of Youth Violence* (New York: Palgrave Macmillan, 2013).

CHAPTER 2

1.   A. Lankford, "Public Mass Shooters and Firearms: A Cross-National Study of 171 Countries," *Violence and Victims*, 31 (2016): 187–99.

2.   J. R. Lott Jr. and C. Moody, "Is the United States an Outlier in Public Mass Shootings? A Comment on Adam Lankford," *Econ Journal Watch* 16 (2019): 37–68.

3.   A. Lankford, "Confirmation that the United States Has Six Times Its Global Share of Public Mass Shooters, Courtesy of Lott and Moody's Data," *Econ Journal Watch* 16 (2019): 69–83.

4.   D. Nass, "How Many Guns Did Americans Buy Last Month? We're Tracking the Sales Boom", *Trace*, March 2, 2021, https://www.thetrace.org/features/gun-sales-estimates/.

5.   A. Karp, "Estimating Global Civilian-held Firearms Numbers", *Small*

Arms Survey, June 2018, http://www.smallarmssurvey.org/weapons-and-markets/tools/global-firearms-holdings.html.

6. D. Hemenway, *Private Guns and Public Health* (Ann Arbor: University of Michigan Press, 2004); A. Kivisto, L. Magee, P. Phalen, and B. Ray, "Firearm Ownership and Domestic Versus Nondomestic Homicide in the U.S.," *American Journal of Preventive Medicine* 57 (2019): 311–20.

7. J. Dilulio, "The Coming of the Super-Predators," *National Review*, November 27, 1995, pp. 23–28.

8. S. Decker, D. Pyrooz, and J. Densley, *On Gangs* (Philadelphia, PA: Temple University Press, 2021).

9. F. E. Zimring and G. Hawkins, *Crime Is Not the Problem: Lethal Violence in America* (New York: Oxford University Press, 1999).

10. E. Monkkonen, "Homicide: Explaining America's Exceptionalism," *American Historical Review* 111 (2006): 76–94.

11. R. Hofstadter, and M. Wallace, *American Violence: A Documentary History* (New York: Alfred A. Knopf, 1970).

12. R. K. Merton, "Social Structure and Anomie," *American Sociological Review* 3 (1938): 672–82.

13. A. Lankford, "Are America's Public Mass Shooters Unique? A Comparative Analysis of Offenders in the United States and Other Countries," *International Journal of Comparative and Applied Criminal Justice* 40 (2016): 171–83.

14. M. J. Ellsworth, *The Bath School Disaster* (1927; repr. Bath, UK: Bath School Museum Committee, 1991).

15. E. Durkheim, *Suicide: A Study in Sociology*, trans. J. Spaulding and G. Simpson (1897; repr. New York: The Free Press, 1951).

16. C. M. Pepper, "Suicide in the Mountain West Region of the United States," *Crisis: The Journal of Crisis Intervention and Suicide Prevention* 38 (2017): 344–50.

17. A. Case and A. Deaton, "Rising Morbidity and Mortality in Midlife Among White Non-Hispanic Americans in the 21st Century," *Proceedings of the National Academy of Sciences* 112 (2015): 15078–83.

18. S. Woolf and H. Schoomaker, "Life Expectancy and Mortality Rates in the United States, 1959–2017," *JAMA* 322 (2019): 1996–2016.

19. S. Dorn, "The COVID-19 Pandemic and Resulting Economic Crash Have Caused the Greatest Health Insurance Losses in American History" (Washington, DC: Families USA, July 13, 2020), https://families usa.org/resources/the-covid-19-pandemic-and-resulting-economic -crash-have-caused-the-greatest-health-insurance-losses-in-american -history/.

20. M. Weber, *Protestant Ethic and the Spirit of Capitalism* (New York: Scribner, 1958).

21. S. Duxbury, L. Frizzell, and S. Lindsay, "Mental Illness, the Media, and the Moral Politics of Mass Violence," *Journal of Research in Crime and Delinquency* 55 (2018): 766–97.

22. C. Weller, "African Americans Face Systematic Obstacles to Getting Good Jobs" (Washington, DC: Center for American Progress, December 5, 2019), https://www.americanprogress.org/issues/economy /reports/2019/12/05/478150/african-americans-face-systematic -obstacles-getting-good-jobs/.

23. https://www.americanprogress.org/issues/economy/reports/2019/12/05/ 478150/african-americans-face-systematic-obstacles-getting-good-jobs/.

24. A. Case and A. Deaton, *Deaths of Despair and the Future of Capitalism* (Princeton, NJ: Princeton University Press, 2020).

25. M. Kimmel, *Angry White Men: American Masculinity at the End of an Era* (New York: Bold Type, 2017).

26. J. Messerschmidt, *Masculinities and Crime: Critique and Reconceptualization of Theory* (Totowa, NJ: Rowman and Littlefield, 1993).

27. B. Cooper et al., "The Divide Over America's Future: 1950 or 2050? Findings from the 2016 American Values Survey" (Washington, DC: PRRI, October 25, 2016), https://www.prri.org/research/poll-1950s-2050-divided -nations-direction-post-election/.

28. J. Carlson, *Citizen-Protectors: The Everyday Politics of Guns in an Age of Decline* (New York: Oxford University Press, 2015).

29. A. Stroud, "Good Guys with Guns: Hegemonic Masculinity and Concealed Handguns," *Gender and Society* 26 (2012): 216–38.

30. F. C. Mencken and P. Froese, "Gun Culture in Action," *Social Problems* 66 (2019): 3–27.

31. M. E. O'Toole, "The Dangerous Injustice Collector: Behaviors of Someone Who Never Forgets, Never Forgives, Never Lets Go, and Strikes Back! *Violence and Gender* 1 (2014): 97–99.

32. G. LaFree, *Losing Legitimacy: Street Crime and the Decline of Institutions in America* (Boulder, CO: Westview Perseus, 1998).

33. R. Roth, "How the Erosion of Trust Leads to Murders and Mass Shootings," *Washington Post*, October 6, 2017, https://www.washington post.com/outlook/how-the-erosion-of-trust-leads-to-murders -and-mass-shootings/2017/10/06/382cc4b2-a91e-11e7-92d1-58c70 2d2d975_story.html.

CHAPTER 3

1. N. Haslam, "Concept Creep: Psychology's Expanding Concepts of Harm and Pathology," *Psychological Inquiry* 27 (2016): 1–17.

2. V. J. Felitti et al., "Relationship of Childhood Abuse and Household Dysfunction to Many of the Leading Causes of Death in Adults: The Adverse Childhood Experiences (ACE) Study," *American Journal of Preventive Medicine* 14 (1998): 245–58.

3. D. C. Biruski, D. Ajdukovic, and A. L. Stanic, "When the World Collapses: Changed Worldview and Social Reconstruction in a Traumatized Community," *European Journal of Psychotraumatology* 5 (2014).

4. C. S. Widom, "The Cycle of Violence," *Science* 244 (1989): 160–66.

5. N. N. Duke et al., "Adolescent Violence Perpetration: Associations with Multiple Types of Adverse Childhood Experiences," *Pediatrics* 125 (2010): 778–86.

6. T. Herrenkohl, H. Jung, J. O. Lee, and M. H. Kim, *Effects of Child Maltreatment, Cumulative Victimization Experiences, and Proximal Life Stress on Adult Crime and Antisocial Behavior*, Office of Justice Programs Research Report, National Criminal Justice Reference Services, 2014, https://www.ojp.gov/pdffiles1/nij/grants/250506.pdf.

7. A. B. Miller et al., "The Relation Between Child Maltreatment and Adolescent Suicidal Behavior: A Systematic Review and Critical Exami-

nation of the Literature," *Clinical Child and Family Psychology Review* 16 (2013): 146–72.

8. H. Dubowitz et al., "Pediatric Primary Care to Help Prevent Child Maltreatment: The Safe Environment for Every Kid (SEEK) Model," *Pediatrics* 123 (2009): 858–64.

9. E. Sama-Miller et al., "Home Visiting Evidence of Effectiveness Review: Executive Summary," OPRE Report #2019–93, September 30, 2017, Office of Planning, Research, and Evaluation, Administration for Children and Families, U.S. Department of Health and Human Services, Washington, DC.

10. A. L. Bruhn, S. Woods-Groves, and S. Huddle, "A Preliminary Investigation of Emotional and Behavioral Screening Practices in K–12 Schools," *Education and Treatment of Children* 37, no. 4 (2014): 611–34.

11. J. S. Merrick et al., "Benevolent Childhood Experiences (BCEs) in Homeless Parents: A Validation and Replication Study," *Journal of Family Psychology* 33, no. 4 (2019): 493–98.

CHAPTER 4

1. President Trump Address on Mass Shootings, *C-Span*, August 5, 2019, https://www.c-span.org/video/?463254–1/president-trump-calls-nation -condemn-racism-bigotry-white-supremacy-mass-shootings.

2. J. W. Swanson et al., "Violence and Psychiatric Disorder in the Community: Evidence from the Epidemiologic Catchment Area Surveys," *Psychiatric Services* 41, no. 7 (1990): 761–70.

3. K. S. Douglas and J. L. Skeem, "Violence Risk Assessment: Getting Specific About Being Dynamic," *Psychology, Public Policy, and Law* 11 (2005): 347–83.

4.   P. Langman, *Why Kids Kill: Inside The Minds of School Shooters* (New York: Palgrave Macmillan, 2009).

5.   D. DeMatteo et al., "Statement of Concerned Experts on the Use of the Hare Psychopathy Checklist—Revised in Capital Sentencing to Assess Risk for Institutional Violence," *Psychology, Public Policy, and Law* 26 (2020): 133–44.

6.   H. M. Cleckley, *The Mask of Sanity: An Attempt to Clarify Some Issues About the So-called Psychopathic Personality* (Saint Louis, MO: C.V. Mosby, 1964).

7.   A. Stark, "I was Almost a School Shooter", *TED*, June 2018, https://www.ted.com/talks/aaron_stark_i_was_almost_a_school_shooter?language=en.

CHAPTER 5

1.   L. M. Pane and S. Dazio, "US Police Assess Rise in Threat Tips After 3 Mass Killings," *Associated Press*, September 21, 2019, https://apnews.com/dd054d08eb904d3a92d9c46cb65c489b.

2.   Wylie, L. E., et al., "Assessing School and Student Predictors of Weapons Reporting," *Youth Violence and Juvenile Justice* 8, no. 4 (2010): 351–72.

3.   J. Gillum and J. Kao, "Aggression Detectors: The Unproven, Invasive Surveillance Technology Schools Are Using to Monitor Students," ProPublica, June 25, 2019, https://features.propublica.org/aggression-detector/the-unproven-invasive-surveillance-technology-schools-are-using-to-monitor-students/.

4.   C. L. Johnson, "Preventing School Shootings: The Effectiveness of Safety Measures," *Victims and Offenders* 12 (2017): 956–73.

CHAPTER 6

1. "1999: The Year of the Net," BBC News, December 30, 1999, http://news.bbc.co.uk/2/hi/business/574132.stm.

2. K. Haslam, "iMac at 20: 10 iMac Facts and History in Pictures", *MacWorld*, August 14, 2018, https://www.macworld.co.uk/news/mac/imac-facts-history-3682354/.

3. J. Raitanen and A. Oksanen, "Global Online Subculture Surrounding School Shootings," *American Behavioral Scientist* 62 (2018): 195–209.

4. M. Follman and B. Andrews, "How Columbine Spawned Dozens of Copycats," *Mother Jones*, October 5, 2015, http://www.motherjones.com/politics/2015/10/columbine-effect-mass-shootings-copycat-data.

5. A. Petridis, "'Columbine Destroyed My Entire Career': Marilyn Manson on the Perils of Being the Lord of Darkness," *Guardian*, September 21, 2017, https://www.theguardian.com/music/2017/sep/21/columbine-destroyed-my-entire-career-marilyn-manson-on-the-perils-of-being-the-lord-of-darkness.

6. G. Tarde, *The Laws of Imitation* (New York: Henry Holt, 1903).

7. R. Cialdini, *Influence: The Psychology of Persuasion* (New York: William Morrow, 1984).

8. M. Chwe, *Rational Ritual* (Princeton, NJ: Princeton University Press, 2001).

9. American Psychological Association, "Resolution on Violent Video Games," Adopted by the APA Council of Representatives, August 2015, http://www.apa.org/about/policy/violent-video-games.aspx.

10. A. Przybylski and N. Weinstein, "Violent Video Game Engagement Is Not Associated with Adolescents' Aggressive Behaviour: Evidence From A Registered Report," *Royal Society Open Science* 6: 171474.

11. S. King, *Guns* (Bangor, ME: Philtrum Press, 2013).

12. M. Gladwell, Thresholds of Violence, *The New Yorker*, October 12, 2015, https://www.newyorker.com/magazine/2015/10/19/thresholds-of -violence.

13. C. L. Jonson, M. Moon, and B. M. Gialopsos, "Are Students Scared or Prepared? Psychological Impacts of a Multi-option Active Assailant Protocol Compared to Other Crisis/Emergency Preparedness Practices," *Victims and Offenders* 15 (2020): 639–62.

14. J. Peterson, E. Sackrison, and A. Polland, "Training Students to Respond to Shootings on Campus: Is It Worth It?" *Journal of Threat Assessment and Management* 2, no. 2 (2015): 127–38.

15. J. Schildkraut, A. B. Nickerson, and T. Ristoff, "Lock, Lights, Out of Sight: Assessing Students Perceptions of Emergency Preparedness Across Multiple Lockdown Drills," *Journal of School Violence* 19 (2020): 93–106.

16. Everytown for Gun Safety Research Report (2020). The Impact of Schools Safety Drills for Active Shootings. https://every townresearch.org/report/the-impact-of-school-safety-drills-for-active -shootings/.

17. S. Towers et al., "Contagion in Mass Killings and School Shootings," *PLOS One* 10 (2015): 112.

18. G. Duwe, "Body-Count Journalism: The Presentation of Mass Murder in the News Media," *Homicide Studies* 4 (2000): 364–99.

19. A. Lankford, "Do the Media Unintentionally Make Mass Killers into Celebrities? An Assessment of Free Advertising and Earned Media Value," *Celebrity Studies* 9, no. 3 (2018): 340–54.

20. K. Ramsland, *Confession of a Serial Killer: The Untold Story of Dennis Rader, the BTK Killer* (Lebanon, NH: University Press of New England, 2016).

21. V. Kappeler and G. Potter, *The Mythology of Crime and Criminal Justice*, 5th ed. (Long Grove, IL: Waveland Press, 2018).

22. *Serial killer* is generally attributed to agent Robert Ressler, a member of the FBI's storied Behavioral Science Unit. The term *serial murderer* first appeared in 1961, in a review of Fritz Lang's film *M*.

23. Data derived from the Radford/FGCU serial killer database of more than five thousand serial killers from 1900 to today, curated by Professors Mike Aamodt, Terence Leary, and Larry Southard, https://www.fgcu.edu/skdb/.

24. A. Liptak, "Facebook Says it Removed 1.5 million Videos of the New Zealand Mass Shooting," The Verge, March 17, 2019, https://www.theverge.com/2019/3/17/18269453/facebook-new-zealand-attack-removed-1-5-million-videos-content-moderation.

25. A. Hern and J. Waterson, "Social Media Firms Fight to Delete Christchurch Shooting footage," *Guardian*, March 15, 2019, https://www.theguardian.com/world/2019/mar/15/video-of-christchurch-attack-runs-on-social-media-and-news-sites.

26. R. Surette, "Performance Crime and Justice," *Current Issues in Criminal Justice* 27 (2015): 195–216.

27. M. Yar, "Crime, Media and the Will-to-Representation: Reconsidering

Relationships in the New Media Age," *Crime, Media, Culture* 8 (2012): 245–60.

28. B. J. Bushman, "Narcissism, Fame Seeking, and Mass Shootings," *American Behavioral Scientist* 62 (2017): 229–41.

29. Y. Uhls and P.Greenfield. "The Value Of Fame: Preadolescent Perceptions of Popular Media and Their Relationship to Future Aspirations," *Developmental Psychology* 48 (2012): 315–26.

30. J. Henderson, "One in Four Millennials Would Quit Their Job to Be Famous," *Forbes*, January 24, 2017, https://www.forbes.com/sites /jmaureenhenderson/2017/01/24/one-in-four-millennials-would-quit -their-job-to-be-famous/?sh=37b4e542c438.

31. A. Lankford, "Fame-seeking Rampage Shooters: Initial Findings and Empirical Predictions," *Aggression and Violent Behavior* 27 (2016): 122–29.

32. T. Teves, "A Call to End the Media Coverage Mass Shooters Want," TED, November 2019, https://www.ted.com/talks/tom_teves_a_call_to _end_the_media_coverage_mass_shooters_want?language=en.

33. P. Krugman, *Arguing with Zombies: Economics, Politics, and the Fight for a Better Future* (New York: W. W. Norton, 2020).

34. A. Lankford and E. Madfis, "Don't Name Them, Don't Show Them, but Report Everything Else: A Pragmatic Proposal for Denying Mass Shooters the Attention They Seek and Deterring Future Offenders, *American Behavioral Scientist* 62 (2017): 260–79.

35. J. Fox. "'No Names or Photos' Won't Stop Mass Shooters, but We Shouldn't Humanize Them with Details," *USA Today*, December 21, 2018, https://www.usatoday.com/story/opinion/2018/12/21/excessive

-details-mass-shooters-killers-humanizes-harmful-report-column/2
378071002/.

36. J. Levin and J. B. Wiest, "Covering Mass Murder: An Experimental Examination of the Effects of News Focus—Killer, Victim, or Hero—on Reader Interest, *American Behavioral Scientist* 62 (2018): 181–94.

37. A. Lankford and E. Madfis, "Don't Name Them, Don't Show Them, but Report Everything Else: A Pragmatic Proposal for Denying Mass Killers the Attention They Seek and Deterring Future Offenders," *American Behavioral Scientist* 62 (2018): 260–279.

38. J. N. Meindl and J. W. Ivy, "Mass Shootings: The Role of Media in Promoting Generalized Information," *American Journal of Public Health* 107, no. 3 (2017): 368–70.

39. S. Every-Palmer et al., "The Christchurch Mosque Shooting, the Media, and Subsequent Gun Control Reform in New Zealand: A Descriptive Analysis," *Psychiatry, Psychology and Law* (2020), DOI: 10.1080/13218719.2020.1770635.

40. "France Gives Online Firms One Hour to Pull 'Terrorist' Content," *BBC News*, May 14, 2020, https://www.bbc.co.uk/news/technology -52664609.

41. J. Schildkraut and G. W. Muschert, "Media Salience and the Framing of Mass Murder in Schools: A Comparison of the Columbine and Sandy Hook Massacres," *Homicide Studies* 18 (2014): 23–43.

CHAPTER 7

1. D. Williams, et al., "Can You Spot a Liar? Deception, Mindreading, and the Case of Autism Spectrum Disorder. *Autism Research* 11 (2018): 1129–37.

2. M. Kinnard, "Feds: Church Shooting Suspect 'Self-radicalized' Pre-attack," *Associated Press*, August 22, 2016, https://apnews.com/article /d9693b0934df490caa059c5e18e27aa3.

3. B. Morlin, "Unrepentant and Radicalized Online: A Look at the Trial of Dylann Roof," *Southern Poverty Law Center*, December 19, 2016, https:// www.splcenter.org/hatewatch/2016/12/19/unrepentant-and-radicalized -online-look-trial-dylann-roof.

4. "On Gab, an Extremist-Friendly Site, Pittsburgh Shooting Suspect Aired His Hatred in Full," *New York Times*, October 28, 2018, https://www .nytimes.com/2018/10/28/us/gab-robert-bowers-pittsburgh-synagogue -shootings.html.

5. M. Fathali, "The Staircase to Terrorism," *American Psychologist* 6 (2005): 161–69.

6. L. Beckett and J. Wilson, " 'White Power Ideology': Why El Paso Is Part of a Growing Global Threat," *Guardian*, August 5, 2019, https:// www.theguardian.com/us-news/2019/aug/04/el-paso-shooting-white -nationalist-supremacy-violence-christchurch?CMP=Share_iOSApp_ Other.

7. C. R. Sunstein and A. Vermeule, "Conspiracy Theories: Causes and Cures," *Journal of Political Philosophy* 17 (2009): 202–227.

8. E. Hoffer, *The True Believer: Thoughts on the Nature of Mass Movements* (New York: Harper, 1951).

9. J. Kyyam, "Opinion: There Are No Lone Wolves," *Washington Post*, August 4, 2019, https://www.washingtonpost.com/opinions/2019/08/04 /there-are-no-lone-wolves/.

10. R. K. Ghansah, "A Most American Terrorist: The Making of Dylann

Roof," *GQ*, August 21, 2017, https://www.gq.com/story/dylann-roof
-making-of-an-american-terrorist.

11. J. Cobb, "Inside the Trial of Dylann Roof," *New Yorker*, January 30,
2017, https://www.newyorker.com/magazine/2017/02/06/inside
-the-trial-of-dylann-roof.

12. M. Juergensmeyer, *Terror in the Mind of God: The Global Rise of Religious
Violence* (Oakland: University of California Press, 2017).

13. K. Dilanian, "There Is No Law That Covers 'Domestic Terrorism.' What
Would One Look Like?," NBC News, August 9, 2019, https://www
.nbcnews.com/politics/justice-department/there-no-law-covers
-domestic-terrorism-what-would-one-look-n1040386.

14. U.S. Department of Homeland Security, *Department of Homeland
Security Strategic Framework for Countering Terrorism and Targeted Violence*, 2019, https://www.dhs.gov/publication/dhs-strategic-framework
-countering-terrorism-and-targeted-violence.

15. D. Holbrook and J. Horgan, "Terrorism and Ideology: Cracking the
Cut," *Perspectives on Terrorism* 13 (2019): 2–15.

16. R. Scrivens, "Exploring Radical Right-Wing Posting Behaviors Online,"
Deviant Behavior (2020), DOI: 10.1080/01639625.2020.1756391.

17. "Psychiatric Examination: Dylann Storm Roof," December 26, 2016,
https://bloximages.newyork1.vip.townnews.com/postandcourier
.com/content/tncms/assets/v3/editorial/d/49/d49ddabc-370d-11e7
-bca9-c3bd2320bb37/5915a96c89fb4.pdf.pdf.

18. J. Taylor, "The Woman Who Founded the 'Incel' Movement," BBC
News, August 30, 2018, https://www.bbc.co.uk/news/world-us
-canada-45284455.

19. "Incels: A Guide to Symbols and Terminology," Moonshot CVE, May 26, 2020, http://moonshotcve.com/incels-symbols-and-terminology/.

20. C. Lord, L. Ross, and M. Lepper, "Biased Assimilation and Attitude Polarization: The Effects of Prior Theories on Subsequently Considered Evidence," *Journal of Personality and Social Psychology* 37 (1979): 2098–2109.

21. B. Nyhan and J. Reifler, "When Corrections Fail: The Persistence of Political Misperceptions," *Political Behavior* 32 (2010): 303–30.

22. L. Festinger, *A Theory of Cognitive Dissonance* (Palo Alto, CA: Stanford University Press, 1957).

23. S. Lewandowsky and J. Cook, *The Conspiracy Theory Handbook*, March 2020, https://www.climatechangecommunication.org/wp-content /uploads/2020/03/ConspiracyTheoryHandbook.pdf.

24. N. F. Johnson et al., "Hidden Resilience and Adaptive Dynamics of the Global Online Hate Ecology," *Nature* 573 (2019): 261–65.

25. M. Squire, "The Question I Get Most . . . ," Twitter, July 10, 2020, https:// twitter.com/MeganSquire0/status/1281621930202849280.

26. C. Newton, "The Trauma Floor: The Secret Lives of Facebook Moderators in America," The Verge, February 25, 2019, https://www.theverge .com/2019/2/25/18229714/cognizant-facebook-content-moderator -interviews-trauma-working-conditions-arizona.

27. R. Mac, "A Kenosha Militia Facebook Event Asking Attendees to Bring Weapons Was Reported 455 Times. Moderators Said It Didn't Violate Any Rules," BuzzFeed News, August 28, 2020, https://www.buzzfeednews .com/article/ryanmac/kenosha-militia-facebook-reported-455-times -moderators.

28. S. Zuboff, *The Age of Surveillance Capitalism* (New York: Public Affairs, 2018).

29. E. Pariser, *The Filter Bubble* (New York: Penguin, 2011).

30. S. Noble, *Algorithms of Oppression: How Search Engines Reinforce Racism* (New York: NYU Press, 2018).

CHAPTER 8

1. T. Abt, *Bleeding Out: The Devastating Consequences of Urban Violence—and a Bold New Plan for Peace in the Streets* (New York: Basic Books, 2019).

2. M. Felson and R. V. Clarke, *Opportunity Makes the Thief: Practical Theory for Crime Prevention* (London: Home Office, 1998); R. V. Clarke, "Opportunity Makes the Thief. Really? And So What?, *Crime Science* 3 (2012): 1, https://doi.org/10.1186/2193-7680-1-3.

3. J. A. Fox, "When It Comes to Mass Shootings, the Panic Is What's Fueling the Crisis," *USA Today,* December 3, 2019, https://www.usatoday.com/story/opinion/2019/12/03/mass-shootings-panic-fueling-crisis-column/4320028002/.

4. R. V. Clarke and P. Mayhew, "The British Gas Suicide Story and Its Criminological Implications," in M. Tonry, ed., *Crime and Justice* 10 (1988): 79–116.

5. E. Emanuel, "A Simple Way to Reduce Suicides," *New York Times,* June 2, 2013, https://opinionator.blogs.nytimes.com/2013/06/02/a-simple-way-to-reduce-suicides/

6. K. Hawton et al., "Long Term Effect of Reduced Pack Sizes of Paracetamol on Poisoning Deaths and Liver Transplant Activity in

England and Wales: Interrupted Time Series Analyses," *BMJ* 346 (2013): f403.

7. M. Miller, D. Azrael, and D. Hemenway, "The Epidemiology of Case Fatality Rates for Suicide in the Northeast," *Annals of Emergency Medicine* 4 (2004): 723–30.

8. T. Nina et al., "Suicide by Firearm in Switzerland: Who Uses the Army Weapon? Results from the National Survey Between 2000 and 2010," *Swiss Medical Weekly* 148 (2018), w14646.

9. E. Markowitz and The Trace, "How Switzerland Accidentally Reduced Suicides," *Atlantic,* September 8, 2016, https://www.the atlantic.com/international/archive/2016/09/switzerland-military-gun -suicide/499028/.

10. G. Lubin et al., "Decrease in Suicide Rates After a Change of Policy Reducing Access to Firearms in Adolescents: A Naturalistic Epidemiological Study," *Suicide and Life-Threatening Behavior* 40 (2010): 421–24.

11. T. Reisch et al., "Change in Suicide Rates in Switzerland Before and After Firearm Restriction Resulting from the 2003 'Army XXI' Reform," *American Journal of Psychiatry* 170 (2013): 977–84.

12. T. Reisch, U. Schuster, and K. Michel, "Suicide by Jumping and Accessibility of Bridges: Results from a National Survey in Switzerland," *Suicide and Life-Threatening Behavior* 37 (2007): 681–87.

13. J. Freilich, S. Chermak, and B. Klein, (2020). "Investigating the Applicability of Situational Crime Prevention to the Public Mass Violence Context," *Criminology and Public Policy* 19 (2020): 271–93.

14. A. Whitaker et al., *Cops and No Counselors: How the Lack of School*

Mental Health Staff Is Harming Students, ACLU Annual Report, 2020, https://www.aclu.org/sites/default/files/field_document/030419 -acluschooldisciplinereport.pdf.

15. J. Peterson, J. Densley, and G. Erickson, "Presence of Armed School Officials and Fatal and Nonfatal Gunshot Injuries During Mass School Shootings, United States, 1980–2019," *JAMA Network* 4, no. 2 (2021): e2037394.

16. A. Kupchik, *Homeroom Security: School Discipline in an Age of Fear* (New York: NYU Press, 2010).

17. D. Gottfredson et al. "Effects of School Resource Officers on School Crime and Responses to School Crime," *Criminology & Public Policy* 19 (2020): 905–940.

18. F. E. Zimring and G. Hawkins, *Crime Is Not the Problem: Lethal Violence in America* (New York: Oxford University Press, 1999).

19. D. Thompson, "California Sues US Regulator in Bid to Deter 'Ghost Guns," *Associated Press,* September 29, 2020, https://apnews.com/article /san-francisco-sacramento-us-news-lawsuits-california-7484255afd9 d73dceee86a28354dac5e.

20. A. Winkler, *Gunfight: The Battle over the Right to Bear Arms in America* (New York: W. W. Norton, 2013).

21. B. Resnick, "How to Make Sense of America's Wildly Different, Confusing Patchwork of Gun Control Laws," the *Atlantic,* December 17, 2012, https://www.theatlantic.com/politics/archive/2012/12/how-to -make-sense-of-americas-wildly-different-confusing-patchwork-of -gun-control-laws/454299/.

22. R. Mukherjee, "How Many Mass Shootings Might Have Been Prevented

by Stronger Gun Laws?," *Los Angeles Times*, February 26, 2020, https://
www.latimes.com/projects/if-gun-laws-were-enacted/.

23.   Q. Bui and M. Sanger-Katz, "How to Prevent Gun Deaths? Where Experts
and the Public Agree," *New York Times*, January 10, 2017, https://www.
nytimes.com/interactive/2017/01/10/upshot/How-to-Prevent-Gun
-Deaths-The-Views-of-Experts-and-the-Public.html.

24.   "Gun Owners Divided on Gun Policy; Parkland Students Having an
Impact," *Monmouth University,* March 8, 2018, https://www.monmouth
.edu/polling-institute/reports/monmouthpoll_us_030818/.

25.   M. Miller, L. Hepburn, and D. Azrael, "Firearm Acquisition Without
Background Checks," *Annals of Internal Medicine* 166 (2017): 233–39.

26.   M. Siegel et al., "The Relation Between State Gun Laws and the Inci-
dence and Severity of Mass Public Shootings in the United States,
1976–2018, *Law and Human Behavior* 44 (2021), 347–60.

27.   K. E., Rudolph et al., "Association Between Connecticut's
Permit to-Purchase Handgun Law and Homicides," *American Journal
of Public Health* 105 (2015): e49–e54.

28.   M., Luca, D., Malhotra, and C. Poliquin, "Handgun Waiting Periods
Reduce Gun Deaths," *Proceedings of the National Academy of Sciences*
114, no. 46 (2017): 12162–65.

29.   N. Nguyen, "Here's What's up with "Smart Guns"—and Why You
Can't Buy One in the US," *BuzzFeed News,* March 13, 2018, https://
www.buzzfeednews.com/article/nicolenguyen/what-is-smart-gun
-technology.

30.   D. C. Grossman et al., "Gun Storage Practices and Risk of Youth Suicide
and Unintentional Firearm Injuries," *JAMA* 293 (2005): 707–714.

31. C. L. Barry et al., "Trends in Public Opinion on US Gun Laws: Majorities of Gun Owners and Non-Gun Owners Support a Range of Measures," *Health Affairs* 38 (2019): 1727–34.

32. C. K. Crifasi et al., "Storage Practices of US Gunowners in 2016," *American Journal of Public Health* 108 (2018): 532–37.

33. D. Azrael et al., "Firearm Storage in Gun-Owning Households with Children: Results of a 2015 National Survey," *Journal of Urban Health* 95 (2018): 295–304.

34. J. A. Simonetti et al., "Firearm Storage Practices Among American Veterans," *American Journal of Preventive Medicine* 55 (2018): 445–54.

35. United States Government Accountability Office, *Personal Firearms: Programs that Promote Safe Storage and Research on Their Effectiveness*, September 2017, https://www.gao.gov/assets/690/687239.pdf.

36. A. Burton et al., "Public Support for Regulating the Lethality of Firearms: Reducing the Opportunity for High-Casualty Mass Murder," *Criminologist* 45 (2020): 7–10.

37. H.R.4296—Public Safety and Recreational Firearms Use Protection Act (1994), https://www.congress.gov/bill/103rd-congress/house-bill/4296.

38. FBI: UCR, "2017, Crime in the United States," https://ucr.fbi.gov/crime-in-the-u.s/2017/crime-in-the-u.s.-2017/topic-pages/expanded-homicide.

38. L. Post, et al. "Firearm Surveillance Informs Gun Control Policy: Regression Lines of Discontinuity." *JMIR Public Health and Surveillance* (2021): 10.2196/26042.

39. D. W. Webster, "Evidence Concerning the Regulation of Firearms Design, Sale, and Carrying on Fatal Mass Shootings in the United States," *Criminology and Public Policy* 19 (2020): 171–212.

40. M. Ferner, "Colorado Republican: It Was Actually 'A Good Thing' Aurora Shooter Had 100-Round Magazine," HuffPost, February 13, 2014, https://www.huffpost.com/entry/bernie-herpin-colorado -magazine_n_4781460.

41. C. Koper, "Assessing the Potential to Reduce Deaths and Injuries from Mass Shootings Through Restrictions on Assault Weapons and Other High-Capacity Semiautomatic Firearms," *Criminology and Public Policy* 19 (2020): 147–70.

42. J. W. Swanson et al., "Implementation and Effectiveness of Connecticut's Risk-based Gun Removal Law: Does It Prevent Suicides?" *Law and Contemporary Problems* 80 (2017): 179–208.

43. "S3E30/Gun Violence in America/What the Swiss can teach us," American Diagnosis with Dr. Celine Gounder, https://podcasts.apple.com /us/podcast/s3e30-gun-violence-in-america-what-the-swiss-can-teach -us/id1282044849?i=1000457471677.

44. N. Rakich, "How Views on Gun Control Have Changed in the Last 30 Years," *FiveThirtyEight,* August 7, 2019, https://fivethirtyeight .com/features/how-views-on-gun-control-have-changed-in-the-last-30 -years/.

CHAPTER 9

1. G. Paulson, *Closing the Asylums* (Jefferson, NC: McFarland, 2012).

2. A. Roth, *Insane* (New York: Basic Books, 2018).

3. D. J. Scholten, A. K. Malla, and R. M. G. Norman, "Removing Barriers to Treatment of First-episode Psychotic Disorders," *Canadian Journal of Psychiatry* 48 (2003): 561–65.

4. J. Peterson, J. Densley, and G. Erickson, "Evaluation of 'the R-Model' Crisis Intervention De-escalation Training for Law Enforcement," *Police Journal* 93 (2020): 271–89.

5. J. Schildkraut, E. Sokolowski, and J. Nicoletti, "The Survivor Network: The Role of Shared Experiences in Mass Shootings Recovery," *Victims and Offenders* 16 (2021): 20–49.

INDEX